CHILDREN'S POCKET ENCYCLOPEDIA

Adrienne Jack

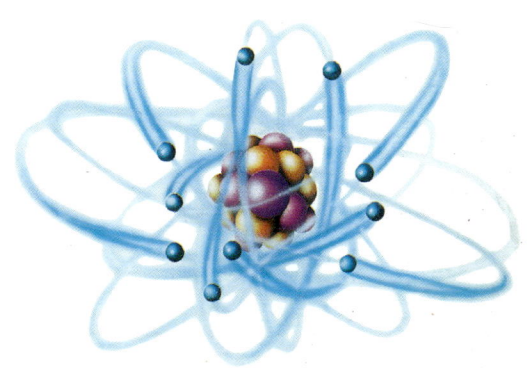

KING*f*ISHER

For Richard and my father Carl L. Norris

KINGFISHER
An imprint of Kingfisher Publications Plc
New Penderel House
283-288 High Holborn
London WC1V 7HZ

First published in 1983
This revised edition published in 1998 by
Kingfisher Books.

10 9 8 7 6 5 4 3 2 1

Copyright © Kingfisher Publications Plc 1998

All rights reserved. No part of this publication may be
reproduced, stored in a retrieval system or transmitted
by any means, electronic, mechanical, photocopying or
otherwise, without the prior permission of the
publisher.

A CIP CATALOGUE RECORD FOR THIS BOOK IS AVAILABLE
FROM THE BRITISH LIBRARY

ISBN 0 7534 0214 9

Produced by Toucan Books Ltd
Printed in Hong Kong

INTRODUCTION

This pocket encyclopedia contains over 500 separate entries. They are arranged in alphabetical order. The information they contain is both interesting and useful.

The encyclopedia can be used in lots of ways. You can look up information on a particular subject for a special project, or you can use it to answer questions that you have been puzzling over, or you can enjoy just browsing through this encyclopedia, stopping when a picture or entry catches your eye.

This is how to look things up:

1. The entries are arranged in *alphabetical order*. Flick through the book until you come to the correct letter for the entry you want to look up.

2. Use the *cross-reference*. 'See also' followed by a word or words in capital letters appear at the end of many articles. These words are separate alphabetical entries that will give you more information about your subject.

3. Use the *index*. Sometimes the subject you are looking for may not have a main entry. Look up your subject in the index at the end of the book. The information you need may be contained in an entry with a different title. For instance, information on the River Amazon appears in the articles on Brazil and South America.

A

Aardvark
The aardvark of Africa is a curious animal. It has no close relatives, although its way of life is like that of the anteater. Aardvarks have strong claws, which they use to break open termites' nests.
See also ANTEATER.

Aardvark: This timid creature is active mainly at night.

Aborigines
Aborigines are the native people of Australia. They arrived there thousands of years ago from southeastern Asia. Traditionally, Aborigines were hunters and foodgatherers, the men hunting emus, kangaroos and game with

Aborigines: A boomerang and shield with traditional decorations.

boomerangs and spears, the women gathering nuts, berries and fruits. This way of life has changed, as today many live and work in the cities or on large farms.

Acids
Acids are sour-tasting chemicals. The sour taste of a lemon is caused by *citric* acid. Sour milk contains *lactic* acid. Vinegar contains *acetic* acid. These are weak acids and are harmless. Strong acids, such as *sulphuric* acid, *nitric* acid and *hydrochloric* acid are poisonous.

Africa
Africa is the world's second-largest continent. Most of the land is a great plateau, or tableland, surrounded by a narrow coastal plain. In the east are volcanic mountains such as Mount Kilimanjaro (5,895m high) and Mount Kenya (5,200m high).

Africa: *The high plains of Africa are home to a great variety of wildlife.*

The equator falls near the middle of Africa. The climate near the equator is hot and wet. Great rainforests grow here. On either side of the equator there are vast savannas. These grasslands are dry for most of the year. Beyond these are areas of scrub, then semi-desert, and then desert. The Sahara desert is in the north and the Kalahari in the south.

Much of Africa is thinly populated. Cocoa, coffee, oil palm, tea, tobacco, cotton and sugar are grown to sell to countries all over the world. The continent is also rich in minerals.

See also COUNTRIES OF THE WORLD; EGYPT; NIGERIA; SOUTH AFRICA.

AIDS

AIDS stands for acquired immune deficiency syndrome, a deadly disease caused by a virus. The virus itself is called the human immunodeficiency virus, or HIV-1 for short. The disease slowly cripples the body's immune system, leaving the victim with no defence at all against infection. In the early 1980s, AIDS spread rapidly from developing countries all through the Western World. It is passed on chiefly through sexual contact and exchanges of infected blood. A cure is still not in sight.

AIR

Air is the substance that fills the 'empty' space around us. It is made up of a mixture of gases, the main ones being nitrogen and oxygen. Oxygen is the gas animals

Aircraft: Military jet aircraft have a streamlined shape to help them fly at supersonic speeds.

must breathe in order to live. Air is invisible and has no taste, but when it moves we can feel it as wind. Water vapour, another invisible substance, is also present in the air.

A layer of air, called the atmosphere, surrounds the Earth. The air in the atmosphere presses down on us. This is called atmospheric pressure.

AIRCRAFT

Two American brothers built and flew the first aeroplane in 1903. They were Wilbur and Orville Wright from Dayton, Ohio. Their first flimsy flying machine was made of wood, cloth and wire. It could fly only a few metres and could not travel much faster than a bicycle.

Modern planes are very different from the Wright brothers' flying machine. They are sleek and streamlined and made of aluminium alloys. With their powerful jet engines they can travel at fantastic speeds.

There are many different types of planes, but, whatever they are like, all planes have certain things in common. They all have wings shaped to enable them to fly. The shape is called an aerofoil, and consists of a thickened and rounded front edge, curving and tapering to a sharper rear edge. All planes have a tail, which helps to keep the plane on a straight course.

To guide a plane through the air a pilot moves hinged panels, called control surfaces, at the rear of the wings and on the tail. By moving these surfaces, the pilot can make the plane's nose tip up or down or turn to the left or right. Many planes today are flown with the help of electronics and computers.

Planes are thrust through the air either by a stream, or jet, of gases or by propellers. In a jet engine fuel is burned to make hot gases. These gases shoot backwards, pushing the plane forwards. Propellers have a twisted shape and 'screw' themselves through the air when they spin.

See also BALLOONS AND AIRSHIPS; BLÉRIOT; HELICOPTER; JET ENGINE; LINDBERGH; WRIGHT.

AIR-CUSHION VEHICLE
See HOVERCRAFT.

ALEXANDER THE GREAT
(356-323BC)
Alexander was king of Macedonia in Greece and a mighty conqueror. His great dream was to conquer the whole world. He subdued his Greek neighbours in 336BC. By 327BC he had conquered the huge Persian Empire to the east. He then led his men into India, but they were exhausted and he turned back. When he reached Babylon he died of a fever aged just 33.

ALGAE
Algae are the simplest plants. They live where there is moisture. Seaweed is a common algae. Another is the green slime that covers the sides of an aquarium.

Like all plants, algae use the energy in sunlight to make their food. In turn, they are food for many water animals, including shellfish and even whales.

There are four kinds of algae. Green algae live near the surface. Lower down live the blue-green, brown and red algae.

See also PLANT.

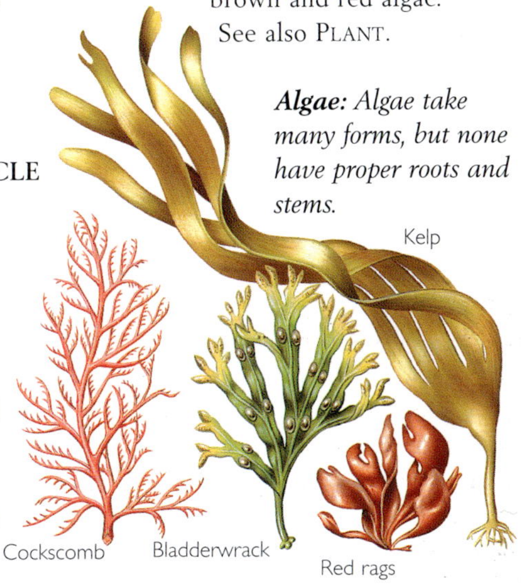

Algae: Algae take many forms, but none have proper roots and stems.

Kelp

Cockscomb   Bladderwrack

Red rags

ALLOY
When two metals are mixed, the result is an alloy. Copper and zinc form the alloy brass. The most common alloy is steel, a mixture of iron and carbon, often with other substances added. Alloys are often used in preference to pure metals because they are stronger.

ALPHABET
An alphabet is a group of letters, or signs, that stand for sounds. It is used to write a language.

The English alphabet comes from the Roman alphabet. It has 26 letters. The letters of the Greek alphabet are used as signs by scientists. The first two Greek letters, *alpha* (A) and *beta* (B), give us our word 'alphabet'.

ALUMINIUM
Aluminium is the most important metal, after iron. It is light, does not rust, and can be made into strong alloys, so is used in the building of aircraft and ships. It conducts heat well and is often used to make pots and pans.

See also ALLOY; METALS.

AMERICAN FOOTBALL
See FOOTBALL.

AMPHIBIAN
Amphibians were the first prehistoric animals to adapt to life on dry land. Modern amphibians, cold-blooded animals such as frogs, toads, salamanders and newts, still spend part of their lives in water and part on dry land.

All amphibians have backbones, and nearly all lay their eggs in water. The young breathe through gills. Adults develop lungs and can leave the water. Amphibians absorb water through their skins, so they must keep themselves moist.

See also FROGS AND TOADS.

Anglo-Saxon: *An Anglo-Saxon helmet decorated with gold.*

ANGLO-SAXON
Anglo-Saxons – the Angles, Saxons and Jutes – were people from Germany who settled in Britain in the 5th and 6th centuries, driving

the original Celtic people into Wales and Cornwall. The Anglo-Saxons ruled in Britain until the Norman Conquest in 1066.

Animal

There are two groups of living things on Earth, animals and plants.

Unlike most plants, most animals can move about. Many have senses, such as sight, hearing and smell, together with a nervous system and a brain. Senses help their owner to find food and escape enemies. Animals use the oxygen they breathe to burn food, which gives them the energy they need. The simplest animals, such as the amoeba, consist of one cell. Other animals are made up of different types of cells joined together.

The animal kingdom is divided into two groups. The larger is the invertebrate group. They include insects, worms, crabs, spiders, snails and starfish.

Animals with backbones are called vertebrates. This group includes fishes, amphibians, reptiles, birds and mammals. Most mammals give birth to live young. Almost all others lay eggs.

All animals behave in certain ways at certain times. This automatic behaviour, such as nest-building, migrating or attacking prey, is called instinct. Invertebrates almost always act instinctively. Vertebrates have more complex brains and they can also learn. Most animals can send each other simple messages.

See also BRAIN; CAMOUFLAGE; CELL; EVOLUTION; MIGRATION; REPRODUCTION; SENSES.

Use the Index to look up animals and animal groups.

Ant

Ants are called social insects because they live in large colonies. There may be as many as a million ants in one nest.

There are three kinds of ant in a colony – a queen, workers and males. The queen mates with a winged male and spends her

Ant: *Eggs, larvae and pupae are tended by workers in a series of chambers inside the nest.*

whole life laying eggs. The female workers cannot lay eggs. They look after the nest, collect food and care for the young. The males mate with the queen.

Ants live in all but the coldest parts of the world. Some have interesting habits. The umbrella ants chew up leaves and use them for growing food. Army ants march in vast columns and eat any living thing in their path.

Antarctic

The Antarctic continent is covered with a sheet of ice thousands of metres thick. It is colder than the Arctic. Even in summer, the temperature rarely rises above freezing point. The South Pole is near the centre of a high, windswept plain.

Algae, mosses and lichens, and some tiny insects live on the continent. The surrounding sea is rich in plankton, fish, seals and whales, and penguins and other birds are also found there.

Anteater

The anteater lives in the forests and savanna of Central and South America. It has a tubular snout and a long, sticky tongue. It feeds on ants and termites, breaking open their nests with its powerful claws.

Antelope

The graceful antelopes are related to cattle. They run swiftly on two-toed hooves and, like cows, chew the cud.

There are antelopes in Africa and Asia. Most live in herds on grassy plains, but some kinds prefer forests or marshes.

See also CATTLE.

Antibiotic

Antibiotics are drugs that either kill bacteria or stop them from spreading. Doctors use them to treat diseases such as pneumonia and tuberculosis that are caused by bacteria. Commonly used antibiotics include penicillin and tetracycline. Many antibiotics, such as penicillin, come from mould; others, such as tetracycline, are produced by bacteria found in the soil.

See also BACTERIA; DISEASE; DRUGS.

Anteater: *The anteater uses its long snout to reach inside insects' nests.*

Ape

Apes include gorillas, chimpanzees, gibbons and orangutans. They are the animals most like humans, with the same number of teeth and the same kind of skeleton. They also have the same kind of blood and catch many similar diseases.

After humans, apes are the most intelligent of all animals. Even so, an ape's brain is only half the size of a human's. Young apes are playful and easily tamed. Apes use their hands and feet skilfully and can solve simple problems.

Unlike monkeys, apes have no tails. Sometimes they stand erect, but usually they move about on all fours, walking on the knuckles of their hands.

Ape: *Apes live in tropical forests and mainly eat leaves, fruit, nuts and insects.*

Archaeology

Archaeology is the study of how people lived long ago through the clues they left behind – their buildings, weapons, ornaments, coins, bones and tools. Often these clues are buried underground.

Archaeologists excavate, or dig out, buried finds. The deeper they dig, the older the objects they find. From human bones, broken pots, kitchen rubbish and other remains they can learn how the people lived, what foods they ate and what skills they had. As a site is excavated, each find is cleaned, labelled and handled with great care as it may be very fragile.

Archaeologists tell the age of an object in several ways. They study the soil and other remains found near it. They can date a find by measuring the amount of natural radioactivity left in certain objects – the carbon-14 method – or by counting the number of tree rings – dendrochronology.

Archaeologists are not just interested in ancient civilization and buried sites. Some, known as industrial archaeologists, study old factories and machinery.

ARCHERY

The use of bows and arrows is called archery. Prehistoric men used bows for hunting and in battle. In the Middle Ages, English archers were famous for their skill with the longbow, which had a

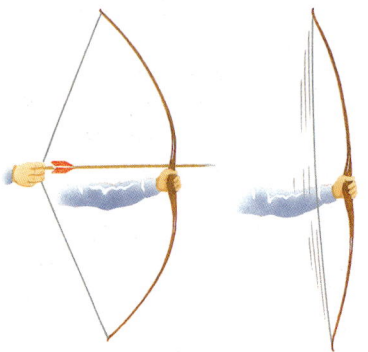

Archery: *A longbow in action.*

longer range than the more complicated crossbow. Bows and arrows became out of date when guns were invented. Today archery is a sport.

ARCHIMEDES (*c.*287-212BC)

Archimedes, a Greek mathematician, lived in Sicily. He discovered that the volume of an object can be measured by the amount of water that it displaces. He also invented the Archimedean screw for lifting water.

ARCHITECTURE

Architecture is the art and science of designing buildings. The architect draws up the plans that the builders follow. Many styles of architecture have been used through the ages. Architecture tells the story of how civilizations grow.

The Greeks tried to be perfect in everything they did. Their system of building was quite simple. Rows of tall marble columns supported stone beams, on which the roof was placed.

Architecture: *The world's skyscrapers include the Empire State Building (left), the World Trade Center (middle) and the Sears Tower (right).*

ARCHITECTURE

Architecture: *Ulm Cathedral in Germany was built in the 19th century, but is Gothic in style.*

Greek architecture was later copied by the Romans. But the Roman architects added two important developments: the arch and the vault, a roof supported by arches. The arch was a good way of spanning a wide distance quickly. Small stones and cement could be used instead of heavy marble beams.

In Europe during the Middle Ages, stone was the natural material for building strong castles and long-lasting cathedrals. At first, architects followed Roman styles. This is called Romanesque architecture. But from around 1150 they began building tall, slender churches and cathedrals, using pointed arches instead of round ones. This is called the Gothic style.

During the Renaissance, architects returned to the Greek and Roman styles. They liked the simple and regular 'classical' designs. They gradually added

PERIODS OF ARCHITECTURE

BC
3200s	Ancient Egyptian begins
600s	Classical Greek begins
100s	Classical Roman begins

AD
400s	Byzantine period begins
950s	Romanesque period in northern Europe
1000s	Norman period in England
1150s	Gothic period begins in France
1400s	Renaissance period in Italy
1600s	Baroque period begins in Italy
1720s	Georgian style begins in England
1750s	Rococo style begins in Italy
1890s	Art Nouveau in Europe
1920s	Modern architecture begins with Functionalism and the International Style

more decoration until, by the 1600s, buildings had become very ornate, inside and outside. Even straight stone columns were twisted into spiral shapes. This was called the baroque style.

An important development in the 1900s was the introduction of steel and reinforced concrete. These materials allowed architects to build more quickly and very much higher than before. The first very tall buildings, called 'skyscrapers' were built in the United States. Now they are built all over the world.

Today's architects use simple shapes. The architect tries to design a new building so that it will fit in well with other buildings near it.

See also CASTLE; CHURCH; EGYPT, ANCIENT; GREECE, ANCIENT; ROME, ANCIENT.

ARCTIC

The Arctic is the cold frozen zone around the North Pole. At the North Pole the Sun never rises in winter. In summer the Sun does not set, even at midnight.

The Arctic Ocean includes both the frozen sea around the North Pole and the unfrozen waters surrounding that. Because so many rivers flow into it from northern Europe, Asia and North America, it is less salty than the world's other oceans.

During the short Arctic summer, grass, flowers and moss grow on the tundra plains of the Arctic. Arctic animals include seals, walruses, whales, polar bears, foxes, owls, weasels, musk oxen and reindeer. The only people native to the Arctic are the Inuit. There are many minerals in the Arctic, including coal, oil and iron.

ARGENTINA

Argentina is the second-largest country in South America. It is a land of farms and ranches, and from these come many different products. Rice, sugar cane and other tropical crops are grown in the north of the country. Cattle and grain come from the central plains, or pampas. Grapes and other fruit are farmed in the west, and fruit and sheep in the cold, dry south.

Argentina was ruled by Spain from 1516 to 1810. In 1966, military leaders took control of the government. In 1982, Argentina and Britain fought a war over the ownership of the Falkland Islands.

See also PAGE 62.

ARISTOTLE (384-322BC)

Aristotle was a Greek philosopher who invented the method of thinking called logic. A student of Plato, Aristotle became tutor to Alexander the Great. His writings

Armour: *Plate armour, designed for medieval knights on horseback, could be very ornate.*

cover many subjects, including politics and nature.

ARMADILLO
This South American mammal looks rather like a small pig, but it is armoured like a tank. It is a timid animal and rolls itself into a ball when frightened. Armadillos eat worms, insects and roots. They use their strong claws to search for food and to dig out burrows.

ARMOUR
Before gunpowder was invented, soldiers fought in hand-to-hand combat. To protect their bodies, they wore armour. Leather made good, light armour and could be made stronger by adding plates of bronze or iron. The Greeks and Romans wore helmets, leg armour and breastplates.

Later armourers learned to link together tiny iron rings to produce coats of mail. Mail gave good protection against swords and spears, but steel plate was even stronger. Plate armour covered the whole of a man's body. But even steel armour was no defence against the cannon. By the 1600s soldiers needed to move more quickly, so they began wearing less armour.

ART
See PAINTING; SCULPTURE.

ASIA
Asia is the largest continent (44,387,000sq km). It stretches from the Arctic to the equator and from Japan in the east to the Middle East and Russia in the west. It contains 48 separate countries and its population of

3,472 million is over half the world's total population.

There are many different types of land and climate in Asia. In the north are evergreen forests, flat grasslands called steppes, and cold tundra plains. In central Asia are the world's highest mountains, including the Himalayas. Some of the world's longest rivers flow across the continent.

Almost all Asia's people live either in the fertile river valleys, or on the coastal plains. Most of them are farmers, scraping a living out of a small patch of land, but more and more people are going to live in the cities.

Rice is the chief crop of the warm, wet monsoon lands of southern Asia. Rice and fish are the main foods of many Asians. Other crops are tea, sugar, cotton, coffee and spices.

Asia has many valuable raw materials. The forests provide timber and rubber. There are minerals such as coal, iron, copper and tin. In the Middle East there is oil beneath the desert. The most important industrial country in Asia is Japan, which manufactures many products to sell in other countries. China, Korea and India are developing rapidly.

Asia has a long history of rich and powerful civilizations. The great religions of Christianity, Islam, Hinduism and Buddhism all began in Asia. Asian peoples reached high levels of progress in the arts and sciences long before the rest of the world.

European explorers came to Asia in the 1400s in search of riches and spices. They set up trading stations, and later founded colonies. Today all the countries of Asia are independent.

See also CHINA; COUNTRIES OF THE WORLD; INDIA; JAPAN; MIDDLE EAST.

ASTRONAUT

An astronaut is a person who travels in space. People had been dreaming of doing this for thousands of years, but it was only in April 1961 that the first person in space orbited the Earth. This was the Russian cosmonaut, Yuri Gagarin. In July 1969, the American, Neil Armstrong, was the first person to set foot on the Moon.

Travelling in space is one of the most exciting and dangerous things people have ever done. The astronauts have to be well trained before they can go. For example, they must learn to withstand the great force caused by the rocket thrust, and to eat, move and sleep in weightless conditions.

In space there is no air to breathe, so astronauts take a supply of air in their spacecraft. To walk in space they wear a spacesuit. This supplies them with

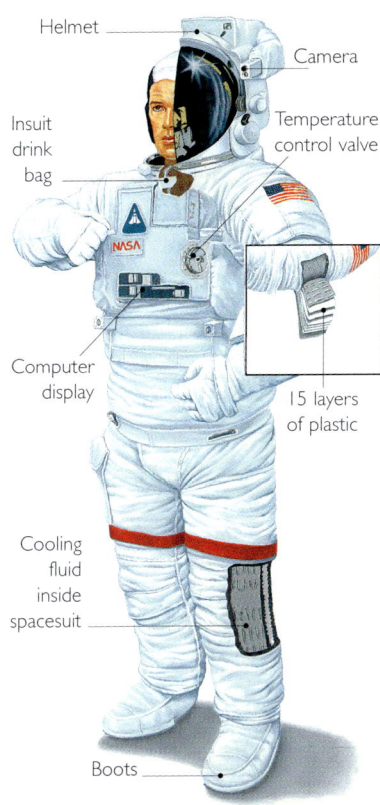

Astronaut: Many controls are built into an astronaut's spacesuit.

air and keeps their bodies at the right temperature.

See also GRAVITY; SPACE EXPLORATION.

ASTRONOMY

Astronomy is the study of the stars, planets and other objects in the universe. People first began to record what they observed in the sky in ancient times. They used these records to predict events such as eclipses. Later records of this sort were used to work out, check and correct calendars.

Astronomers now work with a variety of instruments in well-equipped observatories. Their most useful instrument is the telescope, which gathers and strengthens the feeble light reaching us from the stars. In recent years astronomers have learned much from information collected by spacecraft.

See also COMET; CONSTELLATION; COPERNICUS; GALILEO; METEOR; STAR; TELESCOPE; UNIVERSE.

ATHLETICS

The sport of athletics began with the exercises used to train men for battle. The ancient Greeks loved athletics, and at the Olympic Games young men competed with each other at running, wrestling and throwing.

The modern athlete must train hard to do well. In an athletics event today there are running, or track events; and jumping and throwing, or field events.

ATLANTIC OCEAN

Second only in size to the Pacific, the Atlantic Ocean covers an area of more than 80,000,000sq km and includes many gulfs and seas. Islands include Greenland,

Iceland, the British Isles, the West Indies, the Azores and the Falkland Islands. On the ocean floor are tall underwater mountains, including the Mid-Atlantic Ridge, a mountain chain running from Iceland almost to the tip of South America. Atlantic currents include the Gulf Stream, which warms northern Europe, and the Brazil Current.

ATOM

Every substance is made up of one or more chemical elements. Iron is an element. If you could cut a piece of iron into smaller and smaller pieces, eventually you would be left with tiny particles called atoms. They are the smallest particles of an element that can exist.

At the centre of the atom is a nucleus. This contains two kinds of particles, called protons and neutrons. The protons have a positive electric charge. Circling the nucleus are tiny particles, called electrons. These have a negative electric charge.

Every element is made of a different kind of atom. Atoms of different elements combine to form molecules of a new substance. Two atoms of hydrogen (H) combine with one atom of oxygen (O) to form one molecule of water. We can therefore represent water like this: H_2O.

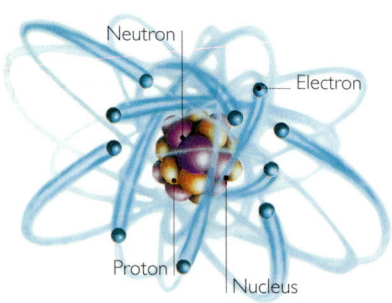

Atom: *An atom is held together by the electrical attraction between protons in the nucleus and electrons circling around the nucleus.*

AUSTRALIA

Australia is the largest island in the world and the smallest continent. Low mountains run all the way down the east coast. Most of the centre is grassy plain, and the western part consists of flat scrubland, barren, rolling hills and desert. About four-fifths of the continent is hot desert.

Along the northeastern coast is a chain of beautifully coloured coral reefs, islands and sandbanks called the Great Barrier Reef. Most people have settled in the southeast, where there is enough water available.

The seasons are the exact opposite of those in the Northern Hemisphere. When it is spring in Britain, it is autumn in Australia. Winters are mild and there is plenty of sunshine.

Although the Dutch discovered Australia in 1606, they did not settle it. Captain Cook claimed eastern Australia for Britain in 1770. In 1788, 800 convicts were landed in Botany Bay. These convicts became Australia's earliest colonists.

Australia is a farming country. It produces wool, dairy foods, meat, fruit and wheat to sell to the rest of the world. Australia mines valuable minerals, too. They include gold, silver, coal, lead, copper, tin and uranium.

It is also the home of many strange plants and animals, such as the platypus and emu, which are found nowhere else in the world. Many of the native animals are marsupials – animals that carry their young around in pouches until they are old enough to look after themselves. These include the kangaroo, koala and wombat.

See also ABORIGINES; KANGAROO; KOALA; PLATYPUS; PAGE 63.

AUSTRIA
See SWITZERLAND AND AUSTRIA.

AUTOMOBILE
See CAR.

AZTEC
The Aztecs were an ancient people who lived in Mexico. Their great city, Tenochtitlán, had huge temple pyramids. The city was built on an island in an area of many lakes, so people travelled about in boats. When the Spanish explorer Cortés entered Mexico in 1519, he was astonished to find such a civilization.

The Spaniards wanted the Aztecs' gold, of which they had a very large quantity. Although their army was small, the Spaniards had guns and horses, and were able to conquer the Aztecs easily.

Aztec: Aztec temples had a chamber at the top where the priests worshipped animal gods and made sacrifices.

B

Bach, Johann Sebastian
(1685-1750)
J. S. Bach is the most famous of a great family of German composers and musicians. He was master of the organ and composed hundreds of pieces of music, including many choral works.

Bacteria
Bacteria are among the smallest living things. Each one is made up of just a single cell, and can be seen only under a microscope. There are millions of bacteria all around us.

Some bacteria feed on dead creatures and waste, causing them to decay. They make the soil rich and help plants grow. Bacteria also turn meat rotten and milk sour; some cause disease.

Badger
The badger is a relative of the weasel. It is a very powerfully built animal with short legs and a black and white striped head.

Badgers dig deep burrows called setts, and emerge from them after dark to find food. They will fight fiercely if attacked but, left alone, they are peaceful animals.

Ballet
See Dance.

Balloons and Airships
Balloons and airships use gases such as helium, hydrogen and hot air to fly. These gases are lighter than air. While balloons can only drift in the wind, airships can be flown with precision.

The first balloon to carry people was built by the Montgolfier brothers in 1783. A fire was built beneath an open-ended bag, filling it with hot air.

Today balloons are used by

Badger: These woodland animals feed on a mixture of plants, insects and small mammals.

BAROMETER

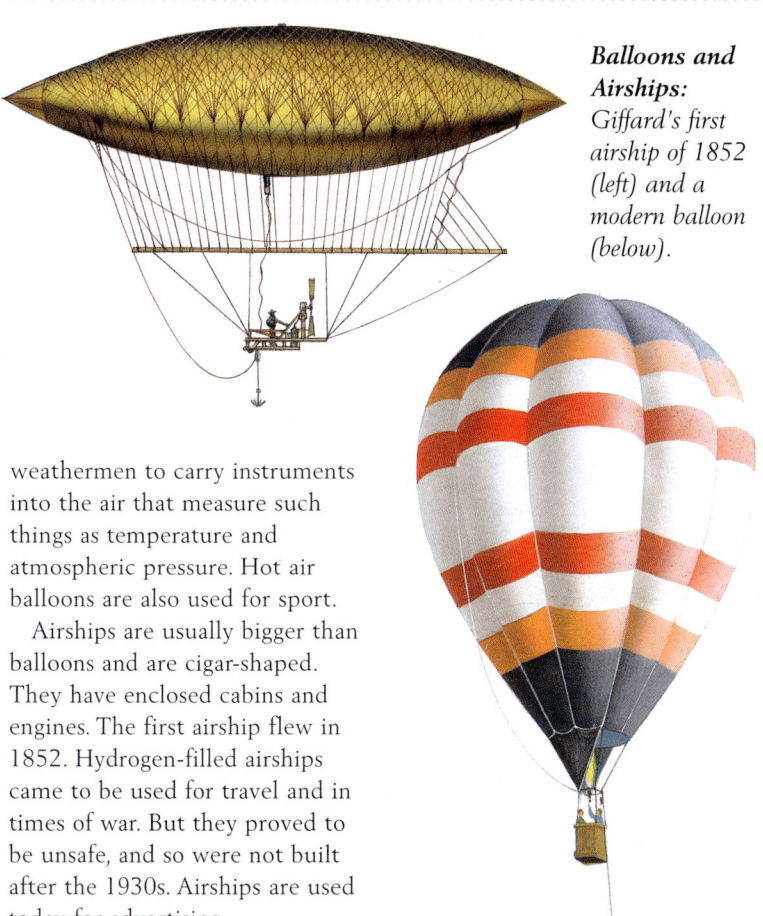

Balloons and Airships: *Giffard's first airship of 1852 (left) and a modern balloon (below).*

weathermen to carry instruments into the air that measure such things as temperature and atmospheric pressure. Hot air balloons are also used for sport.

Airships are usually bigger than balloons and are cigar-shaped. They have enclosed cabins and engines. The first airship flew in 1852. Hydrogen-filled airships came to be used for travel and in times of war. But they proved to be unsafe, and so were not built after the 1930s. Airships are used today for advertising.

BAROMETER

A barometer is an instrument used to measure air pressure. It can help forecast the weather and measure height above sea-level.

There are two major types of barometer: the mercury and the aneroid. The aneroid barometer is the more commonly used. It consists of a drum from which most of the air has been removed. When the air pressure outside the drum changes, the size of the drum changes. This change in size is recorded on a scale.

Generally speaking, if a barometer shows high pressure, it means good weather.

Baseball

Baseball is the American national sport. It may have come from an English game called rounders. Two teams of nine players each take turns to bat the ball and score runs around the baseball diamond. The national championships are decided in the World Series, held each October.

Basketball

Basketball is played on a court by two teams of five players each. Points are made by throwing a ball through a basket. Each

Baseball: The hard leather ball is hit with a cylindrical bat.

'basket' counts as two points. Free throws, for fouls, count as one point. It helps to be tall in this game.

Bat

Bats are the only mammals that can fly. Their large wings consist of thin skin stretched between the fingers of the forelimb and the hindlimb. They sleep by day, hanging upside down in caves or other dark places.
Insect-eating bats cannot see well. Yet they can fly in the dark without bumping into obstacles.

Bat: Bats unfold their powerful wings in order to fly. Their large ears help them pick up echoes from obstacles.

To do this they send out very high-pitched squeaks and listen for the echo that bounces off the things around them.

The vampire bat of South America feeds on the blood of other animals. The largest bats are fruit-eaters.

Bear

Although bears may look cuddly and playful, they are dangerous animals. They are very strong and have sharp claws. Although some bears can be tamed, they may still attack without warning.

Bears live mainly in forests and mountains. They are meat-eaters, but they also eat most kinds of plants and fish. Some bears hibernate (sleep) during the winter, living on fat stored in their bodies.

There are several different kinds of bears. The largest – the grizzly, the Kodiak and the polar – are from North America. The polar bear also lives in northern Europe. The sun bear, from Asia, is the smallest.

Beaver

These rodents have stout bodies and short legs. Their webbed feet and paddle-like tails make them good swimmers. They can stay under water for several minutes.

Beavers live in family groups. They make a home safe from enemies by damming streams and small rivers with branches, stones and mud. In the pool formed behind the dam, the beavers build their lodge, a dome-shaped den of mud and sticks with an underwater entrance.

Bees and Wasps

Bees are very useful insects. They make honey and wax. More importantly, by pollinating plants bees help them to produce seeds.

Some types of bees are solitary. Others, such as the bumblebee and the honeybee, are social insects and live in large colonies. Social insects build a nest or hive. In every beehive there are many worker bees, a few male drones and a queen.

Bees and Wasps: *Bees use the honeycomb cells inside the hive to store food and house larvae.*

Bees and Wasps: *Worker bees collect pollen in sacs on their legs.*

After mating with a drone, the queen bee begins to lay thousands of eggs. The workers are small female bees. They build the wax cells of the comb and gather nectar and pollen from flowers to store inside. Workers also feed the queen and the larvae and guard the hive. Drones do no work and in the autumn they are driven from the hive to die.

Wasps are related to bees, and are hunting insects. Social wasps, like social bees, live in colonies with a queen, drones and workers. Adult wasps eat nectar, but the larvae are fed on insects and caterpillars. In the autumn all the wasps die, except for the young queens. They hibernate through the winter and start new nests in the spring. Solitary wasps live alone and build small nests.

See also INSECT.

BEETHOVEN, LUDWIG VAN (1770-1827)

Beethoven was a German composer who wrote some of the world's greatest music. He began writing music while a boy. In later life he went deaf, but still continued to write music.

See also MUSIC.

BELGIUM

See NETHERLANDS, BELGIUM AND LUXEMBOURG.

BELL, ALEXANDER GRAHAM (1847-1922)

This Scottish-born teacher of the deaf is best remembered as the inventor of the telephone. On March 10, 1876, Bell spoke the

Bell: Bell's telephone used weak electric charges travelling down a wire to transmit sounds.

historic first message over the telephone to his assistant: 'Mr Watson, come here; I want you.'

BIBLE

The Bible is in two parts – the Old and New Testaments. It was written at different times and by different people, but most of it is thousands of years old.

The Old Testament is held sacred by Jews and Christians. It tells the stories of the Jewish people, their kings and prophets. The New Testament is sacred only to Christians. It contains the four gospels of Matthew, Mark, Luke and John. Gospel means 'good news'. Each of these 'evangelists' tells the story of Jesus's life: his birth in Bethlehem, his teaching, his death on the cross and his resurrection. See also CHRISTIANITY; JESUS CHRIST.

BICYCLE

The first bicycle was built in about 1790 by a Frenchman named De Sivrac. Early bicycles were steered by the front wheel and propelled by the rider pushing his feet on the ground. Later bicycles had pedals to propel them. The famous penny farthing bicycle had the pedals attached to its huge front wheel. More and more improvements were made until, by the end of the 1800s, bicycles resembled today's models.

The modern bicycle is propelled by pedals attached to cranks. The

Bicycle: A modern touring bicycle (above) and a penny farthing from the 1880s (right).

BIOLOGY

Bird: *Birds' feathers are their most important asset, being used for temperature control, flying and courtship displays. Their beaks are adapted to the way they feed, acting as seed-pickers, tubes, drills or nutcrackers.*

cranks turn a toothed wheel which turns a chain which drives the rear wheel.

BIOLOGY

Biology is the study of living things – their structure, their development and their relationship to other living things. Within the wide field of biology are many specialized sciences, such as botany (the study of plants), zoology (the study of animals), cytology (the study of cells), genetics (the study of heredity), anatomy (the study of the structures of plants and animals), bacteriology (the study of bacteria), and palaeontology (the study of fossils). Ecologists study the relationship of plants and animals to their environments.

In recent years, space biology has been added to the list. Scientists in this field study what happens to living things when they are taken into space.

Bird

All birds have wings, though some cannot fly. They have feathers, and beaks instead of jaws.

Most birds are perfectly built for flight. Their bones are hollow, light but strong. Their wing muscles are powerful. Their feathers help them fly, and also keep them warm and dry.

Birds rely mostly on eyesight to find food, but their taste and hearing are also good. They are born with the skills they need. Much of their behaviour is not learned but comes from instinct.

Birds reproduce by laying eggs. In order to hatch, the eggs must be kept warm, so parent birds sit on them. When the young hatch, they are helpless and must be fed.

See also EAGLE; HUMMINGBIRD; KIWI; OWL; PENGUIN.

Bison

Bison are wild cattle. They are large, powerful animals with humped shoulders, thick fur and short horns.

The North American bison is sometimes called the buffalo. Vast herds provided food for the Native

Bison: *The North American bison is a protected species.*

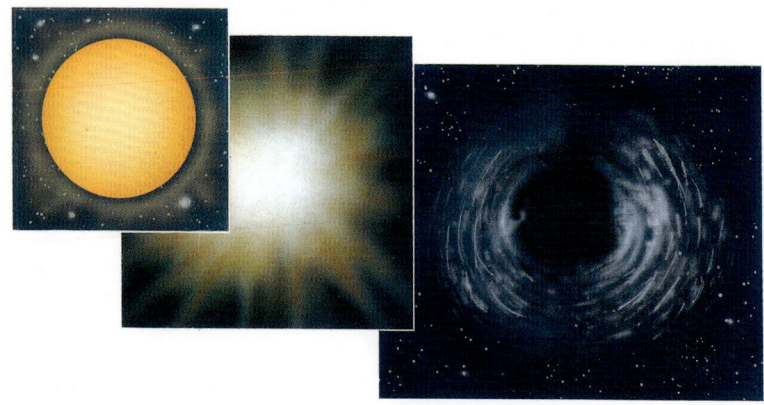

Americans, but European settlers killed so many that the animal nearly died out. The European bison, or wisent, is also rare.

BLACK HOLE

When a star begins to lose its ability to produce energy, it begins a slow process of collapsing in on itself. If the collapsing star is very big it explodes powerfully, and the remaining atoms become very densely packed together as it collapses. The electrons and protons in the atoms combine to become neutrons, and the star is called a neutron star.

If even the neutrons are crushed by gravity, the gravitational force created at the centre is so strong that everything in its gravitational field is drawn in. It is called a black hole because even light cannot escape.

See also STAR.

Black hole: *At the end of its life a massive star explodes (centre) and then collapses. The resulting gravitational pull draws in everything around, even light(right).*

BLÉRIOT, LOUIS (1872-1936)

Blériot, a Frenchman, was one of the great pilots in the history of flying. In 1909 the *Daily Mail* newspaper offered a prize to the first person to fly the English Channel. Blériot accepted this challenge and flew the 40km from Calais to Dover in 37 minutes. He continued to design and later to manufacture aeroplanes.

BLOOD

Blood is made up of red and white cells, and platelets, which all float in a watery liquid called plasma. Blood is pumped around the body by the heart. There are about five litres in an average adult.

Blood serves several important functions. Its main purpose is to carry substances around the body. It takes oxygen from the lungs and nutrients from the intestines and distributes them to body cells. It takes waste products from the cells to the lungs and kidneys. Blood also carries heat around the body from the muscles where most of it is produced.

Finally, blood protects the body. The platelets help the blood to clot when the skin is wounded. The white cells fight infection by attacking germs, and can produce substances to counteract poisons produced by the germs.

See also HEART.

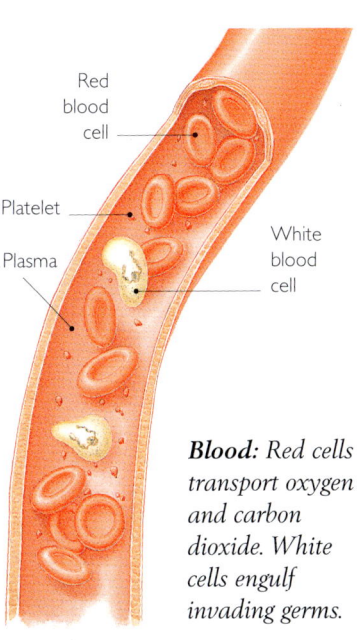

Blood: *Red cells transport oxygen and carbon dioxide. White cells engulf invading germs.*

BOADICEA
(DIED AD60)
Boadicea (or Boudicca) was queen of the Iceni tribe during the Roman occupation of Britain. When the Romans seized Iceni property and ill-treated them, Boadicea and the Iceni rebelled. Many Britons joined them. When they were finally defeated, Boadicea poisoned herself.

BOLÍVAR, SIMÓN (1783-1830)
When Bolívar was born, most of South America was ruled by Spain. 'The Liberator', as he is often known, led the fight for freedom. He headed the armies that drove the Spanish from the northern part of the continent, winning a great victory at the Battle of Boyacá in 1819. Later he helped to drive the Spanish from Peru. At the time he was the most powerful man in South America. The present-day country of Bolivia was named after him.

BONE
Bones make up the framework or skeleton of all vertebrates (animals with backbones). They are very strong. Two-thirds of a bone is mineral, which makes it hard. One-third is animal matter, which makes it difficult to break.

Bones have several functions. They protect important organs such as the brain, heart and lungs, and support the limbs. Some bones are hollow and filled with a red substance called marrow. Marrow makes the red and white cells of the blood.

All bones have names, such as scapula (shoulder blade), patella (knee cap) and skull. There are 206 bones in the human body.

BOOKS

Books are one of the most important inventions. All that we know, and all the ideas, thoughts, beliefs and literature of the past can be found in books. We use them to learn from, for amusement and for inspiration.

The earliest-known books were written by the Egyptians in about 2500BC. They were written on paper made from reeds and were rolled up to form a scroll. The Romans were the first to make modern-looking books. They were inscribed by hand on parchment or vellum made from animal skin.

In 1439, when Johannes Gutenberg invented his printing machine, movable type began to be used and more than one book could be printed at a time.

See also GUTENBERG; PAPER.

BOXING

Boxing is the ancient sport of fighting with the fists. Today the boxers wear gloves, and the matches are divided into three-minute rounds. Boxers are classed by weight. They follow rules set out by the English Marquis of Queensberry in 1872.

BRAHMS, JOHANNES (1833-1897)

This great German composer wrote songs, dances, concertos and symphonies. His *German Requiem* is one of the world's great works for chorus and orchestra. Brahms was a lifelong friend of Robert Schumann, the romantic composer.

BRAILLE

Braille is a form of writing used by blind people. A braille book has raised dots on its page instead of printed letters. By touching the dots with their fingertips, blind people can read. They can also type in braille, using a machine that stamps out the dots through the paper. The braille alphabet was invented by a Frenchman called Louis Braille. He lived from 1809 to 1852, and was blind from the age of three.

BRAIN

The brain and its extension, the spinal cord, are called the central nervous system.

The brain is divided into several different parts, each with its own job. One part, the medulla oblongata, controls breathing, heart-rate and digestion, all of

A	B	C	D	E
F	G	H	I	J
K	L	M	N	O
P	Q	R	S	T
U	V	W	X	Y
Z	and	for	of	the
with	fraction	numeral	poetry	apostrophe
hyphen	dash	comma	semicolon	colon

Braille: *Patterns of raised dots represent letters and can be arranged into words and sentences.*

which you do without thinking. The hypothalamus controls the body's temperature and governs involuntary drives such as hunger and thirst. The cerebellum controls muscular coordination and balance.

The largest part of the brain is the cerebral cortex. Different parts of the body are linked to different areas of the cortex. The senses – sight, hearing and touch –

Brain: *The cerebral cortex fills most of the skull. Activities such as vision, hearing and movement have specific areas within it. It also deals with personality and intelligence.*

– have their own areas, as do memory, thought, movement and language.

The spinal cord receives messages from the nerves and carries them to the brain. It also carries messages from the brain to the nerves in all parts of the body to make them work.

BRAZIL

This is the largest country in South America. It covers 8,511,000sq km. The equator crosses the north of Brazil. Just south of the equator the mighty river Amazon flows from the Andes to the Atlantic.

The Amazon valley is a vast area of tropical plants and animals.

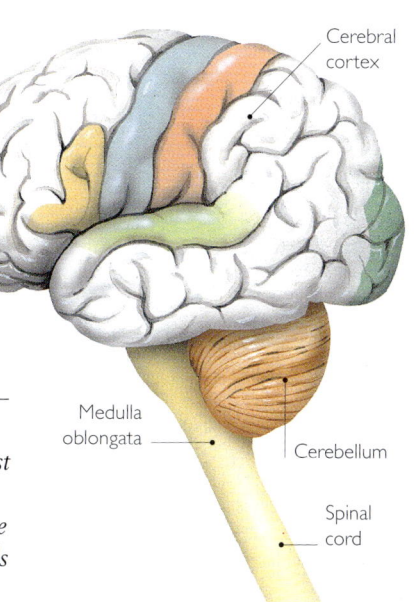

Today many of the trees are being cut down, destroying this important natural area.

Most of Brazil's 161,790,000 people live in cities. It is the world's largest producer of coffee. Beef, cocoa, maize, sugar cane and tobacco are also produced. Oil has been discovered and there are many industries.

The Portuguese ruled Brazil from 1500 to 1825. It became a republic in 1889.

See also PAGE 62.

BREATHING

All animals breathe. They need oxygen from the air in order to burn the food they eat and make energy from it.

Humans breathe through lungs. Lungs are spongy bags inside the body that fill with air when we breathe in. Oxygen from the air goes into the blood, and we breathe out carbon dioxide.

Fishes breathe through gills, which trap the oxygen dissolved in water. Insects breathe through tiny holes in the hard outer casing of their bodies.

BRIDGE

There are three basic types of bridge – girder, arch and suspension. These types can be combined in many ways and can be made of wood, stone, bricks, iron, concrete or steel.

The kind of bridge used for a site depends upon three factors: the hardness of the ground, the width and depth of the valley or river to be spanned, and the weight to be carried.

The Romans built marvellous arch bridges, some of which still stand. Coalbrookdale, the first iron bridge, is an arch bridge. It was built in Britain in 1779.

The first major suspension bridge was the Menai Bridge in North Wales, built by Thomas Telford in 1826. The suspension bridge with the longest span is the Akashi-Kaikyo bridge between the Honshu and Awaji islands in Japan.

BRITISH ISLES

There are about 5,000 islands in the British Isles, the largest of which are Great Britain and Ireland. Great Britain consists of England, Scotland and Wales, which together form the United Kingdom. Northern Ireland is also governed by the United Kingdom, but most of Ireland is an independent republic. The climate of the British Isles is mild, with heavier rainfall in the west.

The UK has natural resources of oil and gas, which lie beneath the North Sea. The North of England, Scotland and South Wales have traditionally been home to heavy industries such as mining and ship-building. These are gradually being replaced by newer ones such as the electronics, food processing and chemical industries. Many people work in service industries such as education, healthcare and tourism. Much of the countryside in the UK is intensively farmed.

Many people in the Republic of Ireland also work in the service industries or in manufacturing industries. Farming is vital to the economy, with exports including butter, cheese and other dairy products, natural fibres, whiskey and beer.

England was conquered by the Romans and later by the Normans. It conquered Wales in the 1200s. England and Scotland have had the same monarch from 1603 and the same parliament from 1707. Ireland joined the union in 1801, but southern Ireland broke away in 1921.

BRONZE AGE

The Bronze Age followed the Stone Age. During this time, people used bronze instead of stone, flint, wood and bone for their weapons and tools.

Bronze is a mixture of copper and tin. It can be hammered into many shapes to make weapons, tools and jewellery. It was used by the great early civilizations in the Middle East and Egypt. The Bronze Age lasted in Britain from 2500BC until about 500BC.

BUDDHA AND BUDDHISM

Buddhism is one of the world's great religions. Its founder was Gautama, who lived from 563BC to 483BC. He was rich, yet he was sad for he knew the world was full of suffering. So he gave away his riches, and spent many years trying to find the answer to the world's unhappiness. He taught

Bronze Age: Bronze Age metal-workers hammered out complex patterns on their pots.

Buddha and Buddhism: *Buddha in a characteristic pose, with legs folded. His restful expression reflects a state of peace.*

that there are eight 'paths' to nirvana, or perfect peace. For this he was called Buddha, meaning 'Enlightened One', and today millions of Buddhists around the world follow his teachings.

Buffalo

Buffalo are wild cattle of Africa and Asia. There are several kinds. The Indian water buffalo likes muddy swamps. It is a useful working animal, and gives meat and milk. The African or Cape buffalo cannot be tamed. It has massive horns and can be dangerous.

Bulb

Plants make their own food, and some are able to store this food in special leaves, called bulbs.

An onion is a bulb. If you cut one open, you can see the closely packed layers of leaves. Daffodils, tulips and hyacinths also have bulbs. In spring they use food from the bulb to make new leaves.

Butterflies and Moths

Butterflies are among the most beautiful insects. They fly by day and their scaly wings are often brilliantly coloured. Most moths are less colourful. Moths usually fly at dusk. Butterflies and moths belong to the same family. Moths have hairier bodies, and they fold their wings flat when resting, whereas butterflies hold their wings upright.

Female butterflies and moths lay eggs, which hatch into larvae, called caterpillars. Caterpillars eat almost non-stop and grow by shedding their skins. Some, like that of the cabbage butterfly, are harmful to crops. Others, like the silkworm, are useful.

When the caterpillar is fully grown, it stops eating. It fastens

Butterflies and Moths: *Butterflies are identified by their wonderfully patterned wings. In many species, the adults live only a few weeks.*

Painted Lady (flying)

Painted Lady (resting)

Small Tortoiseshell (resting)

Small Tortoiseshell (flying)

itself to a leaf or twig and becomes a chrysalis. Inside the hard case of the chrysalis the caterpillar changes its shape. Soon the chrysalis splits and out crawls the adult insect. As soon as its wings are dry, it flies away.

BYZANTINE EMPIRE

In AD330 the Roman Emperor Constantine made the city of Byzantium the capital of the Roman Empire. He renamed it Constantinople. It later became the centre of the rich and powerful Byzantine Empire.

This empire became the storehouse of Greek learning and Roman law because it was not plundered by barbarians, as Rome was after AD476. It was here, also, that the Greek Orthodox Church was formed.

The empire finally fell to the Turks in 1453.

Camberwell Beauty

C

CAESAR,
JULIUS (100-44BC)

Julius Caesar was a Roman soldier, writer and statesman. He was also a brilliant general. He conquered Gaul – what is today France, the Netherlands and Germany – and in 55BC he successfully invaded Britain. He wrote a book about his military experiences.

He brought his army back to Italy in 49BC. After three years of civil war, he captured Rome and was declared dictator in 46BC. Caesar had many enemies. They thought he would make himself emperor, and assassinated him on the Ides (15th) of March, 44BC.

See also ROME, ANCIENT.

CALCULATOR

Calculators are machines that help you to solve mathematical problems. One of the first calculators was the abacus, which was used in the Middle East over 5000 years ago. Today most calculators are electronic and work very fast indeed.

See also COMPUTER.

CALENDAR

A calendar is a way of dividing up the year into months, weeks and days. Practically everyone in the world uses the same kind of calendar. The Romans worked out our present calendar nearly 2000 years ago. They based it on the movements of the Earth around the Sun, and the Moon around the Earth. In 1582, Pope Gregory XIII made some minor changes to the Roman calendar. This calendar, called the Gregorian calendar, is used today.

CAMEL

For thousands of years this strange-looking animal has been used to carry people and their goods. The camel is well adapted

Camel: *The camel can withstand extremes of heat and cold, and can survive on salty vegetation.*

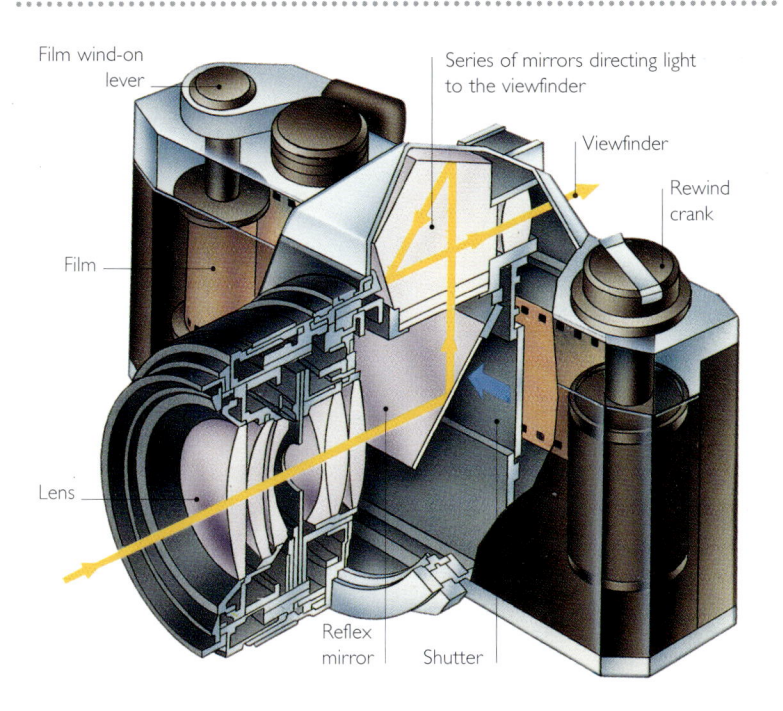

Labels on diagram:
- Film wind-on lever
- Series of mirrors directing light to the viewfinder
- Viewfinder
- Rewind crank
- Film
- Lens
- Reflex mirror
- Shutter

to desert life. It stores fat in its hump and can go for days without water. Its wide, padded feet do not sink into the sand.

The Bactrian camel from Asia has two humps. It can live in quite cold regions. The Arabian camel has only one hump.

CAMERA

A camera is a light-tight box with a window, or lens, at the front. When you take a picture, a shutter moves aside and lets light from the object you are photographing pass through to the back of the camera, where it falls

Camera: In a single-lens reflex camera, a mirror directs light entering the lens up to the viewfinder, allowing the image through the lens to be seen. When the shutter button is pressed, the mirror swings out of the way to allow light to reach the film.

on a strip of light-sensitive film, forming an image of the object.

When the film is treated with certain chemicals, or developed, the image shows up. The developed film is called a negative. The process of printing changes the negative image into a

37

positive picture on specially coated paper. The result is a photograph. It may be in black and white or in colour, depending on the type of film used.

To take a clear photo, the right amount of light must hit the film, and the lens must be focused on the subject. Some cameras make these adjustments automatically. Others have controls to allow you to do it more accurately yourself.

Cassettes and cartridges record moving images. Videocassettes carry reels of tape that record both sound and pictures. A film cartridge is similar to a cassette but contains photographic film. The cartridge slots into a camera and, when exposed, is removed without any manual re-winding.

CAMOUFLAGE

Many animals are coloured or shaped to match their background. We call this camouflage. Camouflage makes an animal difficult to see, and so protects it from enemies.

Spots or stripes help to hide an animal by breaking up the outline of its body. The zebra's stripes blend with the long grass on which it grazes. The leopard's spots conceal it among the sun-dappled leaves of a tree.

Most fishes have dark backs and light undersides. This makes them harder to see from above and from below. Some animals trick

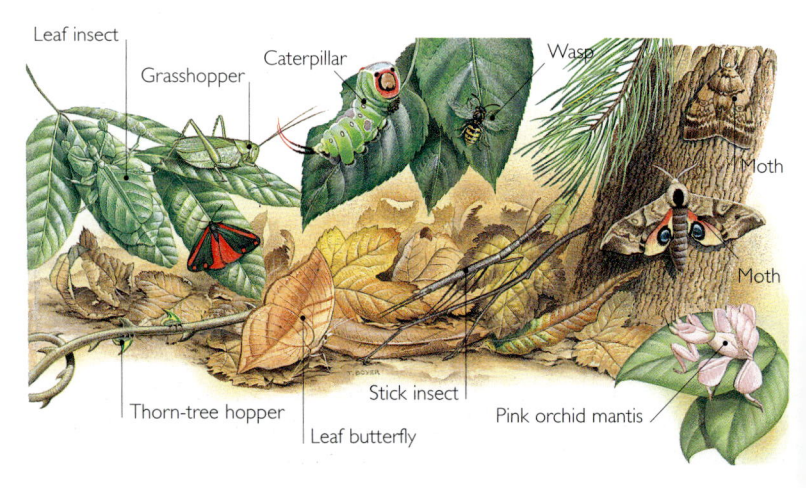

Camouflage: Many insects mimic a feature of their surroundings, or another insect. Some look like leaves; stick insects look like twigs. Some flies look like stinging wasps, and some moths have an off-putting pattern on their wings.

Leaf insect
Grasshopper
Caterpillar
Wasp
Moth
Moth
Thorn-tree hopper
Stick insect
Leaf butterfly
Pink orchid mantis

their enemies by looking like something else. This ability is called mimicry.

Many insects and reptiles are so well camouflaged that it is hard to spot them until they move.

CANADA

Canada is a massive country. It covers the northern part of North America, stretching from the Atlantic Ocean in the east to the Pacific in the west and to the Arctic Ocean in the north. Altogether, it has an area of 9,976,130sq km. Yet the population is very low – about 29 million people – and most of the country is empty.

Canada is a land of high mountains, thick forests and vast plains. It has so many large lakes and rivers that more than 7 per cent of its area is made up of fresh water.

Because of its size Canada has a variety of climates. The west coast has cool summers and mild, wet winters. On the plains and in the east, the summers are hot and the winters cold. The north has short, cool summers and cold winters.

The land is very rich. The plains produce wheat and dairy products and timber comes from the forests. There are many minerals, such as coal, oil, natural gas, gold and uranium. The rivers provide hydroelectricity.

Canada is divided into ten provinces and two territories. Each has its own government. The federal (central) government in the capital, Ottawa, makes laws for all Canada. Canada is a member of the Commonwealth of Nations.

See also PAGE 62.

CANAL

Canals are man-made rivers. Some are built to carry cargo boats, barges and ships. Others provide water for irrigating the land. In some low-lying countries, canals drain the land. In Venice, in Italy, canals form the 'roads' of the city.

Some canals were built a very long time ago. Parts of the Grand Canal in China are over 2,000 years old.

Today, the most important canals are the ship canals of Suez, Panama and the St Lawrence.

CANCER

Cancer is a dangerous disease that occurs through the uncontrolled growth of body cells. After heart disease, it is the leading cause of death in the world today.

Scientists everywhere are trying to find a cure for cancer. Many lives have been saved by educating people to spot cancer symptoms at an early stage, and through treatment by surgery, radiation and drugs.

CAR

Two German engineers, Karl Benz and Gottlieb Daimler, built the first cars in 1885 and 1886. These had a petrol engine, like most modern cars. Later, some cars were built with steam engines; others were driven by electricity from batteries. In the end, the petrol engine proved to be the most successful.

At first, cars were hand-made and expensive. It was not until 1908 that they began to be made cheaply. In that year Henry Ford started to mass produce his Model T, called the 'Tin Lizzie'. It marked the beginning of the modern car industry, which now produces over 25 million cars a year throughout the world.

A modern car is a collection of 10,000 or more separate parts. These parts make up several basic units: the body, the engine and the transmission are the main units. The transmission carries power from the engine to the driving wheels. The other units are the steering, the braking and the suspension.

See also FORD, HENRY.

CARBON

Carbon is one of the chemical elements. All living things contain carbon. If you hold a plate above a candle flame, a black deposit of carbon forms on it. Both charcoal and coke are forms of carbon. The 'lead' in pencils and diamonds are natural forms of carbon.

CARIBBEAN

The islands known as the West Indies lie between the Caribbean Sea and the Atlantic Ocean. The many islands are divided into more than 20 countries. The largest are Cuba, Jamaica, Haiti and the Dominican Republic.

Most of the islands have a tropical climate and people grow sugar, tobacco, cocoa, coffee, coconuts, bananas and other fruits. There is not much industry but iron ore, bauxite and asphalt are mined. Many islands have a busy tourist industry.

The West Indies were discovered in 1492 by Christopher Columbus. Spain conquered the islands in the 1500s and later the British, French and Dutch set up colonies there. African slaves were brought to work on plantations. Today most islands run their own affairs. Most West Indians speak English, French or Spanish.

See also PAGES 62-63.

CASTLE

Hundreds of years ago a castle was the safest place in time of war. The earliest castles were wooden forts. They were built on hilltops and surrounded by banks of earth

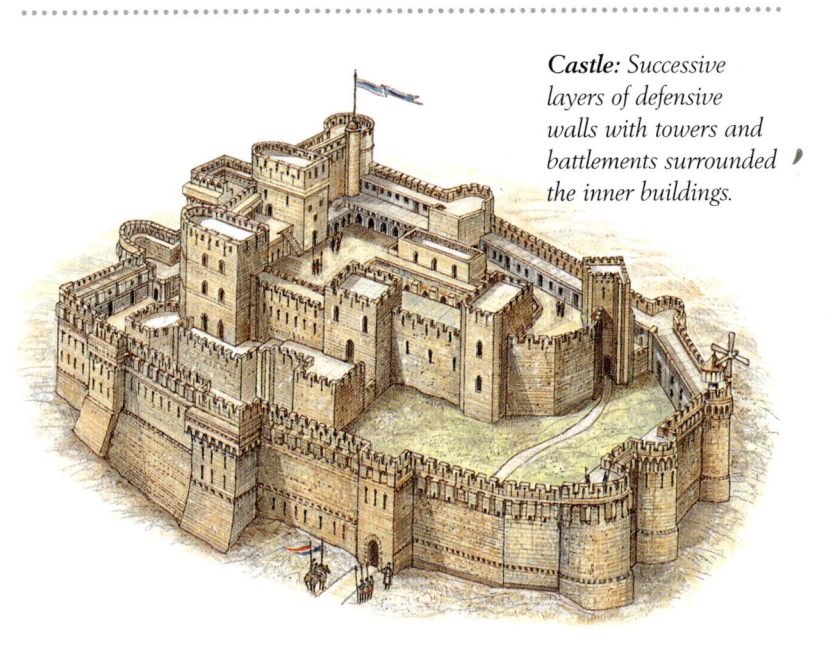

Castle: *Successive layers of defensive walls with towers and battlements surrounded the inner buildings.*

and ditches. Inside there was room for the local people and their animals to take shelter.

In the Middle Ages castles were built of stone. The outer walls were high and thick. There were towers along the walls, with slits through which archers could fire arrows. Around the walls was a ditch, or moat, filled with water. In the centre of the castle was a massive tower called a keep. Inside the keep, or in a separate building, was a great hall where the nobleman and his family lived, and a chapel. Elsewhere in the castle were kitchens, storerooms, barracks for soldiers, stables for animals and a well.

It was difficult to capture a castle once the defenders had pulled up the drawbridge over the moat. Inside, they stored enough food and water to last for weeks. From the shelter of the castle walls they could shoot at the attackers, or drop boulders and boiling oil on top of them.

When an army laid siege to a castle, they surrounded the castle walls. If they failed to force their way in, they would try to starve the occupants out.

Although they must have been cold and damp to live in, castles were good strongholds until cannons were invented. Cannon balls easily smashed stone walls.

CAT

A fluffy, playful kitten does not look very fierce. But it is a close relative of the mighty tiger. All cats are flesh-eating mammals. They hunt by stealth, usually alone. They move soundlessly because their claws retract into soft pads on their feet. They can see well, even at night, and they have a keen sense of smell.

Domestic cats are descended from the African wild cat. The cat was sacred to the ancient Egyptians. In Europe, cats did not become common mousehunters until the 1700s.

There are many kinds, or species, of cats, and they make good pets. They are independent animals, however, and can go back to living in the wild quite easily.

Abyssinian

Red Point Siamese

Cat: Although there are many different breeds of cat, they do not vary very much from one another in overall shape and size. The main differences between breeds are largely those of coat length, colour and texture.

Maine Coon Cat

CAT

Cats can breed twice a year. The female usually gives birth to a litter of five or six kittens each time. The young of the big cats, such as lions and tigers, are called cubs. All cats, even well-fed pets, are hunters, and the big cats are the fiercest hunters of all.

Spotted Short-hair

Cornish Rex

Peke-faced Persian

CATHEDRAL
See CHURCH.

CATTLE
Cattle is the term applied to animals such as buffalo, bison and yaks, and bulls, oxen and cows.

Cattle are kept to supply milk, meat and hides. In many parts of Asia and Africa, they are also used to carry loads and pull carts.

People have kept cattle since ancient times. Pictures of them appear in Egyptian tomb drawings and reliefs.

CAVE
Caves are found in the sides of hills and cliffs. They are hollowed out of the rock by the sea or by underground streams.

Some caves were used by early people as dwelling places and often contain relics and fossils.

See also STALACTITE AND STALAGMITE.

CELL
All living things are made up of cells. Most cells can only be seen under a microscope.

The animal called an amoeba has only one cell. The human body, on the other hand, has millions of cells, each with a job to do.

The centre of a cell is the nucleus; around the nucleus is a blob of jelly called protoplasm.

Cave: *Many cave systems occur in layered rock. People enter them via vertical cavities called potholes.*

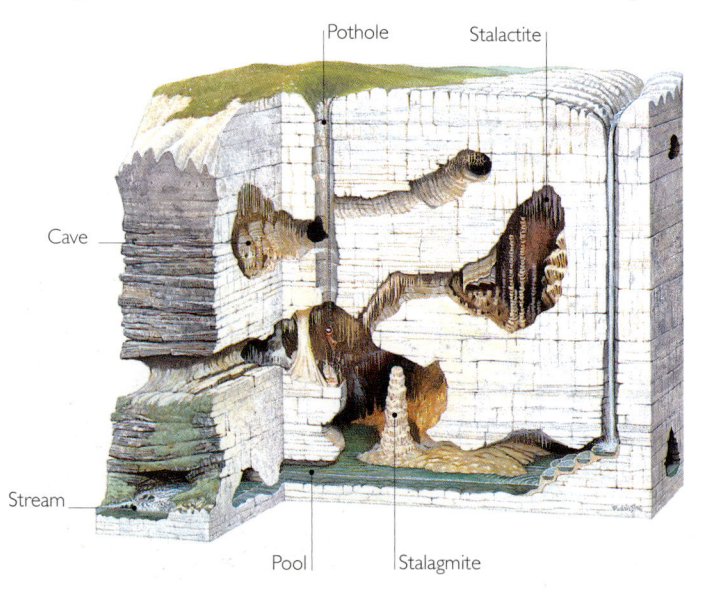

Cell wall

Protoplasm

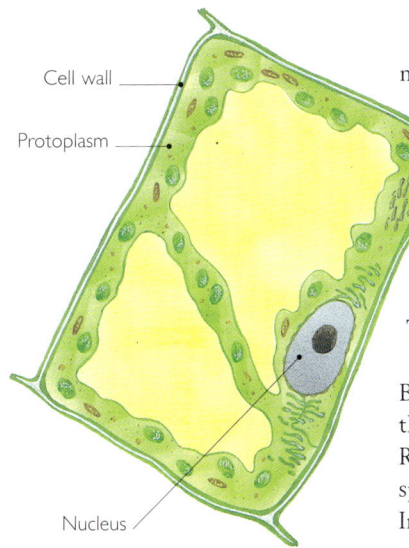

Nucleus

Cell: The nucleus is surrounded by a gel-like substance where particles store and transform proteins and dispose of waste.

Cells join together to make tissues – the materials from which our bodies are built. Different cells build skin, bone, blood, nerves, muscles and glands. Cells reproduce by dividing. In this way, worn out cells are replaced by new cells as we grow. Plants are also made up of cells.

CELTS

When we speak of Celts, we are really talking about people who speak Celtic languages. They are not all alike physically.

The ancient Celts lived in northwestern Europe. They had loosely organized tribes made up of a chief, nobles, free men and slaves. They were very warlike and fought among themselves. They were good metal-workers and gifted musicians and poets. Their religion was Druidism.

Celts may have arrived in Britain as early as 600BC. Later they were conquered by the Romans. Today the largest Celtic-speaking groups are found in Ireland, Scotland and Wales.

CENTRAL AMERICA

Central America forms a bridge between North and South America. It consists of the independent republics of Costa

Celts: The Celts were skilled craftsmen, and their work often used animal forms.

Rica, El Salvador, Guatemala, Honduras, Panama, Nicaragua and Belize. It was created millions of years ago by volcanic activity and its landscape ranges from desert to rainforests, swamps and beaches.

Most people in Central America are *mestizos*, a mixture of Spanish and Native American. Spanish is the main language, but English and Native American are also spoken. Tropical crops, such as sugar, bananas, cotton and coffee, are the main produce.

CEREALS

Cereals are important food crops. They belong to the grass family. The fruit or seed of the plant is

***Cereals:** The different types of cereals are all high in nourishment.*

called a grain. In tropical lands the most important cereals are rice, maize and millet. In cooler climates the chief cereals are wheat, oats, barley and rye.

Rice is the main food for over half the people in the world. It grows in warm and wet climates and needs plenty of water.

Much of the world's wheat is grown on the plains of Canada, the USA, Australia and Russia. The grain is ground into flour and used to make bread, pasta and breakfast foods.

CHARLEMAGNE (742-814)

The name Charlemagne means Charles the Great. He was king of a people called the Franks and he conquered and ruled a huge empire in Europe. This Christian

Rice   Wheat   Rye   Oats   Barley

empire was the greatest since the time of Rome, and became known as the Holy Roman Empire.

Charlemagne and his warriors fought against many enemies, including the Moors in Spain. As well as being a great soldier, Charlemagne also built schools and libraries. Scholars from all over Europe came to his court.

CHAUCER, GEOFFREY
(*c*.1342-1400)
Chaucer was a great English poet whose most famous work is *The Canterbury Tales*. He was the first important author to write in English rather than Latin.

The Canterbury Tales is a collection of stories told by an imaginary group of people on a pilgrimage to the tomb of St Thomas à Becket at Canterbury.

CHEESE
Cheese is made from the solid part, or curd, of sour milk. Bacteria are added to milk to make it sour, and the curd is separated from the watery part, or whey. The curd is then heated, pressed, and allowed to cool.

There are many different kinds of cheese. Some famous English cheeses are Cheddar, Cheshire and Stilton. Cheeses such as Roquefort (France) and Gorgonzola (Italy) have blue veins in them. These are caused by special moulds.

CHEMISTRY
Chemistry is one of the main branches of science. The people who practise chemistry are called chemists. They look into the properties and make-up of matter. They try to find out what substances are made of, how they are put together, and how they react with other substances.

CHESS
This is a game that has been played for hundreds of years. It probably came from India, where it was known in the 7th century, and had reached Europe by the 11th century.

Chess is played by two players on a board with 64 squares. Each player has 16 pieces, and the pieces move in different ways. They attack and defend, and can be captured and taken out of play. The king is the most important piece and the game is won when one player takes the other's king.

CHINA
China is the world's third-largest country. About one-fifth of the world's people are Chinese. For much of its history, China was cut off from the rest of the world.

China became a united empire more than 2,000 years ago. The land was ruled by royal families called dynasties. To keep out nomadic enemies, the emperor Shih Huang Ti built the Great Wall of China. Writing, music and painting flourished. Wise men studied the works of such teachers as Confucius and Lao Tse.

Cities and roads were built, and merchants sailed as far as Africa and India. The Chinese invented paper and printing, and discovered how to make silk and gunpowder. Their fine pottery, or porcelain, was so famous that we still call all crockery 'china'.

For centuries the Chinese did not want anything to do with the outside world. But gradually China was made weak by civil wars and bad government. Europeans started trading in China in the 1800s and tried to run things for their own advantage. China even had to give bits of land to them. For example, it gave the island of Hong Kong to the British in 1842.

At first the Chinese were unable to stop the Europeans. Then, in the early 1900s, they overthrew the last of the emperors and set up a republic. Later, China was split by fighting between Communists and Nationalists. Before World War II Japan invaded China. By 1949, the Communists had won the civil war and China, led by Mao Zedong, became a Communist state. By the late 1900s China was becoming powerful once more. In 1997 it took back Hong Kong from the British.

See also PAGE 62.

CHRISTIANITY

Christianity is one of the world's great religions. Christians follow the teachings of Jesus Christ, whom they believe is the son of God who came to live on earth in human form.

There are over a billion people on earth who call themselves Christians. They belong to many different sects, or groups. But all accept the Bible as their holy book. The most important Christian festivals are Christmas, which celebrates Christ's birth, and Easter, which marks his death and resurrection. Christian worship takes place on Sunday, a holy day and day of rest.

Christianity is almost 2,000 years old. We date our calendar from the year in which it is thought Jesus was born.

See also JESUS CHRIST.

CHURCH

Christians began to build churches when the Roman emperor Constantine was converted in the 4th century and they no longer had to worship in secret. These early buildings were patterned after the Roman basilica – an oblong hall with aisles and an

spires, tall, narrow arches, richly stained-glass windows and lots of stone carvings. Such churches were meant to inspire awe and wonder in the worshipper.

The most splendid churches are often cathedrals. A cathedral is the most important church in an area called a diocese, headed by a bishop. The cathedral contains the bishop's *cathedra* (seat), or throne. Many magnificent cathedrals were built in Europe in the Middle Ages. Most have beautiful carvings, statues and stained-glass windows. Built to glorify God, they demanded the best engineering skills of their time.

Church: Florence cathedral was started in 1296, and is mainly Gothic in style. Its huge dome was built in the 15th century.

apse, or rounded part, at the end. Later, a transept or two wings were often added to make the shape of a cross.

From the 5th to the 12th centuries, many churches adopted the Romanesque style, which had round arches and thick walls. In the Middle Ages the Gothic style appeared. This featured pointed

CHURCHILL,

WINSTON LEONARD SPENCER (1874-1965) Churchill was Prime Minister of Britain during World War II.

One of Churchill's ancestors was a great English general, the Duke of Marlborough (1650-1722). Churchill led an adventurous life as a soldier and newspaper reporter before becoming a politician. But his greatest years were from 1940 to 1945, when his stirring speeches and strong leadership encouraged people during the war against Hitler's Germany.

Civil Rights Movement
See KING, MARTIN LUTHER.

Civil War
A war fought between citizens of the same country is called a civil war. Sometimes a civil war produces a great change in a country's history.

In England the last civil war was fought from 1642 to 1649. It was a battle for power between the king, Charles I, and Parliament. Charles thought that he had a divine, or God-given, right to rule the country. Parliament thought he was too extravagant. Charles finally dismissed Parliament in 1642 and called his supporters to arms. They were called Royalists.

The parliamentary soldiers were the Roundheads. Led by Oliver Cromwell, they defeated the Royalists and captured the king. Charles was put on trial and executed in 1649. England became a monarchy once more in 1660, but the king never again had as much power as before the Civil War.

The American Civil War (1861-1865) was fought between the government (Union), backed by the northern states, and the southern states (Confederacy). The war was fought over the rights of each state to make its own laws, in particular the laws regarding slavery. In 1860 the southern states thought that the

Union flag
Union soldier
Confederate flag
Confederate soldier

Civil War: In the American Civil War the Union (the northern states) and the Confederacy (the southern states) each had their own uniform and flag.

new Republican president, Abraham Lincoln, would abolish slavery. The large farms, or plantations, of the South depended on slave labour, and the owners thought that the abolition of slavery would ruin them.

In 1861 the 11 southern states decided to break away, or secede, and form a separate nation, the Confederate States of America. War broke out in April, when the Confederates fired on Fort Sumter in Charleston harbour, South Carolina. At first the war went well for the South. Under their brilliant commander, Robert E. Lee, the South won a victory at the Battle of Bull Run in July 1861. But in 1863 the tide turned after the Battle of Gettysburg, in Pennsylvania. In 1864 General Ulysses S. Grant took command of the Union armies, and in April 1865 Lee surrendered. Both sides had suffered tremendous losses.

In the late 20th century there have been many civil wars in Africa, Latin America and South-east Asia.

CIVILIZATION

Civilization began when people no longer had to spend all their time searching for food. Farming and trade developed as people settled in one area. As they grew more prosperous, they built cities, temples and roads. They developed languages, and expressed themselves through art, music and theatre. Most civilizations in ancient times had strong armies and spread their way of life by conquest.

Only the ruins of these great civilizations of the past now remain. But they have left their mark on our lives. Civilization in Europe today, for example, owes a great deal to the ideas of the Greeks and Romans. The modern world is a mixture of civilizations.

CLEOPATRA (69-30 BC)

Cleopatra, Queen of Egypt, was one of the most beautiful and fascinating women in history. Two famous Roman rulers, Julius Caesar and Mark Antony, fell in love with her. Antony even gave parts of the Roman Empire to Cleopatra. The angry Romans made war on Antony, and defeated him. Antony killed himself, and Cleopatra also took her own life.

CLIMATE

Climate means the typical weather of a place over a long period of time.

Several factors affect climate. One is latitude – a place's distance from the equator. The Sun's rays are most direct at the equator, so it is hotter there. At the poles the rays spread over a large land area

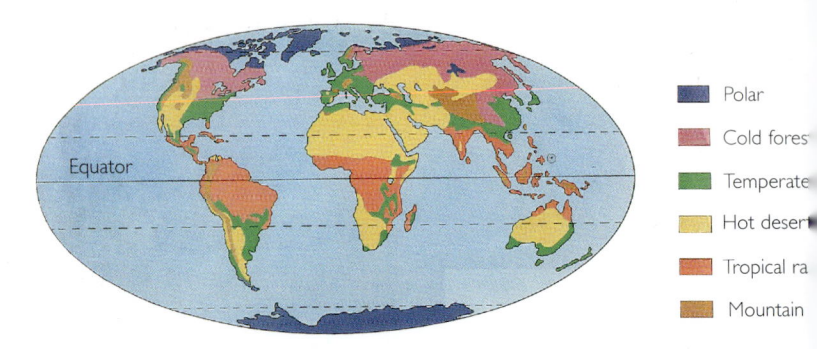

Polar
Cold forest
Temperate
Hot desert
Tropical ra[in]
Mountain

Climate: *The world is divided into climate zones. Places all round the world that are in the same zone have a similar kind of climate.*

and it is cool. A second factor is how close a place is to the sea. Water heats and cools more slowly than land. Away from the sea, land becomes much hotter in the summer and colder in winter.

The chief elements of climate are temperature and rainfall. The world's climatic regions are based on average temperatures and rainfall figures over many years.

CLOCKS AND WATCHES

A clock is an instrument for measuring the time. A watch works in a similar way and is small enough to carry around.

Although the Chinese probably had clocks as early as AD 600, the earliest European clocks were made about 1200. They were made by blacksmiths and were often crude and clumsy. They worked by the force of gravity (weights) and were not accurate. A more accurate clock was developed when Galileo discovered that the pendulum could be used to regulate time. Since then, clocks have been continuously improved and ordinary clocks are accurate to within a few minutes a year.

Today, two very precise clocks are used. One is the quartz crystal clock. The second is the caesium atomic clock, which keeps time to within a second in a million years.

See also GALILEO.

CLOUD

After it has rained, the puddles soon dry. The water has turned into invisible water vapour.

Water vapour rises into the air, and the higher it rises, the cooler it becomes. As it cools, the vapour turns back into water. Millions of tiny drops of water, so light they float in the air, make clouds.

When the air can hold the water droplets no longer, they fall as rain.

When the air is very cold, they turn to ice and fall as hail or snow.

By studying the different kinds of cloud, scientists can tell what sort of weather to expect.

See also FOG; RAIN, SLEET AND HAIL; WATER.

COAL

Coal is one of our most important fuels. It can be burned to heat buildings. At power stations it is burned to make electricity. Coal is also made into coal gas and coke, which are both good fuels. A lot of coke is used in the steel industry. Many chemicals can be produced from coal to make dyes, plastics, medicines and explosives.

Coal is mined from the ground. It is formed from the remains of forests of huge ferns and strange trees that grew millions of years ago. When these died, they became covered by mud and sand. In time, the mud and sand changed into rocks. The dead plants were squeezed until they changed into coal. Most coal is deep underground and mining it is expensive and dangerous.

See also MINING.

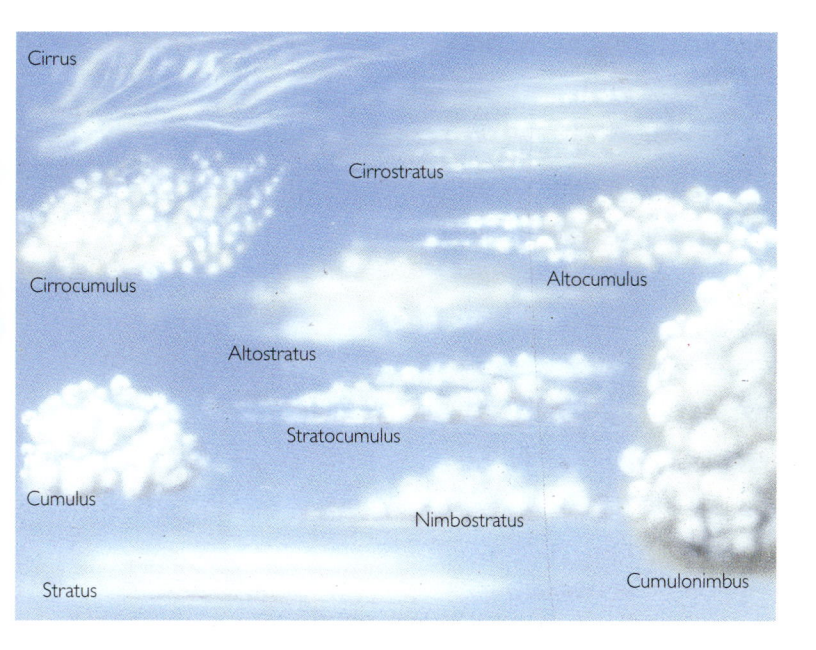

Cloud: Cumulus, stratocumulus, altocumulus and cirrus are fair-weather clouds; altostratus, cirrostratus, nimbostratus and cumulonimbus are rain-bearing.

Cirrus
Cirrostratus
Cirrocumulus
Altocumulus
Altostratus
Stratocumulus
Cumulus
Nimbostratus
Stratus
Cumulonimbus

Cocoa

Cocoa comes from the seeds of the cacao tree, which is grown in West Africa, the West Indies and South America. Chocolate is made from cocoa and was first introduced, as a drink, to Europe from the Spanish in the 16th century.

Coffee

Coffee is made from the roasted and ground beans of the coffee plant. Coffee bushes grow best in warm, wet highland areas, such as in Brazil and Kenya. Inside each red berry are one or two beans. At harvest time, the beans are removed and dried in the sun. Then they are roasted until they are brown, and sold, either ground or whole.

Colour

White light is actually a mixture of all colours. It is only when white light is split up, as it is in a rainbow, that we see its range of different colours.

The first person to understand light and colour was Sir Isaac Newton. In 1666, by passing light through a glass prism (a triangular solid block of glass), he obtained all the colours of a rainbow. This band of colour is called the spectrum. Newton then combined the colours again by passing them

Cocoa: A South American woman harvests cocoa. The beans are dried, roasted and ground into a thick brown liquid which, when dried, makes cocoa powder.

Colour: *When light beams in the three primary colours are mixed, they make white light. But when the same colours are mixed in the form of paint, they make black.*

through a second prism to form white light. The colours of the spectrum are always in the same order – red, orange, yellow, green, blue, indigo and violet.

We see the colour of an object, such as a yellow flower, because all the other colours are absorbed and only the yellow is reflected. A white flower gives back all the colours of light.

COLUMBUS, CHRISTOPHER (1451-1506)

This Italian explorer discovered America by accident. He believed he could reach the Indies (Asia) by sailing west, instead of east, for he was sure the Earth was round. He persuaded the King of Spain to let him try, and in 1492 he set out with three ships, *Santa Maria*, *Pinta* and *Nina*, across the Atlantic Ocean. When he reached the Caribbean islands, Columbus thought he had reached Asia, so he called them the 'Indies'.

Comet: *A comet gives off a trail of dust and gas, which can be seen as a tail streaming away from it.*

COMET

Comets are heavenly bodies. They are glowing balls of gas and dust that travel in an orbit, or path, around the Sun. Some of them have long tails, but they only start to glow when they get near the Sun. Some comets take only a few years to circle the Sun, others take thousands of years. The most famous comet is Halley's comet, which orbits the Sun about every 76 years.

COMMONWEALTH

Most of the countries that were part of the British Empire now belong to the Commonwealth of Nations. It includes huge countries, such as Australia, Canada and India, and tiny islands. Nearly all the members are self-governing, but their laws, schools and way of life are often similar. Some still trade mainly with Britain. The richer members try to help the poorer countries, and Commonwealth leaders meet regularly to discuss their economic and financial problems.

COMMUNICATION

The exchange of information, ideas, or feelings is called communication. Animals communicate with one another, but people have the most complicated forms of communication.

Speech was the earliest means of human communication. The Sumerians were the first to invent writing, and the Phoenicians developed the first alphabet sometime before 1000BC.

Until the 1400s, all books in Europe were handwritten. Then Johannes Gutenberg invented a system of printing from movable type. Communication took a giant step forward, with the printing of many copies of books, newspapers, and eventually magazines. The invention of photography brought about visual communication through pictures and films, and electricity made communication over huge distances possible, by means of the telegraph, telephone, radio and television. Computers have revolutionized modern communications because they can store, sort and provide information at amazing speed.

Communism

The main idea behind Communism is that wealth should be shared. So Communist governments control all factories, mines, farms and shops.

Karl Marx and Friedrich Engels put forward Communist ideals in the 1800s. The first country to have a Communist government was the USSR, after the 1917 revolution. Later, much of eastern Europe and Cuba also became Communist, along with China.

The situation changed quickly after 1990, when the USSR and other eastern European countries abandoned Communism.

Compass

A compass is an instrument used to find directions. A simple compass has a needle that always points in the same direction – north and south. This is a magnetic compass, and it works the way it does because the Earth itself acts like a big magnet. The compass needle lines up parallel with the Earth's magnetic field.

Most ships and planes use a gyrocompass. This device contains a spinning drum and, once set, its axis always points in one direction, no matter which way the ship or plane turns.

Computer

Computers are electronic machines, like calculators. But computers do more than work out mathematical problems. They can process information. This means that they can be given information, store it and sort through it in order to carry out a task. What is more, they can work at incredible speeds.

Computers cannot think. They have to have instructions, called programs, to tell them what to do with the information they are given. These programs can be changed so that computers can do an enormous number of different things. Today computers are found in offices, hospitals, factories, schools and homes. They can send spacecraft to outer planets, help forecast the weather, run machines and play exciting games.

Every computer has four main parts. The input is where the computer receives instructions and information; the central processing unit (CPU) is where calculations are carried out; the

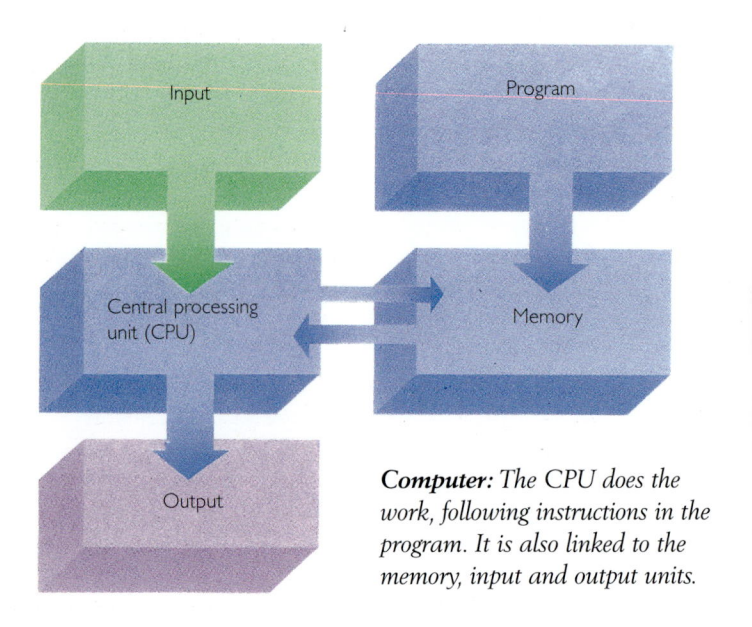

Computer: The CPU does the work, following instructions in the program. It is also linked to the memory, input and output units.

memory is where information and instructions are stored; and the output is where the result is displayed or printed out.

The first computer, ENIAC, was built in 1946. It filled a whole room. Today the programs to run a computer can be held electronically on tiny silicon chips. The largest computers are called mainframes. They can service several hundred users. The smallest are called laptops. The internet is a vast network that allows people with computers to communicate anywhere in the world.

See also CALCULATOR; ELECTRONICS; INTERNET; SILICON CHIP.

CONFUCIUS (*c.*551-479BC)

China's most famous thinker and teacher was born in poverty. Confucius hated the misery and disorder he saw all around him and wanted to do something about it. He did this by gathering together groups of followers and teaching them how to lead good lives. He taught them that all people should try to love others and understand them. People should become rulers because they were good, not just because they were strong or came from powerful families. His followers helped to spread his teachings long after he died at the age of about 70.

Conifer

Conifers are plants that have cones instead of flowers for making pollen and seeds. They are all trees or shrubs, and are mostly found in the cool parts of the world. Conifers include cedars, larches, pines, firs and spruces. Most of them have thin, needle-like leaves, which they do not shed in winter.

Conservation

Conservation is the protection of nature, including natural resources such as water, soil, minerals, forests and wildlife.

For centuries people have made use of these resources without any thought of preserving them. Conservationists work to prevent the pollution of our earth, air and water and the destruction and disappearance of rare animals and their habitats.

Constellation

From earliest times people have studied the night sky. It did not take them long to realize that the sky had a systematic pattern of stars in fixed groups, or constellations. People saw the shapes of animals and the heroes of their myths, and named groups of stars after them.

Some constellations always come up in the east in a certain order just before sunrise and seem to travel in the same path as the Sun. These are the 12 figures or signs of the zodiac.

There are 88 constellations. The Greeks identified and named 48 of them. Some constellations can be seen only in the Northern Hemisphere and some only in the Southern Hemisphere.

See also ASTRONOMY; STAR; UNIVERSE.

Cook, Captain James (1728-1779)

James Cook made three voyages of discovery to the Pacific and Antarctic oceans. The first was an expedition to the South Seas in 1768. He sailed to Tahiti and then to New Zealand. In 1770 he reached Botany Bay in Australia and claimed it for Britain.

On his second voyage (1772-1775), he sailed more than 100,000km, going right round the world. On his third expedition he discovered the Hawaiian Islands. He was killed there by the inhabitants.

See also EXPLORERS.

Copernicus, Nicolaus (1473-1543)

Copernicus was a Polish astronomer. He showed that the Earth was not the centre of the universe. He stated that the Earth revolves once every 24 hours, that it travels around the Sun once a year and that it and the other planets form the Solar System.

See also ASTRONOMY.

COPPER

Copper was one of the first metals to be used. To begin with, people used pure copper, which they found in the ground. Later, people learned how to extract it from ore by smelting.

Pure copper is very soft. It is often mixed with other metals to make a harder alloy such as brass.

See also ALLOY; METALS.

CORTÉS, HERNAN

(1485-1547)
Cortés was a Spanish soldier who conquered the Aztec Empire in Mexico between 1519 and 1521 with less than 600 men. Cortés had guns, which gave him great power over the people, and they thought he was a god.

Cortés: Cortés governed Mexico for nine years.

COTTON

Cotton is a very useful plant. Inside its round fruits, called bolls, are masses of white fibres. When the fruits ripen, they split open and the fibres are blown away, spreading the seeds. On cotton plantations the bolls are picked before this can happen, and the fibres are processed into the different types of cotton fabrics.

Cotton grows best in warm, wet lands, including Asia, the southern United States, India, China, Egypt and Brazil.

COUNTRIES OF THE WORLD

There are over 180 independent countries in the world, and they exist in all shapes and sizes. The following list shows the situation at the end of 1997.

EUROPE

Country	Population	Capital
Albania	3,441,000	Tirana
Andorra	62,500	Andorra-la-Vella
Austria	7,968,000	Vienna
Belarus	10,141,000	Minsk
Belgium	10,113,000	Brussels
Bosnia-Herzegovina	3,459,000	Sarajevo
Bulgaria	10,319,000	Sofia
Croatia	4,495,000	Zagreb
Czech Republic	10,296,000	Prague
Denmark	5,215,718	Copenhagen
Estonia	1,530,000	Tallinn
Finland	5,107,000	Helsinki
France	57,981,000	Paris
Georgia	5,457,000	Tbilisi
Germany	81,591,000	Berlin
Gibraltar	29,000	Gibraltar
Greece	10,451,000	Athens
Hungary	10,115,000	Budapest
Iceland	269,000	Reykjavík
Ireland	3,553,000	Dublin
Italy	57,023,000	Rome

Country	Population	Capital
Latvia	2,557,000	Riga
Liechtenstein	30,629	Vaduz
Lithuania	3,700,000	Vilnius
Luxembourg	401,000	Luxembourg
Macedonia*	2,571,000	Skopje
Malta	370,402	Valletta
Moldova	4,432,000	Kishinev
Monaco	31,000	Monaco-Ville
Netherlands	15,503,000	Amsterdam; The Hague (seat of government)
Norway	4,337,000	Oslo
Poland	38,388,000	Warsaw
Portugal	9,823,000	Lisbon
Romania	22,835,000	Bucharest
Russia	147,000,000	Moscow
San Marino	25,000	San Marino
Slovakia	5,353,000	Bratislava
Slovenia	1,946,000	Ljubljana
Spain	39,621,000	Madrid
Sweden	8,780,000	Stockholm
Switzerland	7,202,000	Bern
Ukraine	51,380,000	Kiev
United Kingdom	58,258,000	London
Vatican City	1,000	Vatican City
Yugoslavia* (Serbia-Montenegro)	10,849,200	Belgrade

AFRICA

Country	Population	Capital
Algeria	27,939,000	Algiers
Angola	11,072,000	Luanda
Benin	5,409,000	Porto Novo
Botswana	1,487,000	Gaborone
Burkina Faso	8,769,000	Ouagadougou
Burundi	6,393,000	Bujumbura
Cameroon	13,233,000	Yaoundé
Cape Verde Is.	359,500	Praia
Central African Republic	3,315,000	Bangui
Chad	6,361,000	N'djaména
Comoros	544,000	Moroni
Congo	2,590,000	Brazzaville
Côte d'Ivoire	14,253,000	Yamoussoukro

*Not internationally recognized

Country	Population	Capital
Djibouti	586,000	Djibouti
Egypt	62,931,000	Cairo
Equatorial Guinea	400,000	Malabo
Eritrea	3,531,000	Asmara
Ethiopia	55,053,000	Addis Ababa
Gabon	1,320,000	Libreville
Gambia	1,118,000	Banjul
Ghana	17,453,000	Accra
Guinea	6,700,000	Conakry
Guinea-Bissau	1,073,000	Bissau
Kenya	28,261,000	Nairobi
Lesotho	2,050,000	Maseru
Liberia	3,039,000	Monrovia
Libya	5,407,000	Tripoli
Madagascar	14,763,000	Antananarivo
Malawi	11,129,000	Lilongwe
Mali	10,759,000	Bamako
Mauritania	2,274,000	Nouakchott
Mauritius	1,117,000	Port Louis
Morocco	27,028,000	Rabat
Mozambique	16,004,000	Maputo
Namibia	1,540,000	Windhoek
Niger	9,151,000	Niamey
Nigeria	111,721,000	Abuja
Rwanda	7,952,000	Kigali
Säo Tomé & Príncipe	131,100	Säo Tomé
Senegal	8,312,000	Dakar
Seychelles	73,000	Victoria
Sierra Leone	4,509,000	Freetown
Somalia	9,250,000	Mogadishu
South Africa	41,465,000	Pretoria (administration) Cape Town (legislature) Bloemfontein (judiciary)
Sudan	28,098,000	Khartoum
Swaziland	855,000	Mbabane
Tanzania	29,685,000	Dodoma
Togo	4,138,000	Lomé
Tunisia	8,896,000	Tunis
Uganda	21,297,000	Kampala
Zaire	43,901,000	Kinshasa
Zambia	9,456,000	Lusaka
Zimbabwe	11,261,000	Harare

ASIA

Country	Population	Capital
Afghanistan	20,141,000	Kabul
Armenia	3,599,000	Yerevan
Azerbaijan	7,558,000	Baku
Bahrain	568,000	Manama
Bangladesh	120,433,000	Dhaka
Bhutan	1,638,000	Thimbhu
Brunei	284,500	Bandar Seri Begawan
Cambodia	10,251,000	Phnom Penh
China	1,221,462,000	Beijing (Peking)
Cyprus	729,800	Nicosia
Hong Kong	6,189,800	Victoria
India	935,744,000	Delhi
Indonesia	197,588,000	Jakarta
Iran	67,283,000	Tehran
Iraq	20,449,000	Baghdad
Israel	5,629,000	Jerusalem
Japan	125,095,000	Tokyo
Jordan	5,439,000	Amman
Kazakhstan	17,111,000	Alma-Ata
Korea (N)	23,917,000	Pyongyang
Korea (S)	44,995,000	Seoul
Kuwait	1,547,000	Kuwait
Kyrgyzstan	4,745,000	Bishkek
Laos	4,882,000	Vientiane
Lebanon	3,009,000	Beirut
Macao	395,300	Macao
Malaysia	20,140,000	Kuala Lumpur
Maldives	238,000	Malé
Mongolia	2,410,000	Ulan Bator
Myanmar	46,527,000	Rangoon
Nepal	21,918,000	Katmandu
Oman	2,163,000	Muscat
Pakistan	140,497,000	Islamabad
Philippines	67,581,000	Manila
Qatar	359,000	Doha
Saudi Arabia	17,880,000	Riyadh
Singapore	2,848,000	Singapore
Sri Lanka	18,354,000	Colombo
Syria	14,661,000	Damascus
Taiwan	21,200,000	Taipei
Tajikistan	6,101,000	Dushanbe
Thailand	58,791,000	Bangkok
Turkey	61,945,000	Ankara
Turkmenistan	4,099,000	Ashkhabad
United Arab Emirates	1,904,000	Abu Dhabi
Uzbekistan	22,843,000	Tashkent
Vietnam	74,545,000	Hanoi
Yemen	14,501,000	San'a

SOUTH AMERICA

Country	Population	Capital
Argentina	34,587,000	Buenos Aires
Bolivia	7,414,000	La Paz (seat of government) Sucre (legal capital)
Brazil	161,790,000	Brasília
Chile	14,262,000	Santiago
Colombia	35,101,000	Bogotá
Ecuador	11,460,000	Quito
French Guiana	98,000	Cayenne
Guyana	835,000	Georgetown
Paraguay	4,960,000	Asunción
Peru	23,780,000	Lima
Surinam	412,000	Paramaribo
Uruguay	3,168,000	Montevideo
Venezuela	21,844,000	Caracas

NORTH AND CENTRAL AMERICA THE WEST INDIES

Country	Population	Capital
Anguilla (Br.)	8,960	The Valley
Antigua and Barbuda	64,166	St John's
Bahamas	275,700	Nassau
Barbados	264,300	Bridgetown
Belize	215,000	Belmopan
Bermuda	72,000	Hamilton
Canada	29,463,000	Ottawa
Costa Rica	3,424,000	San José
Cuba	11,041,000	Havana
Dominica	74,200	Roseau
Dominican Republic	7,823,000	Santo Domingo

El Salvador	5,768,000	San Salvador
Greenland (Dan.)	55,000	Godthaab
Grenada	96,000	St George's
Guadeloupe (Fr.)	387,000	Basse-Terre
Guatemala	10,621,000	Guatemala City
Haiti	7,180,000	Port-au-Prince
Honduras	5,654,000	Tegucigalpa
Jamaica	2,447,000	Kingston
Martinique (Fr.)	359,600	Fort-de-France
Mexico	93,674,000	Mexico City
Nicaragua	4,433,000	Managua
Panama	2,631,000	Panama City
Puerto Rico (US)	3,300,000	San Juan
St Kitts-Nevis	41,000	Basseterre
St Lucia	141,000	Castries
St Vincent and the Grenadines	111,000	Kingstown
Trinidad and Tobago	1,306,000	Port-of-Spain
United States of America	263,250,000	Washington DC

AUSTRALASIA

Country	Population	Capital
Australia	18,088,000	Canberra
Fiji	784,000	Suva
Kiribati	80,000	Baraiki
Marshall Islands	54,000	Majuro
Micronesia	121,000	Kolonia
Nauru	11,000	Nauru
New Caledonia	171,000	Nouméa
New Zealand	3,575,000	Wellington
Niue	2,500	Alofi
Palau	17,000	Koror
Papua New Guinea	4,302,000	Port Moresby
Solomon Islands	378,000	Honiara
Tonga	98,000	Nuku'alofa
Tuvalu	9,000	Fongafale
Vanuatu	165,000	Port Vila
Western Samoa	169,000	Apia

CRAB

Along with shrimps, prawns and lobsters, crabs belong to the group of animals called crustaceans.

Most crabs live in the sea. They have jointed legs, like insects, and walk sideways. They seize food in their strong pincers, or claws.

There are about 5,000 different kinds of crabs. They vary in size from tiny pea crabs less than 1cm across to giant crabs measuring 30cm or more.

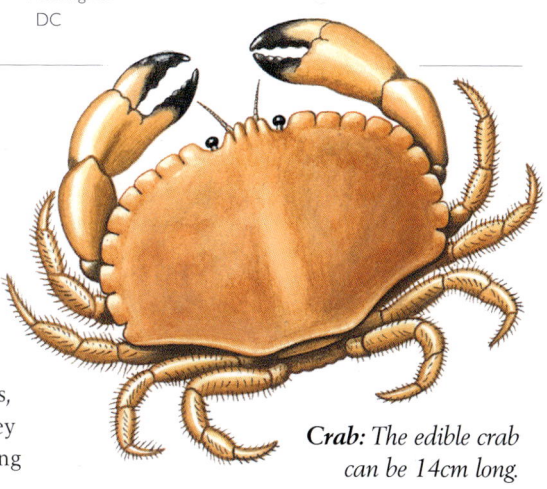

Crab: The edible crab can be 14cm long.

CRICKET

The game of cricket began in the 1700s. It is played by two teams of 11 players, using a wooden bat and a leather ball. Each team takes it in turn to 'bat' and to 'field'. The batsmen try to score 'runs' by hitting the ball when it is bowled to them. The bowler, helped by fielders, tries to get the batsmen 'out'.

CROCODILES AND ALLIGATORS

These reptiles are related. They both have tough, armoured skin and their ears, eyes and nostrils are located at the top of their heads. Unlike most reptiles, crocodiles and alligators lay their eggs in a nest or heap of dead leaves and plants. As the plants rot, they provide heat, which helps to hatch the eggs.

Crocodiles live in Africa, Asia and Australia. They eat fish, birds, turtles and water mammals. They vary in size from 1.5m to 6m and have narrow, pointed heads.

Alligators live in America and China, where they can grow as big as crocodiles. They eat mostly fish.

Crocodiles and Alligators:
Crocodiles use their long, pointed teeth to spear fish and to grasp the flesh of prey animals.

CROMWELL, OLIVER (1599-1658)

Cromwell was one of the most famous men in English history. He helped to lead Parliament's army to victory over the Royalists in the Civil War, and became Lord Protector from 1653 to 1658. He was one of those who signed the warrant for the execution of Charles I.

See also CIVIL WAR.

CRUSADES

The Crusades were wars in which Christian armies fought to win back the Holy Land of Palestine from the Muslims.

The First Crusade began in 1096 after Pope Urban II had called on the Christians of Europe to capture Jerusalem, which was a sacred city to the Muslims as well as the Christians. Many knights answered the call, and the First Crusade was a great success. The crusaders captured Jerusalem in 1099. The Muslims were not beaten, however. In 1187, led by the great sultan Saladin, they recaptured Jerusalem.

There were eight Crusades in all, and thousands of crusaders went to the Holy Land. Before the Muslims finally defeated them in 1303, many crusaders had died of sickness or in battle.

The Crusades brought Europeans into contact with the way of life of the East. They learned Eastern medicine and science, and were encouraged to trade for the riches of the East.

CURIE, MARIE (1867-1934) AND PIERRE (1859-1906)

The Curies, who were husband and wife, were among the earliest workers in the science of radioactivity, the powerful rays given off by some rare materials.

In 1898 the Curies discovered and worked on the radioactive elements, polonium and radium. They shared a Nobel prize in physics in 1903 with Henri Becquerel for their work. Madame Curie was awarded a second Nobel prize, in chemistry, in 1911 for her further work on radium.

See also RADIOACTIVITY.

CUSTER, GEORGE (1839-1876)

George Armstrong Custer was an army officer and Indian fighter who died at the Battle of the Little Big Horn. A graduate of West Point (1861), he became the youngest general in the Union army during the Civil War. Custer later commanded the Seventh Cavalry in many attacks on the Sioux and Cheyenne tribes before the famous battle in which he and all his men were killed.

CYCLONE

See HURRICANE AND TORNADO.

D

Dam

A dam is a barrier built across a river or lake. Some dams are built to create a reservoir for storing water, others to control flooding or to produce water power for making electricity.

Some dams are made from earth or rock fill, others are made from concrete. There are two main types of concrete dam: gravity dams resist the horizontal thrust of the water through the weight of the dam itself; arch dams curve upstream in the centre, enabling them to resist the force of the water. At 335m high from its foundations, the Rogun dam in Tajikistan is the world's highest dam.

Dance

People have danced to music since the beginnings of history, and many different countries and regions of the world still have their own special traditions of 'folk' dance – for example, Scottish reels and Irish jigs.

In modern times dance crazes have often swept across the Western World. One of the first was the craze in the early 1800s for dancing the waltz, which started in Germany. In the early 1900s there were crazes for the tango, which started in South America, and many other dances. Nowadays the most popular kind of social dancing is probably disco dancing to recorded pop music.

In folk dances people usually dance in small groups. For dances like the waltz and tango, people usually dance in pairs, and in disco dancing they sometimes dance without a partner at all.

Dance can also be performed by trained dancers on a stage. An example of this is ballet. Classical ballet is based on a number of set positions and movements that are arranged by a choreographer in different combinations and sequences to tell a story or act out an idea or feeling. Ballet was first recognized in France, where the Royal Academy of Dancing was founded in 1661. Modern ballet allows dancers more freedom of movement and expression.

Ballet steps are recorded on paper using special symbols, so the same ballet can be danced by different ballet companies at different times. Some of the ballets performed today were first presented 140 years ago.

Darwin, Charles Robert (1809-1882)

Darwin was a great naturalist whose theory of evolution sought to explain why there are so many different kinds of plants and animals. Darwin said that those animals and plants whose slight differences made them better able to live in their environment would survive and pass on their differences to their offspring.

Darwin put forward this idea of natural selection in his book, *On the Origin of Species*, in 1859.

Deer

Deer are hoofed mammals, and run swiftly to escape their enemies. Like antelope and cattle, deer chew the cud. Usually only the stags (males) have horns, or antlers. Females are called hinds.

Deer live in cooler climates than antelopes. Most deer live in woodland, feeding on grass and leaves. The reindeer, or caribou, lives on the cold northern tundra. The largest deer is the moose, or elk, found in North America and Europe.

Democracy

The word democracy comes from two Greek words and means 'government by the people'. In ancient times emperors and kings had great power to make laws and collect taxes. In a democracy a group of men and women elected by the people make the laws.

Some democracies are republics, in which the head of state is a president elected by the people. Others have a king or queen, although the country is governed by parliament. If the people living in a democracy do not like their government, they vote against it at an election.

Desert

Not all deserts are hot and sandy. Some are cold. Many are rocky. But all get very little rain and snow. About one-fifth of the Earth's land surface is desert.

Most deserts are in the middle of continents. There is little rain,

Deer: *The stag sheds his antlers each year and grows a new, larger pair. He uses them for fighting other stags.*

Desert: *Cacti survive in the desert because they store water in their fleshy stems.*

because the moist winds from the sea are dry by the time they reach these areas. As there are no clouds, a desert may get very hot during the day. At night, the ground loses heat and the desert becomes cold.

Desert: *Oases occur in the desert where there is an underground supply of water.*

Strong winds blow away the soil, leaving bare rock, or sweep the sand into great waves called dunes. It is difficult for plants to live in such conditions. Many desert animals shelter from the sun by day and come out at night. Some never drink, but get moisture from their food.

The world's largest desert is the Sahara in Africa. There are other huge deserts in central Asia (the Gobi), in southern Africa, Australia, India, and in North and South America.

DICKENS, CHARLES JOHN HUFFAM (1812-1870)

Dickens is one of the greatest English novelists. He created many famous characters, like the miser Scrooge in *A Christmas Carol*, and often wrote about children. In *David Copperfield* he described his own boyhood. Though his books contain many humorous characters, they also tell of the poverty, crime and cruelty of his day. Dickens's writing encouraged people to do something about these problems.

DIGESTION

The food we eat must be broken down inside the body before it can be absorbed by the blood and used for nourishment and energy. This happens in the digestive system.

Digestion begins in the mouth, where food is chewed into small pieces and mixed with saliva, before being pushed down into the stomach. The stomach churns the food, mixing it with gastric juices, and turns it into a soft paste, which passes slowly into the small intestine.

Inside the small intestine it is mixed with bile from the liver and juice from the pancreas, which break it down further. Much of this fluid passes through the wall of the small intestine into the blood. The waste passes into the large intestine and leaves the body as faeces.

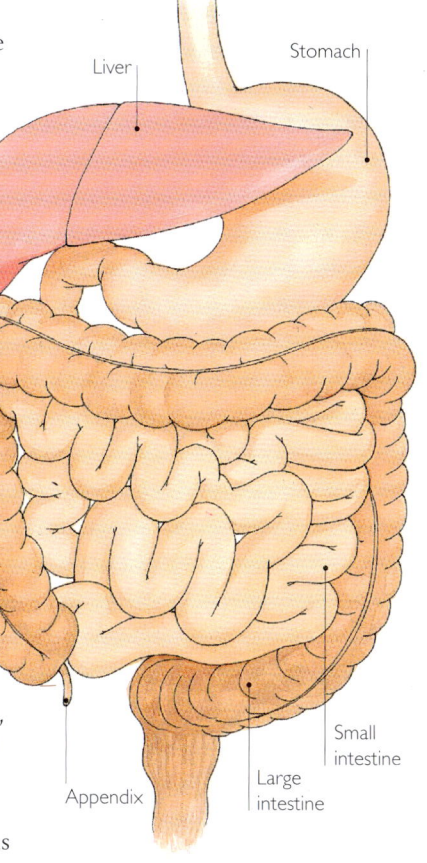

Digestion: *A meal takes between 10 and 20 hours to travel through the different parts of the human digestive system.*

DINOSAUR

See PREHISTORIC ANIMALS.

Disease

When something goes wrong with a part of your body, you may be suffering from a disease.

Many diseases are infectious. They are caused by attacks on the body by tiny living things. Bacteria cause diseases such as typhoid and tuberculosis. Viruses give us influenza, measles and the common cold.

Diseases can also be caused by poor diet and lack of vitamins. Sometimes glands can go wrong and upset the way the body works. Other diseases are hereditary, being passed on from parents to children.

Drugs can cure many diseases. And vaccination can protect us from others.

See also BACTERIA; DRUGS; MEDICINE; VITAMIN.

Diving, Underwater

To remain under water for more than a few minutes, divers must wear breathing apparatus. In fairly shallow waters divers use a device called an aqualung. It supplies them with compressed air through a mouthpiece. Deep-sea divers wear a special pressure suit pumped up with air.

DNA and RNA

See GENETICS.

Dog

The dog was the first animal to be tamed by human beings. Cave men probably reared wild dog pups and trained them to hunt.

Today, there are many different kinds, or breeds, of dog. Each breed has qualities that suit it to particular tasks. Spaniels and retrievers are good at retrieving

Field spaniel

Shihtzu

Pug

game. Alsatians and dobermanns make excellent guard dogs. Hounds follow a scent. Sheepdogs control a flock of sheep. And many breeds make excellent companions.

Even though the dog has lived close to people for so long, it still has the instincts of a wild animal. Before going to sleep, a dog will turn round and round – as if making a bed in dry leaves. Because wild dogs live in packs, or groups, the dog's instinct is to follow and obey the pack leader. This makes it easy to train, as its master becomes the 'pack leader'.

The wild members of the dog family include coyotes, foxes, jackals and hunting dogs.

Dobermann

French bull dog

Boston terrier

Greyhound

Dog: *Dogs come in a huge range of shapes and sizes, depending on the purpose for which they were originally bred.*

Dolphin

Dolphins are small whales. They live in the sea or in big rivers, and they eat fish. Dolphins are mammals, so they have to come to the surface to breathe. They are marvellous swimmers and often play by leaping right out of the water and twisting about.

Dragon

A dragon is a fabulous invented monster. It is often represented as a gigantic reptile with a lion's claws, the tail of a serpent, wings and a scaly skin, and breathing fire.

Mostly we think of dragons as being evil, fearful creatures, but this is not so in all cultures. The Chinese think the sign of the dragon can protect them from evil or injury.

Drugs

Herbs and chemicals that are used to cure diseases are called drugs. Some mosses and herbs contain healing substances that have been known to people since earliest times. By the 1600s nearly every town had an apothecary, or chemist, who made up pills and mixtures. Many of these did no good at all.

In the 1800s the first man-made drugs, produced from chemicals, were used to treat disease. A great step forward was the discovery of penicillin in 1928. This was the first antibiotic drug, the type that kills harmful bacteria.

Drugs can be dangerous if they are not used properly. People can become addicted to certain drugs and cannot live without them.

See also DISEASE.

Dye

Dyes are substances used to colour fabrics and other materials. Some dyes come from plants and animals. A red dye called madder comes from the roots of the madder plant. Cochineal is a scarlet dye obtained from the cochineal insect. Most dyes used today are made from chemicals. Many of these man-made dyes have brilliant colours.

Dynamite

In 1866 Alfred Nobel, a Swedish chemist, accidentally made an important discovery. He mixed a very dangerous explosive called nitro-glycerine with a kind of sandy earth called *kieselguhr*. The mixture turned into a solid cheesy substance that could be handled safely but was still a powerful explosive. He called it dynamite.

Nobel made a fortune from explosives. With some of the money he set up a fund to give yearly prizes to scientists and writers whose work has helped mankind. These are known as Nobel prizes.

See also NOBEL PRIZE.

E

EAGLE

These birds of prey are the kings of the bird world. Eagles can fly to great heights. The largest eagles, such as the golden eagle, can carry off lambs and even young deer in their strong claws.

Today, eagles are protected by law. Eagles are becoming rare because people have shot and poisoned many of them.

EAR

Any sound causes vibrations which are passed by the outer ear down to the ear drum. The ear drum then vibrates, just like the skin of a musical drum. Three tiny bones in the middle ear pick up and pass on the vibrations. Inside the inner ear is a shell-like tube full of fluid called the cochlea.

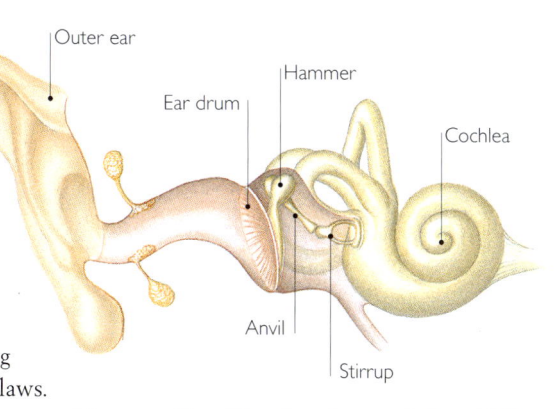

Ear: The three bones of the middle ear are the hammer, the anvil and the stirrup. They magnify sounds about twenty times.

The vibrating air makes the fluid vibrate, too. Nerves send messages about the vibrations to the brain. And when the brain has worked out what the messages mean, we 'hear' the sounds.

The inner ear also helps us keep our balance by means of fluid-filled tubes.

Eagle: Some eagles are huge, with wingspans of more than 2m.

Earth

The Earth we live on is one of nine planets that orbit the Sun. Scientists think the Earth was probably formed from a spinning cloud of gas and dust. From the age of the oldest rocks we know that the Earth is more than four billion years old.

The Earth has an invisible outer covering called the atmosphere. The atmosphere lies in several layers. The outer edge is about 1,600km from the Earth. The lowest layer, the troposphere, is where life exists.

The Earth is the only planet with large amounts of surface water. Oceans and seas cover 70 percent of its surface. The water was formed by chemical reactions after the Earth had become a solid ball of rock.

The Earth is rocky, and very rugged in places. It is made up of igneous, or crystallized, rocks and sedimentary, or deposited, rocks. The surface is called the crust.

Earth: The Earth gets hotter towards its centre. Temperatures in the inner core are probably around 5000°C.

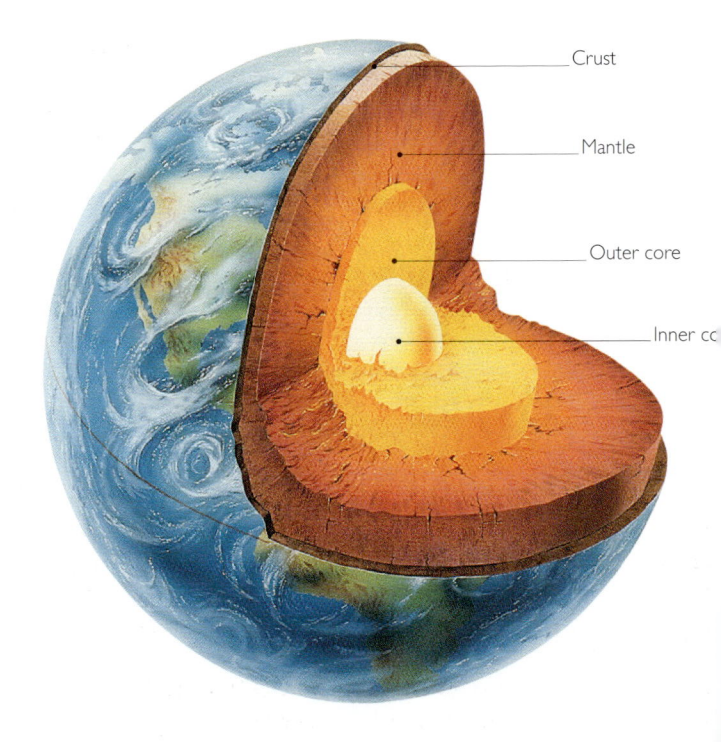

- Crust
- Mantle
- Outer core
- Inner core

Epicentre

Hypocentre

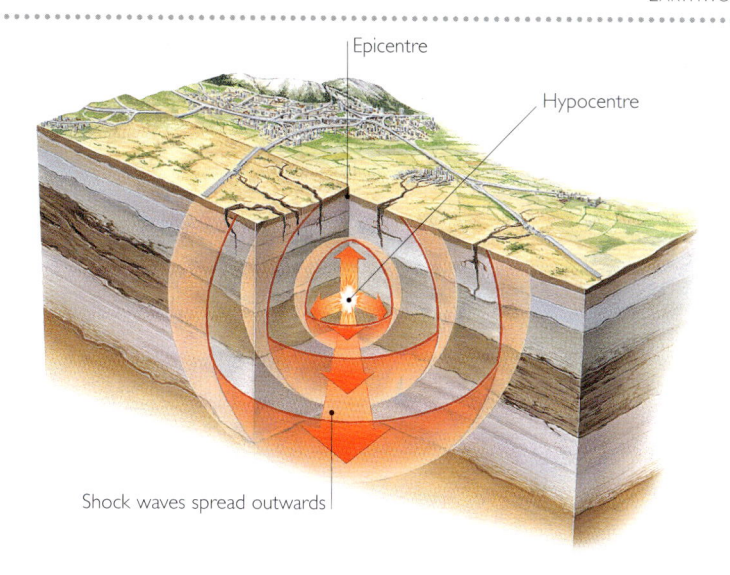

Shock waves spread outwards

Below the crust is the mantle. This is a thick layer of heavier rocks, up to 2,900km deep. Below this the rocks are molten (melted) because it is so hot. At the centre of the Earth is a core of solid rock, probably made of nickel and iron. The core acts as a giant magnet.

See also CALENDAR; FOSSIL; MOUNTAIN; OCEANS; RIVER; ROCK; SOLAR SYSTEM; VOLCANO.

EARTHQUAKE

The Earth's crust is made up of plates of rock, which can move and crack. When they shift like this, the ground shakes causing an earthquake.

Not all earthquakes are major, destructive movements. About twenty severe earthquakes occur

Earthquake: The hypocentre is where the rock plates shift suddenly. The epicentre is the point above it on the Earth's surface.

each year. But there are about a million minor tremors as well. Earthquakes are detected by instruments called seismometers.

When an earthquake occurs on the ocean floor it produces great waves called tsunamis. They travel long distances at speeds of up to 800km/h. In the open ocean they may be only 1m or so high, but when they run into shallow water and slow down they rise rapidly to heights of from 10m to 30m.

See also VOLCANO.

EARTHWORM
See WORM.

Eastern Europe and the Balkans

The countries of Eastern Europe include Poland, Hungary, the Czech Republic, Slovakia, Romania, Bulgaria, Albania, the former states of Yugoslavia, and the western states of the former Soviet Union – Ukraine, Moldova and Belarus. Much of the region is mountainous and much of it has large forests and fertile plains. Agriculture plays an important role in all economies and many of the countries have large industries. The region has natural resources such as timber, oil, coal, natural gas and iron ore.

For much of the late 20th century all of the countries were under Communist rule. The first democratic elections did not take place until the late 1980s and 1990s. While some countries re-established themselves peacefully, there have been devastating wars in others, such as the former states of Yugoslavia.

Echo

Sometimes when we shout, the sound of our voice comes back again a few seconds later. This is an echo. It happens when the sound is reflected by an object some distance away. Bats use sound echoes to find the insects they eat. Ships and submarines use sound echoes (sonar) to detect objects under water. Airports use echoes of radio waves (radar) to track aircraft.

Eclipse

When one heavenly body passes in front of another and blots out its light, we say an eclipse is taking place. The Moon can cause an eclipse of the Sun. This happens when the Moon passes in front of the Sun and blots out the Sun's light. The Moon's shadow falls on the Earth and the sky goes dark. Then, as the Moon's shadow passes by, daylight returns. An eclipse of the Moon occurs when it moves into the shadow of the Earth.

Eclipse: In a solar eclipse the Moon comes between the Sun and the Earth.

Edison: *Thomas Edison invented the phonograph in 1877. It was the ancestor of the gramophone and all modern sound systems.*

Ecology

Ecology is the study of plants and animals and how they live in their natural communities. This science shows how living things make use of their surroundings, or environment, and how they affect one another.

Most plants and animals can live only in a particular kind of environment such as a desert, a pond, a marsh or a forest. Each plant is suited to the temperature, soil and water supply of the ground it grows in. Animals eat the plants or other animals. This link between plants and animals is called a food web.

Edison, Thomas A. (1847-1931)

Edison was one of the world's greatest inventors. He patented nearly 1,300 inventions. Among these were the phonograph, the electric light and an electric generating station. He said he owed his success not to genius but to hard work.

Eel

The life story of the common eel is very strange. These eels live in rivers in Europe and North America. But they migrate to the sea to breed. They make an amazing journey, swimming downstream and even wriggling overland until they reach the sea. The eels lay their eggs far out in the Atlantic Ocean. Then they die. The young eels, called elvers, swim back to the rivers. The long journey can take three years.

Some eels, such as the conger eel, spend all their lives in the sea.

EGG

All animal life comes from some sort of egg. Some are laid by the female and develop outside her body before they hatch. Most mammals develop inside the mother's body. The egg, or ovum, must be joined with a sperm cell from the male in order to develop.

EGYPT

Modern Egypt is a country of more than 62 million people. Nearly all of them live in only four percent of the country's total area (1,002,000sq km). This is the land irrigated by the Nile. The rest is desert.

Most Egyptians work on the land. They produce cotton, rice, fruits, grain and vegetables. In some areas modern irrigation has been so successful that two or three crops are grown a year.

Egypt is an independent Arab republic. The major religion is Islam and the language is Arabic.

See also PAGE 61.

Egg: The different fluids inside a bird's egg provide the embryo with the nutrients it needs.

EGYPT, ANCIENT

The civilization of ancient Egypt was centred on the river Nile. The Nile valley is hot and dry, but each year the river floods and spreads a rich silt over the land, making it fertile. The ancient Egyptians worshipped the Nile as a god.

The pharaohs (kings) of Egypt were very powerful. The people thought the pharaoh was a god. He owned everything and everyone had to obey his commands. The pharaohs built huge tombs, often in the form of pyramids. The dead pharaoh was buried inside, surrounded by treasure and by all the things he would need in the next world, such as food, clothes, furniture and weapons. The dead body was

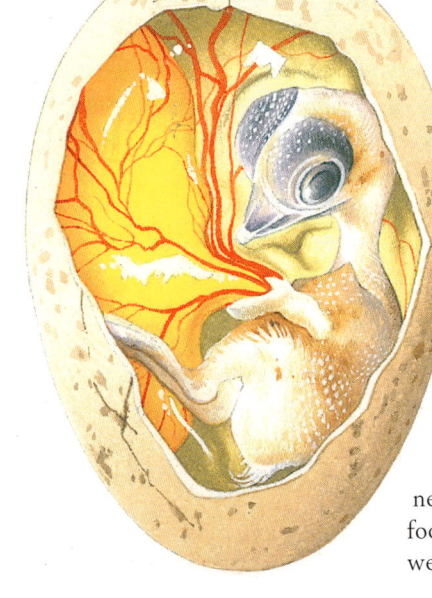

Egypt, Ancient: *Important people's bodies were preserved using special chemicals. The preserved bodies are called mummies.*

preserved, or mummified, before being buried.

Rich Egyptians enjoyed lives of luxury. They had servants, slaves, dancers and musicians. Ancient Egyptian civilization began around 3200BC and lasted until 30BC, when Egypt was finally conquered by the Romans.

EINSTEIN, ALBERT (1879-1955)

Einstein was one of the most brilliant thinkers of modern times. He completely changed our ideas about space, time and motion, and about matter and energy. Einstein said that nothing can travel faster than light, and that mass and energy are different forms of the same thing. His ideas were set out in his famous laws of relativity.

ELECTRICITY

Electricity is a form of energy. The electricity we use in our homes is produced by generators in power stations. A battery is a portable supply of electricity.

Electricity flows through wires as electric current. It is a flow of electrons, tiny particles present in all atoms. They flow easily in metals, which are called good conductors of electricity. Current

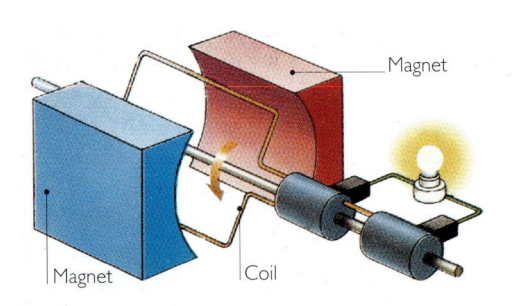

Electricity: *In a simple electrical generator, a coil of wire is turned between the poles of a magnet, generating an electrical current.*

can only flow if a wire makes a complete loop or circuit. Switches operate gaps in the circuit to start or stop the flow of electricity.

Electronics

Electronics is the study of the way electrons act as they flow through certain crystals, gases or a vacuum. Electrons are tiny particles found in all atoms. Electronic devices like transistors and silicon chips are used in radios, televisions and computers.

See also COMPUTER; RADAR; RADIO; SILICON CHIP; TELEVISION; TRANSISTOR.

Elements and Compounds

Elements are the building blocks from which all substances are formed. When a chemist splits up salt, he finds that it is made up of two substances called sodium and chlorine. No matter how hard he tries, he cannot split sodium and chlorine any further. They are chemical elements. In nature there are 92 elements. And scientists have made another 17.

Elements are made up of atoms. Groups of atoms joined together are called molecules. For example, a molecule of oxygen consists of two oxygen atoms. A substance whose molecules contain more than one kind of atom is called a compound. Most elements are found as chemical compounds.

Elephant

The elephant is the largest living land animal. A big male, or bull, may weigh 7 tonnes. Elephants

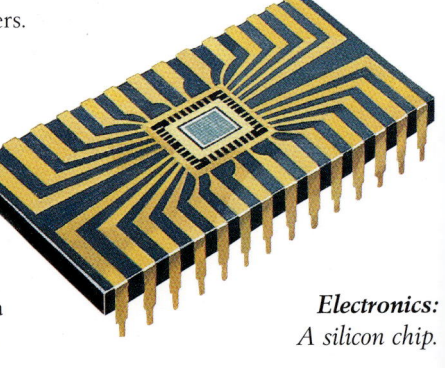

Electronics: *A silicon chip.*

Elephant: *African elephants, like this one, have larger ears than their Indian cousins.*

live in herds. If one elephant is injured, the rest will help it. Elephants eat huge amounts of grass and tree leaves every day.

There are two kinds of elephant. The Indian one can be trained to work. The larger African elephant is not easily tamed.

Elizabeth I (1533-1603)

When Elizabeth was born, her father, Henry VIII, was furious. He wanted a son to succeed him as King of England. But when Elizabeth became queen in 1558, she proved a strong ruler. She never married, and for 45 years successfully protected England against its chief enemies, France and Spain. Daring seamen, such as Francis Drake, and brilliant writers, like William Shakespeare, made her reign one of the most exciting in English history.

Energy

When a piece of wood is set alight, it burns and gives out light you can see and heat you can feel. Heat and light are two common forms of energy.

Wood is one kind of fuel, which releases energy when burnt. Coal, petrol and natural gas are other fuels. When petrol is burned in a car engine, the energy produced makes pistons turn the car wheels.

The chemical energy in the fuel has been changed into mechanical energy to turn the car wheels. When the car is moving it has kinetic energy, the energy of motion. A rock balancing on top of a cliff has potential energy – the energy of position.

Energy: Wind generators harness wind power to make electricity – but they are expensive.

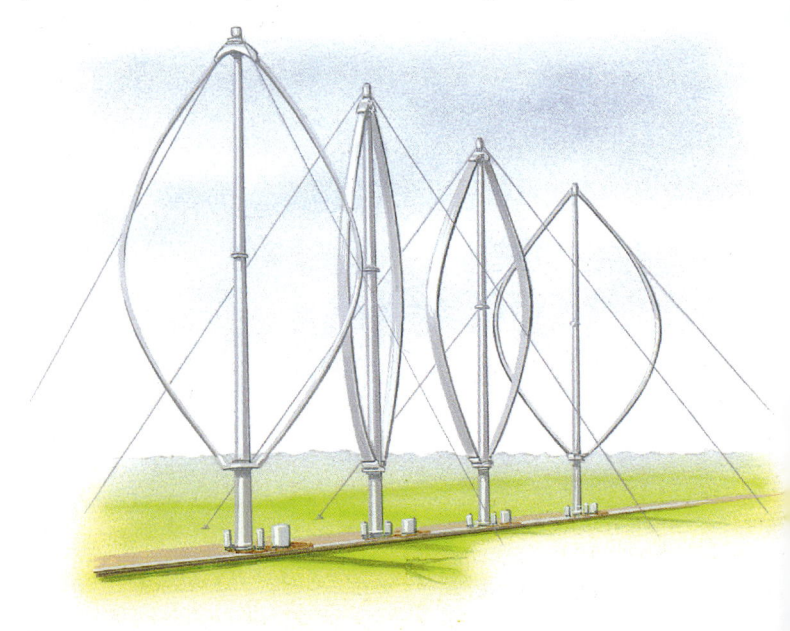

Engine

We use many kinds of engine in the modern world to work the machines in our homes and factories, and the ones that transport us in the air and on sea and land. Most engines burn a fuel to produce energy. A car engine burns petrol, while lorries and buses have diesel engines, which burn oil. Aircraft have jet engines, which burn kerosene (paraffin). There are all kinds of internal combustion engines, in which fuel is burned in an enclosed space. Steam engines and turbines burn fuel outside the engine.

See also ENERGY; FUEL; JET ENGINE.

Erosion

Erosion happens when parts of the Earth's surface are worn away or shaped by water, wind or ice. The sea beating against a coast, for example, often wears it away or erodes it. After rain, water pours down a mountainside and may wear away or erode the soil covering it. Winds, too, may erode soil, whipping it into the air and carrying it away. The ice in glaciers grinds away at rock, eroding it. Erosion is a problem for farmers because it carries away the soil in which they plant their crops. Mountain farmers often build step-like terraces down mountain slopes to stop this from happening.

Europe

The continent of Europe is smaller than any of the other continents except Australia. Yet a fifth of the world's people live in Europe.

Most of Europe has fertile soil and good rainfall. Europe's farmers produce meat, grain, fruit and vegetables. Most farms use modern machinery. Europe is rich in coal, iron ore and other raw materials.

Europe lives by trade. It has good roads, railways, airports and canals. Ships carry goods across the Baltic Sea, the North Sea and the Mediterranean Sea, and to all parts of the world.

The people of Europe are made up of many different nationalities. Each has its own language and customs. In the past, European countries fought with each other. European wars affected the rest of the world, because European countries were so powerful. Two world wars in the 20th century have begun in Europe.

For many years after World War II there was hostility between Communist Eastern Europe and the democratic West. But that ended with the sudden decline of Communism in the late 1980s and early 1990s. In recent years, most of Europe has worked together to bring peace to the region.

European Economic Community

See European Union.

European Union

The EU, or European Union (which used to be known as the European Community or Common Market), is a group of countries mostly in western Europe. In 1997 there were 15 members: Austria, Belgium, Denmark, Finland, France, Germany, Greece, Ireland, Italy, Luxembourg, the Netherlands, Portugal, Spain, Sweden and the United Kingdom. These countries all work and trade together. The EU has a civil service and a parliament. There is also a European Court of Justice.

Evolution

Evolution is the gradual process by which all living things have changed since life began millions of years ago. Fossils show us how creatures have changed.

The first creatures were very simple forms of life. They evolved into more complicated plants and animals. Fishes evolved from smaller sea creatures. Some fish began breathing air and crawled onto dry land. These were the first amphibians. The amphibians evolved into reptiles. All birds and mammals, including man, evolved from reptiles.

Explorers

People have always had the urge to explore the unknown. Some explorers have gone in search of lands to settle. Others were greedy for riches, while some explorers journeyed only in search of knowledge.

To the ancient peoples of Europe, 'the world' meant the lands around the Mediterranean Sea. Only the Phoenicians dared to sail out into the grey Atlantic Ocean beyond.

In the 900s the Vikings sailed in their small, fragile ships as far as North America. But until the invention of the magnetic compass in the 1300s, long sea voyages were very dangerous.

To reach the East, with its gold, spices and silks, European merchants had to travel overland. Marco Polo reached China in 1275. Then the Portuguese discovered they could reach India by sailing round the coast of Africa. In 1492 Columbus reached America, the 'New World'. By 1522 Magellan's sailors had proved that the world was round by sailing round it.

After this, explorers went out from Europe eager to find lands to settle as colonies. The last continent to be explored by Europeans was Africa. During the 1800s several explorers crossed this unknown continent.

Explorers: *Columbus and the other explorers of his time sailed the world's oceans in small but sturdy ships called caravels.*

In 1909 Peary reached the North Pole, and in 1911 Amundsen beat Scott to the South Pole. Today few parts of the Earth are unexplored.

See also COLUMBUS; COOK; GAMA; MAGELLAN; MARCO POLO; VIKING.

EYE

Our eyes are very delicate. Each eye is a ball full of liquid. In the centre of the front is a black hole called the pupil. This lets in light. Behind the pupil is a lens. The lens focuses an image of whatever we are looking at onto a screen called the retina. Then messages are sent along a nerve to the brain. The brain arranges the messages into a picture again, and we 'see'.

The coloured part of the eye is called the iris. It is a ring of muscle which makes the pupil larger or smaller. In bright light, the pupil gets smaller. But in dim light, it gets larger to let in as much light as possible.

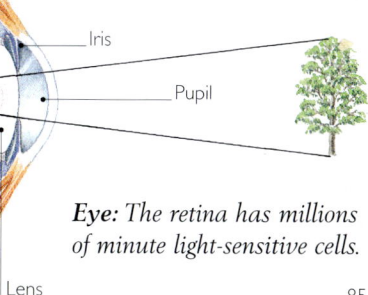

Eye: *The retina has millions of minute light-sensitive cells.*

F

Farming

Farming is the world's most important industry. By raising animals and growing crops, farmers provide us with the food we eat. Civilization became possible only when people stopped being nomadic and settled down to farm.

Gradually, people learned how to plant seeds and grow crops, and how to keep and breed animals such as chickens, cattle and sheep. Slowly, tools were devised to help.

In the 1800s and 1900s machines were invented to do the work of people and animals. There were better ploughs, seed drills, threshers and reapers, and tractors replaced the horse and ox. Discoveries about crop rotation, fertilizers and chemicals allowed farmers to grow larger crops.

Fertilizers were important because they add vital plant food to the soil. Plants grown for their crops need some substances, such as nitrogen, phosphorus, and potassium, in greater amounts than are usually found in the soil. Fertilizers top up the levels of these substances. Some are made from natural substances; others are mainly chemicals.

Fern

Ferns are primitive plants. There have been ferns on the Earth for more than 300 million years. Many prehistoric ferns were as tall as trees; a few tree ferns still grow in tropical forests.

Ferns have no flowers or seeds. Instead they have tiny cells called spores under their leaves. The wind scatters the spores onto the ground and they eventually grow into new ferns.

Fibre Optics

An optical fibre is a glass or plastic strand along which light, including laser light, can be sent on a curved path. Each fibre can be as little as 0.013mm to

Fibre Optics: Optical fibres have many uses. Doctors use them to see inside the body.

0.15mm thick. The fibres are most often used together in bundles. Fibre optics are more and more being used instead of metal wires for telephone systems, since a single fibre can carry thousands of telephone conversations at the same time.

See also LASER.

FIELD HOCKEY
See HOCKEY.

FILM
'Moving pictures' were first shown in the 1890s. People crowded into cinemas to watch them. During the 1930s, because of its good weather and varied scenery, Hollywood in the USA became the centre of the film industry. At first films were silent and rather jerky. 'Talking pictures' appeared in 1927.

The person who decides how a story is made into a film is the director. The producer takes care of the business side. And, apart from the actors and cameramen, there are people to look after scenery, lighting, costumes, make-up and 'stunts'. Sometimes a studio set, with artificial scenery, is used. But films are often 'shot' (filmed) out of doors 'on location'. When filming is over, the best parts of the film are edited (cut up and run together) to make the finished film.

FINGERPRINTS
The tiny ridges and furrows arranged in patterns on the tips of the fingers and thumbs are called fingerprints. No two people have the same fingerprints. Even if the

Fingerprints: Police experts classify fingerprints by their basic patterns and by the numbers of ridges.

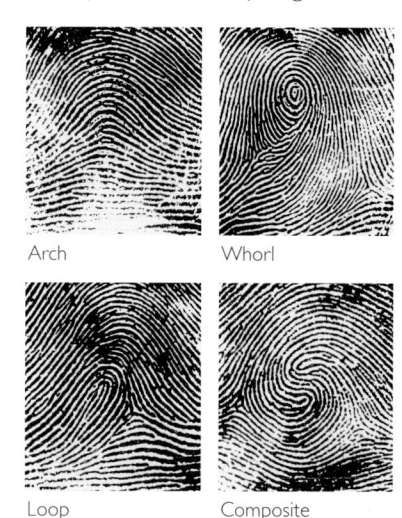

Arch

Whorl

Loop

Composite

outer skin is damaged, the pattern does not change. This is why fingerprints are so helpful to the police in identifying criminals.

FISH
Fishes are animals that spend their lives in water. Some fishes live in saltwater and some live in freshwater. Some spend part of their lives in the sea, and part in the rivers.

Fish: *These North American freshwater fishes have also been introduced in parts of Europe.*

Most fishes have bony skeletons. But a small group, including sharks, have skeletons made of gristle, or cartilage. Like all animals, fishes have to breathe oxygen. Their gills take oxygen out of the water. Some fishes breathe through their skins as well, and a few have lungs.

Fishes eat water animals, including other fishes, and plants. They swim by bending their bodies from side to side, and by moving their tails. They use their fins to keep them upright and for steering and braking.

Most fishes are covered with scales. Some fishes have a line of special scales along each side of the body. This is called the lateral line. It helps the fish detect underwater vibrations. Most fishes have an air bladder inside their bodies to keep them at any level they choose. But the more primitive cartilage fishes do not have this 'swim bladder'. If they stop swimming they sink.

During the breeding season some fishes migrate long distances to reach their spawning grounds.

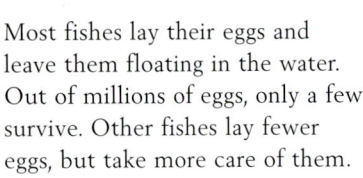

Rock bass

Pumpkinseed

Most fishes lay their eggs and leave them floating in the water. Out of millions of eggs, only a few survive. Other fishes lay fewer eggs, but take more care of them.

See also EEL; SEA HORSE; SHARK.

FISHING

Most fish are caught in the sea, but in some countries river and lake fisheries are important. The best fishing grounds are in the Atlantic and Pacific oceans.

The most important food fish are cod, mackerel, haddock, herring, flatfish (such as plaice and sole), sardine, tunny (or tuna) and salmon. Shellfish, such as prawns, lobsters and oysters, also make valuable catches.

Most sea fish are caught in nets. Trawls are long, bagshaped nets towed along under water. A purse-seine net is drawn round a shoal of fish, then pulled up. Gill nets look rather like curtains: the fish swim into them and are caught in the mesh. Fish can also be caught on baited lines. This method is known as trolling.

FLAG

Every country has its own flag. Organizations such as the United Nations and the Red Cross have flags, and kings and queens have their own personal flags.

The first flags were ornamental streamers. In battle, flags or standards, raised high on poles, were rallying points for soldiers.

In the Middle Ages there were several flags of different shapes, (gonfalons, banners and pennons) but today most are rectangular. Flags are also used at sea to identify ships and to send messages.

FLOWER

Most plants have flowers. The flower is the part of the plant where the seeds develop. Without it, the plant could not reproduce itself. Inside each seed is all the 'information' needed to make a

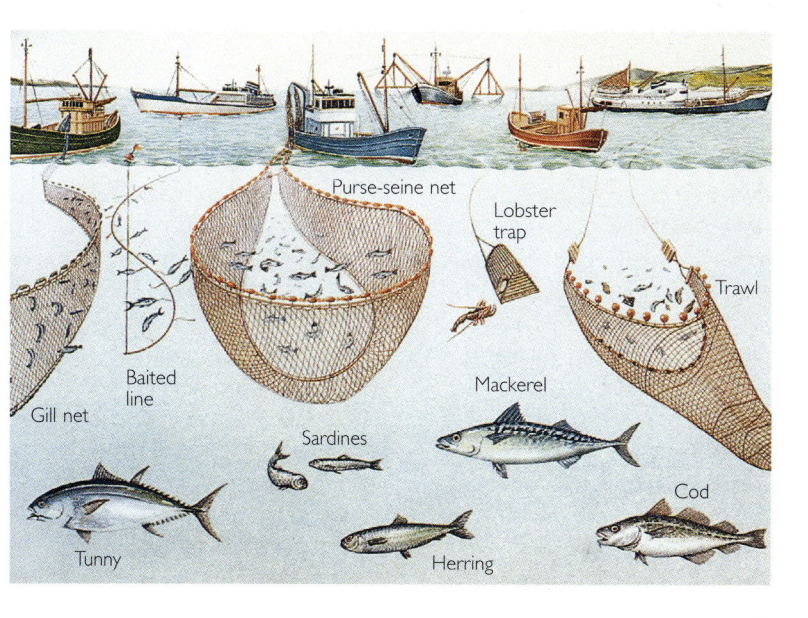

Fishing: Most fish are caught using trawl nets. Seine nets are good with fish like herrings that gather in shoals near the surface.

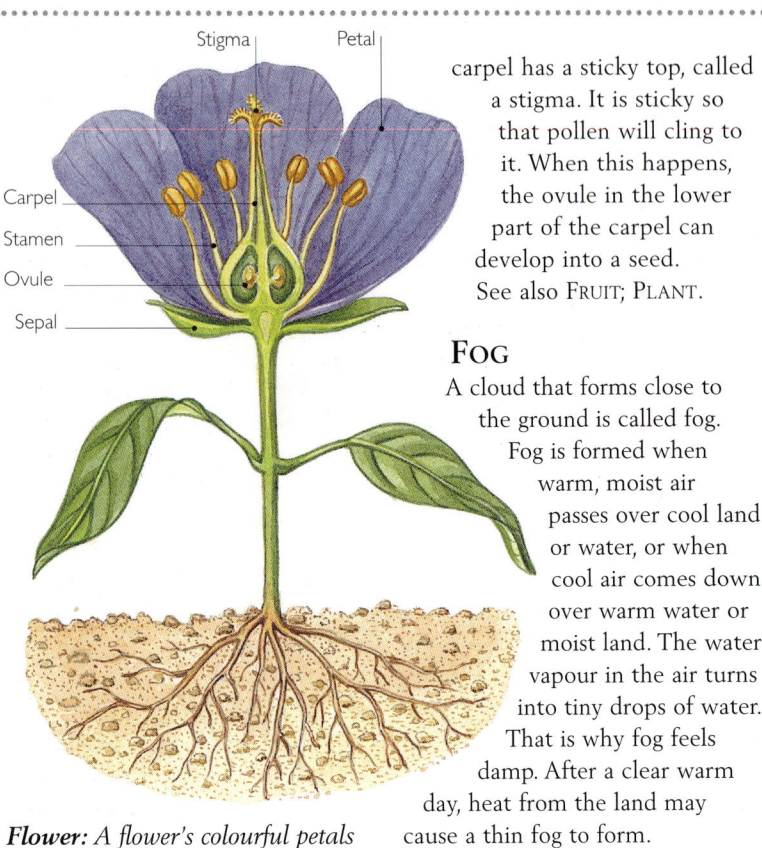

Flower: A flower's colourful petals attract birds and insects, which then help to spread the powdery pollen onto the sticky stigma.

new plant grow. Most flowers appear in the summer when the plant is fully grown. Flowers come in all shapes and sizes, but they all have the same basic parts.

The most important parts are called stamens and carpels. The stamens are male parts, which produce a powder called pollen. The carpels are female parts. Each carpel has a sticky top, called a stigma. It is sticky so that pollen will cling to it. When this happens, the ovule in the lower part of the carpel can develop into a seed. See also FRUIT; PLANT.

FOG

A cloud that forms close to the ground is called fog. Fog is formed when warm, moist air passes over cool land or water, or when cool air comes down over warm water or moist land. The water vapour in the air turns into tiny drops of water. That is why fog feels damp. After a clear warm day, heat from the land may cause a thin fog to form.

FOOD

Our bodies need energy to live and grow. This energy comes from the food we eat. The three most important substances in food are carbohydrates, fats and proteins. Carbohydrates are food 'fuels'. They give us energy to work, move and keep warm. Sugar and starch are carbohydrates. We eat carbohydrates in bread, potatoes, rice, sweets and cakes. Cream, butter and the fat in meat provide us with fats. These are also good fuels. But if we eat too many carbohydrates or fats, our bodies store what they cannot use. Then we get fat. Proteins build the body's cells and are vital to good health. Protein-rich foods are eggs, lean meat, cheese, fish and beans.

FOOTBALL

There are seven different games of football: Australian Rules, Canadian, American, Gaelic, Rugby League, Rugby Union and Association (or soccer). They all come from a rough game played in England as long ago as the Middle Ages. Any number of players took part and there were no rules.

Nowadays, soccer is played in more places and by more people than any other kind of football. It is the only one of the seven games in which handling the ball is not allowed. Each team has 11 players.

In Rugby, players are allowed to use their hands to catch, throw or run with the ball. There is very little difference between Rugby League and Rugby Union, except that, until recently, the players in Rugby League were professionals, while Rugby Union players were amateurs. In Rugby League each team has 13 players; in Rugby Union each team has 15.

In American football each team has 11 players, all wearing heavily padded clothing. The game is similar to Rugby but in American football, unlike Rugby, players are allowed to pass the ball forward. Canadian football is very close to American, except that each team has 12 players.

Gaelic football is played in Ireland and the USA. Players, 15 in each team, are not allowed to throw the ball but they can punch it. In Australian Rules football, played as its name suggests in Australia, each team has 18 players. They may kick or punch the ball but are not allowed to run with it for more than 10m.

FORD, HENRY (1863-1947)

Henry Ford was an American automobile manufacturer. He was the first man to develop assembly-line methods of production. In

Ford: Model T.

mass-production the parts of the car are added to the car body on a conveyor belt. Ford could produce many cars very cheaply. Between 1908 and 1927 he mass-produced 15 million Model T cars alone.

FOREST

Land that is covered with trees is forest. Today about a third of the Earth's land surface is covered by forests. There are about 20,000 different kinds of tree, and about 1,000 of them produce good timber.

In cold lands the forests are mainly of conifers, such as pines and firs. The largest coniferous forests are in northern Europe, Canada and Siberia.

Milder countries have forests of broad-leaved trees, such as oaks,

Forest: Countries like New Zealand have mixed forests with both conifers and broad-leaved trees.

elms, beeches, birches and maples. These trees are deciduous, that is, they shed their leaves every year.

In the hot, wet lands close to the equator there are tropical forests of trees such as ebony and mahogany, whose wood is very hard. There are vast rainforests in South America, central Africa and Southeast Asia. Near the coasts are often found swamp forests of mangroves.

FOSSIL

Fossils are the hardened remains of dead animals and plants that lived thousands of years ago. They

Fossil: *By studying fossils, experts can discover much about the far-distant history of the Earth and the creatures that have inhabited it.*

tell us what life was like before written records were kept.

Some fossils are the impressions made by remains that have since disappeared. They are often found in rock because the plants and animals were covered by mud or sand which later turned into rock.

Sometimes a whole body is preserved including the hair and skin. Sometimes the body has dissolved away and the space it left filled with mud or sand that slowly turned into rock. Most commonly, though, fossils are just the remains of the hard parts of animals such as bones or shells.

Fox

Foxes belong to the dog family. They hunt by night for rabbits, mice and voles. The female fox is called a vixen. She rears her cubs in an underground den.

Fox: *Foxes can adapt to most environments, even nowadays to city life.*

Farmers dislike foxes, because they kill other animals. In Britain and some other countries the fox is hunted by foxhounds. Silver and blue Arctic foxes are bred on special farms for their fur. The little fennec fox lives in the desert.

FRANCE

France is the largest country in Western Europe. Its beautiful scenery includes forests, plains, valleys, high mountains and great rivers.

France has fertile soil and a mild climate. Many of its people are farmers. In many parts of France grapes are grown to make wine; French cheeses are also famous. France has many industries and is a member of the EU. Its capital city is Paris.

In 1789 the French people overthrew their king and set up a republic. This important event is called the French Revolution.

See also PAGE 60.

FREUD, SIGMUND (1856-1939)

Sigmund Freud was a Viennese doctor who made a great contribution to the study of the human mind. He taught that the subconscious, the activity of the mind that we are not aware of, provides clues to a person's mental state. He also developed the system of psychoanalysis, a kind of examination of the mind.

FROGS AND TOADS

These animals are amphibians. They can live on land, but must return to the water to lay eggs.

Frogs and Toads: Tree frogs have suction pads on their toes that help them to cling to branches.

Fruit: *Many fruits are sweet and juicy, so that animals will carry them away as food and help to spread the seed.*

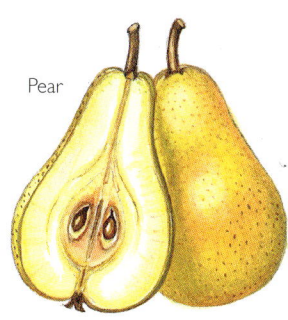

Plum

Pear

Orange

Frogs and toads look rather alike. But frogs use their long back legs to hop. Toads crawl or run. Both eat insects and worms, catching their prey with their long, sticky tongues.

In spring frogs and toads travel to ponds and streams to breed. They lay eggs called spawn. The eggs hatch into tadpoles. Tadpoles swim like fish and breathe through gills. But soon they grow legs, lose their tails and develop lungs. Finally, they become tiny frogs or toads.

FRUIT

We all recognize apples, oranges, plums and pears as fruits. But pea pods, walnuts, tomatoes, cucumbers, acorns and dandelion 'clocks' are also fruits. Many fruits are good to eat and growing them is an important industry.

The fruit is the part of a plant that protects the seed. It helps to spread the seed, so that new plants can grow. Some fruits have wings (such as the sycamore) or light, fluffy heads (such as the dandelion) so that the seeds will blow away. Burrs are fruits that cling to the fur of passing animals. Many fruits split when ripe, letting their seeds fall. Some fruits, like the coconut, float on water and are dispersed that way.

See also FLOWER; PLANT.

FUEL

Fuels are substances that release energy when burnt. The process of burning is called combustion.

Fuel may be solid, liquid or gas. Coal, wood, charcoal and peat are solid fuels. The most important liquid fuels come from petroleum. Natural gas, a compound of hydrogen and carbon, is often found near petroleum.

G

GALAXY
Our Sun is part of a great family of stars. We call this family the Milky Way galaxy. A galaxy is a big group of stars held together by gravity. A galaxy like ours contains about 100 billion stars and probably many planets. Some stars are grouped together in giant clusters. The galaxies also contain great clouds of gas and dust called nebulae.

GALILEO (1564-1642)
Galileo was an Italian astronomer. In 1609 he became the first person to look at the sky through a telescope. He saw the mountains on our Moon and the moons of the planet Jupiter.

Galaxy: The Milky Way, our galaxy, is a huge spiral. We are part of the solar system, which lies towards the edge of the galaxy.

Galileo was skilled at mathematics and carried out scientific experiments. He discovered how a pendulum swings and showed that different weights fall to the ground at the same rate.

GAMA, VASCO DA (c.1469-1524)
This Portuguese explorer was the first man to find a sea route to India. He sailed from Lisbon in July 1497, rounded the Cape of Good Hope in November and went on to land in southwestern India in May 1498. He returned to Portugal with two ships laden with spices.

GANDHI, MOHANDAS KARAMCHAND (1869-1948)
Gandhi helped to free India from British rule. Known as the Mahatma or 'Great Soul', he believed that all violence was wrong. So he used 'peaceful non-cooperation' as a weapon.

He was born in India. From 1893 to 1915 he worked in South

Africa. When India became independent in 1947, Muslims and Hindus began fighting. Gandhi failed to make peace between them, and was shot by a Hindu fanatic on January 30, 1948.

GARIBALDI,
GIUSEPPE (1807-1882)

Garibaldi was an Italian patriot. In his time Italy was made up of several separate states, and large parts of northern Italy belonged to Austria. Garibaldi fought to make Italy one country from 1834 until 1860. Then Victor Emmanuel became king of the whole of Italy.

GEM

Some rocks contain crystals that can be cut to show great brilliance and sparkle. They are called gems or gemstones. They can be set in gold or silver to form jewellery.

The finest gems are diamonds. They are a form of carbon. Diamonds are expensive because they are rare and difficult to cut.

Gem: *About a hundred different kinds of gemstone are found in the Earth's rocks.*

They are the hardest of all the minerals. Some diamonds are made into cutting tools.

Some gems are not crystals, but lovely stones. They include opal and lapis lazuli. Pearls are gems that oysters produce in their shells.

GENETICS

The science of genetics explains why living things look and behave as they do. Advanced animals have two sexes, male and female. Each individual produces sex cells. If a male and female sex cell join, the

Turquoise

Diamond

Ruby

Opal

Amethyst

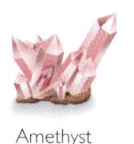

Lapis lazuli

Emerald

Jade

female cell grows into a new individual. Each parent passes on characteristics to its offspring. This process is called heredity.

Heredity works in an amazing way. Inside every cell are tiny chromosomes, largely made of the chemical DNA (deoxyribonucleic acid). Different parts of each chromosome carry different 'coded messages'. Each part is called a gene. The genes carry all the information needed to make a new plant or animal. They decide its sex and what characteristics it inherits. Some characteristics are stronger than others. They are 'dominant'. Weaker ones are 'recessive'.

DNA is one of two kinds of nucleic acid – special molecules in cells that play an important part in growth and reproduction. DNA is found only in the nucleus of the cell. RNA (ribonucleic acid) is found throughout the cell, where it controls protein-making.

Genetics: Genes for brown eyes are 'dominant' – they dominate over weaker, 'recessive' genes for blue eyes. So you have blue eyes only if you inherit two blue-eye genes. Here are the combinations possible in children if both parents have one brown-eye and one blue-eye gene (below) and if one parent has both a blue-eye and a brown-eye gene and the other parent two blue-eye genes (bottom).

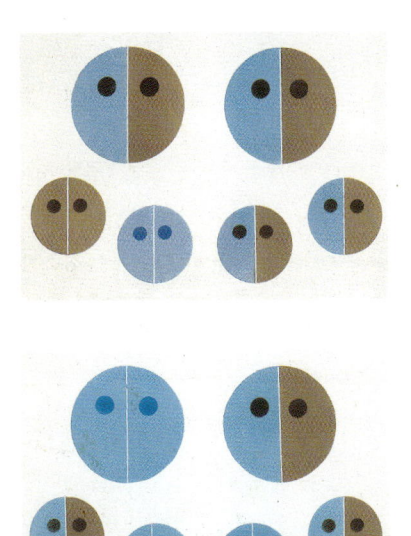

GENGHIS KHAN (1167-1227)

Genghis Khan was one of the most feared men in history. He was born Temujin, son of a Mongol prince, but became known as Genghis Khan, meaning 'conqueror of the world'. The Mongols came from central Asia. Wherever Genghis Khan led his Mongol army, terrible tales were told of his cruelty. He conquered many tribes in China, Russia, Afghanistan and Persia.

GEOLOGY

Geology is the study of the substances that make up the Earth and of the forces that act upon it to change it. Geologists work to find what kinds of rocks the Earth is made of and how they got there. They study volcanoes and earthquakes for clues about the underground movements of the Earth. To understand the Earth as it is today, geologists study the history of the planet from its beginnings four billion years ago.

GERMANY

Germany has had a troubled history during this century. It has begun two devastating wars – World War I (1914-1918) and World War II (1939-1945).

After World War II, Germany split into two. The eastern sector became a Communist state – the German Democratic Republic. The western sector was renamed the Federal Republic of West Germany. In 1990, with the collapse of Communism, the two became a single country again.

Only northern Germany has a sea coast – on the North and Baltic Seas. Here the land is mostly low and flat. Central Germany is hilly and wooded, and in the south are high mountains and thick forests. In eastern Germany the Elbe and Oder rivers flow north towards the Baltic.

Germany has fertile soil and a mild climate. Farmers grow cereals, potatoes and sugar beet, and make wine. They raise cattle and pigs. The country has plenty of coal,

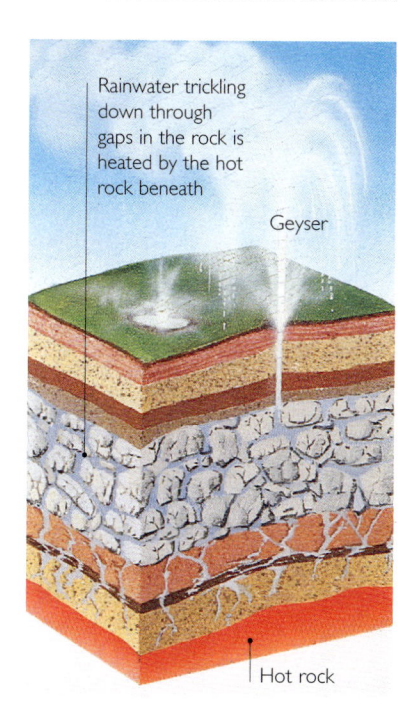

Geyser: *In a geyser, steam and superheated water spout into the air through a crack in the rock.*

iron ore, timber and hydroelectric power. There are many factories, especially in the Ruhr region.

See also HITLER; PAGE 60.

GEYSER

A geyser is a spring which spouts hot water and steam into the air from time to time. It is a small sign of the searing heat deep inside the Earth.

A geyser consists of a hole which goes down to a layer of hot rock (usually uncooled lava) and water. When the water is superheated by the rocks, it erupts or shoots into the air.

Geysers are found in many volcanic regions. The most famous are in Japan, the USA, Iceland and New Zealand.

See also VOLCANO.

GIRAFFE

The giraffe is the tallest animal in the world. It may reach nearly 6m in height. Giraffes live in Africa. They eat leaves, not grass, and when they drink, they have to spread their legs wide in order to reach the water. They can run fast to escape from their enemies.

GLACIER

A glacier is a slow-moving river of ice. It flows down the slopes of mountains from an icecap or high snowfield. Glaciers push stones and boulders along with them. They scrape the soil from the land, smooth the hills and scour out valleys. The rocky mounds piled up by glaciers are called moraines.

During the Ice Ages glaciers spread across the Northern Hemisphere. Boulders carried with the ice can still be seen.

See also ICE AGE; ICEBERG.

GLASS

Glass is a useful material. It is transparent, easy to shape, and cheap to make. It can be made as flat sheets for windows, or into curved lenses for cameras. It can be blown to make bottles, tumblers and other objects.

Glass is made from some of the cheapest materials you can think of – sand, limestone and soda ash. These are mixed together and heated in a very hot furnace. They melt and become glass.

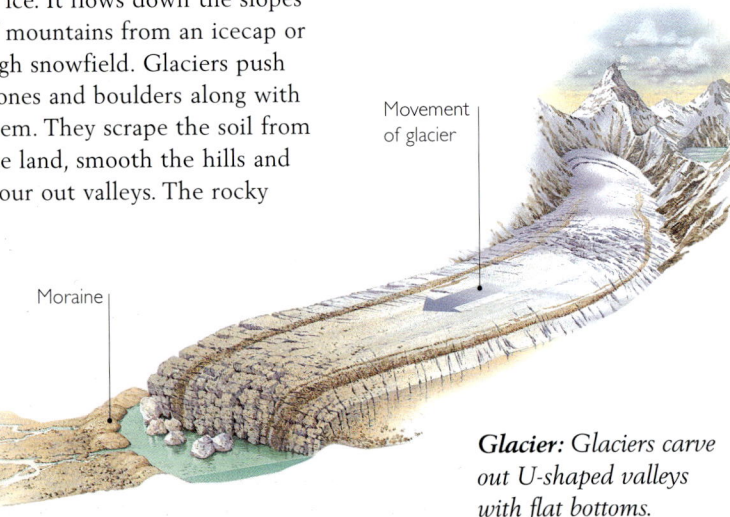

Glacier: *Glaciers carve out U-shaped valleys with flat bottoms.*

Goat

The goat was one of the earliest animals to be tamed. Its milk, meat, wool and skin have been useful to people for thousands of years.

The goat is tougher than its relative the sheep. It can live in dry, rocky country. It climbs well and can eat almost anything. Herds of hungry goats have turned good pastures into deserts. Wild goats live on high mountain crags.

Gold

Gold is a heavy, yellow metal. It has been used for thousands of years to make jewellery and ornaments because it is beautiful and does not lose its shine. It is also easy to shape. Gold is precious because it is scarce.

Sometimes large lumps of gold, or nuggets, are mined in rocks. But usually gold is found in lodes or veins in rocks. Half the world's gold is mined in just one part of South Africa.

See also METALS.

Government

People living together in a group need government. They have to agree on what jobs must be done and who should do them.

In a primitive tribe the best hunter or strongest warrior might become the ruler or chief. The ancient Greeks tried a form of government called democracy or 'rule by the people'. The people met to discuss new laws and to decide what taxes should be paid. This was the beginning of the modern parliament.

Today every country has a head of state. Britain is a monarchy, so the head of state is the Queen.

Goat: *The Toggenburg is a domesticated goat from Switzerland. Angora goats are raised for their silky hair. This is made into mohair, a kind of cloth in which angora wool is mixed with cotton or sheep's wool.*

But the country is ruled by a government of ministers. The head of the government is the Prime Minister. Parliament is divided into two parts, the House of Commons and the House of Lords.

The President of the United States is head of state and government. Presidents are elected every four years. The US parliament, called the Congress, is divided into the House of Representatives and the Senate.

See also COMMUNISM; DEMOCRACY.

GRASS

Most grasses are slender, with hollow stems and pointed leaves. The plants keep growing even when the leaves are cut.

Cereals are grasses that are also foods. Many farm animals eat grass, fresh in summer and dried as hay in winter. Sugar cane is a kind of grass.

GRAVITY

Throw a ball into the air and it falls back to the ground. This is because the Earth pulls it back. The Earth's pull is called gravity. It is one of the basic forces in the universe. Magnetism is another. Isaac Newton first stated the laws of gravity. He said that every object has an attraction for every other.

Gravity is what keeps all the heavenly bodies in their paths through space. It keeps the Moon moving in a circle around the Earth. It keeps the Earth moving around the Sun. If there were no gravity, the Moon and Earth would fly off into space.

GREECE AND TURKEY

Greece includes hundreds of islands in the Aegean and Ionian seas. It has natural harbours, mountains and valleys, a rocky landscape of limestone and a warm, sunny climate. The islands are peaceful, but Greece's cities are busy with people and traffic. In Athens, the capital, air pollution is eating away at its mixture of ancient and modern buildings. Greece's main industries are agriculture and tourism.

Turkey is partly in Europe and partly in Asia. Much of the land is mountainous and dry, but the coastal plains are fertile and farming is the main industry. Turkey was once the centre of the mighty Ottoman Empire which lasted for 500 years but collapsed after World War I.

See also PAGE 60; PAGE 62.

GREECE, ANCIENT

The ancient Greeks built one of the greatest of all civilizations. It began some 4,000 years ago when wandering tribes from central Europe came to the land that we now call Greece.

Over the centuries, the Greek civilization developed. Cities were built. Craftsmen made gold ornaments and bronze weapons. Art, music and poetry developed.

Democracy, 'rule by the people', started about 2,500 years ago in Athens. The Athenians also built fine temples and public buildings. For entertainment, the Athenians played music on flutes and lyres or they went to the theatre. The Athenians loved to hear stories of great Greek heroes and their deeds. The greatest of these stories were told by the poet Homer in two long poems, called the *Iliad* and the *Odyssey*. The beauty of life in Athens can be seen from the ruins that still remain.

Athens was only one of a number of city states in Greece. The states often quarrelled. The greatest rival of Athens was Sparta, and the two states were

Greece, Ancient: *Greek artists carved beautiful sculptures to decorate their public buildings.*

very different. Sparta was a military state. Its people were soldiers and the Spartans had no use for art, philosophy or comfortable homes.

The Greeks were very fond of athletics, such as running, javelin throwing, discus throwing and wrestling. The first Olympic Games, held in a place called Olympia, took place in 776BC. The Greeks had many gods, but the greatest was Zeus, king of the gods.

The age of the city states in Greece ended in 338BC. Then, King Philip of Macedonia brought all of Greece under his rule.

Greek ideas have survived many centuries, and have had great influence. The way we live and think today owes a great deal to the civilization of ancient Greece.

GULF STREAM

The Gulf Stream is a very important warm-water ocean current. It is surface water which flows in a clockwise movement around the North Atlantic Ocean. It begins near the equator and drifts past Florida up the coast of the United States towards Newfoundland and then moves towards Europe.

Part of the Gulf Stream washes the shores of France, the British Isles, Norway and Iceland. Because it is warm, winter in these countries is much milder than that of other places as far north.

GUN

Guns are weapons that fire bullets or shells. Small arms, also called firearms, include pistols, revolvers, shotguns and rifles. Big military guns – artillery pieces – include field guns, howitzers and mortars.

All guns work in roughly the same way. A gun has a long, hollow, metal barrel. The bore of a gun is the width of the hole in the barrel. One end of the barrel, the breech, is closed; the other end, the muzzle, is open. When the gun is fired, an explosive charge inside a cartridge sends a bullet down the barrel and out of the muzzle with great force.

GUTENBERG, JOHANNES (c.1398-1468)

Gutenberg invented movable type for printing in about 1439. His invention meant that books could be produced cheaply. Knowledge, once available only to a few people, could now be studied by many.

GYMNASTICS

Gymnastics consists of exercises to develop and strengthen the body. There are two main types – Swedish and German. They were developed in the 19th century. Both systems help make people supple, strong and agile. Gymnasts use apparatus such as beams, rings, and horizontal and parallel bars.

Gutenberg: In early printing presses the type was positioned on a wooden base, the paper laid over it, and the wooden screw turned to press the paper onto the type.

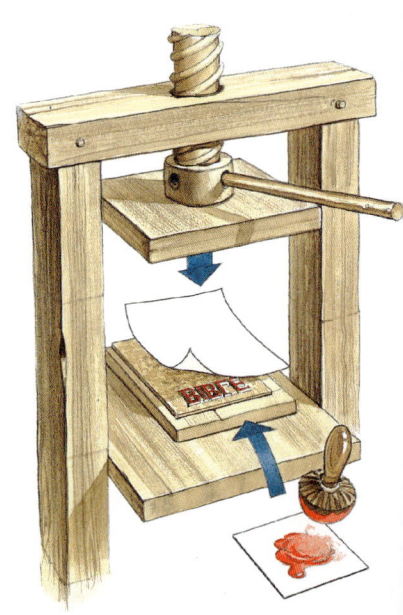

H

HANDEL, GEORGE FREDERICK (1685-1759)
Handel was a German-born English composer who was famous for his operas, concertos and oratorios. His best known works are the *Messiah*, *Music for the Royal Fireworks* and *Water Music*.

HANNIBAL (247-183BC)
Hannibal, a general and statesman, was one of ancient Rome's greatest enemies. He came from Carthage in North Africa. In 218BC he invaded Italy by crossing the Alps with his entire army including war elephants. He fought against the Romans for 15 years but was never able to crush them.

HARVEY, WILLIAM (1578-1657)
Harvey was an English physician who showed how the heart functioned and proved that the blood goes around the body in a circular motion.

HEART
Your heart beats about 70 times every minute. It is a pump – a bag of extra strong muscle that pumps blood around the body.

The pump is divided into four parts: a left and right atrium above a left and right ventricle. The two sides of the pump work quite independently. Blood fresh from the lungs enters the left atrium and is forced through a valve down to the left ventricle. From there it is forced into the body's main artery, the aorta, and out of the heart ready to flow around the body.

On the other side, 'stale' blood from the body enters the right auricle, passes into the right ventricle and is forced out towards the lungs where it will dump its carbon dioxide and pick up vital oxygen.

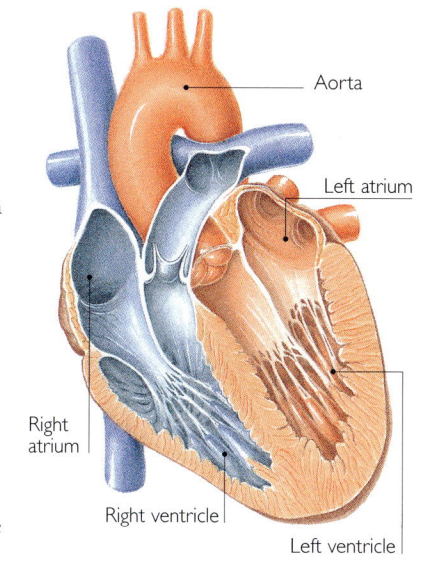

Heart: *Over the course of an average life, the human heart beats some 2,000 million times.*

HEDGEHOG
The hedgehog is one of a group of mammals called insectivores. Although the word insectivore means it eats insects, the hedgehog will eat almost anything. It rolls itself into a prickly ball when frightened and hibernates in winter.

HELICOPTER
A helicopter is a machine that can fly forwards, upwards, downwards, and sideways. This is because it has a rotor, or rotating (turning), wing. Ordinary aircraft have fixed

Rotor blade

Helicopter: A helicopter has spinning rotor blades, which provide both lift and thrust.

wings and their engines can drive them forwards only. The helicopter's rotor consists of metal blades mounted on top of the body. Turned by the engine, the rotor screws itself into the air to lift the helicopter off the ground. When a helicopter is flying forwards, the rotor blades are angled so that they push the air backwards.

HERCULES
Hercules is a hero of ancient Greek and Roman mythology. In a fit of madness, he killed his wife and children. The god Apollo ordered Hercules to perform Twelve Labours in punishment. Today the word 'Herculean' is used to describe a mammoth or difficult task.

HIBERNATION
In winter when food is scarce, many animals go into a long deep sleep. This is called hibernation. During late summer and autumn, while food is still plentiful, the animal eats until its body is fat. Then it digs itself into the ground or finds a sheltered place to sleep. While the animal is asleep, its heartbeat and its breathing slows. It uses so little energy that it can live solely on the fat in its body.

HIEROGLYPHIC
This was a system of writing used in ancient Egypt. Hieroglyphics began before 3000BC with a very simple kind of picture writing, in which each picture stood for an object. Later, pictures came to represent ideas. Finally, pictures were used to represent sounds in the spoken language.

Hieroglyphics fell into disuse

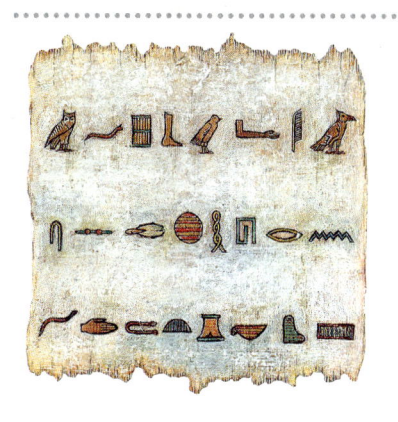

Hieroglyphics: Egyptian scribes used a form of picture writing with about 700 different hieroglyphs.

and remained unread until a Frenchman called Champollion deciphered inscriptions on a stone slab, the Rosetta Stone, in 1822.

HINDUISM

Hinduism is a religion. Hindus believe that God is present in all things. Their most important holy books are the *Vedas*. Hindu priests or Brahmins worship the supreme God. Ordinary people worship lesser gods, such as Vishnu, God of Life.

HIPPOPOTAMUS

The huge hippopotamus lives in the rivers of Africa. Its name means 'river horse', but it is actually related to the pig.

Despite their gaping jaws and tusks, hippos eat only plants. They spend the day in the water, floating or walking along the river bottom, and come ashore at night. They love to wallow in mud. Hippos can be dangerous if they are annoyed.

HISTORY

History is the story of the past. Historians are mostly interested in famous people and great events, because these affect nations. But history is also concerned with ordinary people's lives.

Science, medicine, art, religion and architecture all have histories of their own. History is revealed in many ways: by digging for it, by reading about it in old books and manuscripts, and by listening to people talking.

See the history chart overleaf.

Hinduism: Shiva is one of the most important Hindu gods.

HISTORY

BC	AFRICA
c.8000	Farming begins
c.4000-3500	Wheel, plough and sail in Egypt
c.3500	Early writing in Egypt
c.2700-c.2200	Age of Pyramids in Egypt
2050-1800	Middle Kingdom under Theban rulers
670	Assyrians conquer Egypt
525	Persians conquer Egypt
500	Nok civilization founded
332	Alexander the Great conquers Egypt
306	Ptolemy I founds new dynasty in Egypt
30	Death of Antony and Cleopatra. Rome conquers Egypt

AD	
100	Kingdom of Ethiopia founded
429-444	Vandals occupy North Africa
533-534	Belisarius reconquers North Africa for Justinian
800s	Civilization of Ghana
969	Fatimids conquer Egypt

BC	ASIA
c.6000	Rice cultivation in Far East
c.4000	Farming, plough, wheel in Mesopotamia
c.3000	Civilization of Sumeria
c.2700-1750	Harappan civilization in Indus Valley
c.2000-c.1200	Hittite civilization in Turkey
c.1750-1000	Shang dynasty in China
c.1200-650	Domination of Assyrian Empire
1000-c.500	Chou dynasty in China
551	Birth of Confucius
c.550-330	Achaemenid Empire in Persia
530s	Buddha preaching
334-23	Campaigns of Alexander the Great
c.320	Mauryan Empire in India
c.200BC-c.AD220	Han dynasty in China
c.6	Birth of Jesus

AD	
c.30	Crucifixion of Jesus, founder of Christianity
226-636	Sassanid Empire in Persia
304-308	Huns invade China
c.320	Gupta Empire in Ganges Valley: 'Golden Age' of Hindu culture
c.300-500	Main spread of Buddhism in China
c.520	Decimal system invented in India
540	Persian-Byzantine War begins
618-906	T'ang dynasty in China
622	Muhammad founds religion of Islam
636-750	Arabs conquer an empire from Spain to the Indus Valley
794	Japanese capital moves to Kyoto
?960-1280	Sung dynasty in China
1096	First Crusade

HISTORY

BC	EUROPE
c.6500	Farming begins in Greece and the Aegean
c.2000	Bronze Age in north Europe
c.2000-1200	Minoan and Mycenaean civilization in Crete and Greece
753	Rome founded
c.750-c.550	Greeks and Phoenicians colonize Mediterranean and Black Sea
490-479	Battles of the Persian Wars
431-404	Peloponnesian War
c.380-300	Works of Plato, Euclid and Aristotle
c.327-300	Main Roman expansion
27	Octavian takes title of Augustus: end of Roman republic

AD	
c.43	Romans occupy Britain
284-305	Roman Empire reorganized and divided into East and West
313	Freedom of Christian worship in Roman Empire
378	Valens defeated by Visigoths at Adrianople
410	Sack of Rome
496	Baptism of Clovis, king of the Franks
c.600	Slavs move into Balkans
711	Muslims invade Spain
768-814	Charlemagne builds Frankish Empire
800s	Vikings invade and settle north-west Europe
1054	Break between Greek and Roman Churches
1066	Norman conquest
1096-1300	The Crusades

BC	AMERICA AND AUSTRALASIA
c.48 000	Aborigines begin to arrive in Australia from Southeast Asia
c.33 000-13 000	People start to cross the Bering Straits from Asia into North America
c.7000	Agriculture begins in Middle America
c.6000	People living at the southernmost tip of South America
c.1200-100	Olmec tribe of Middle America develop counting system and calendar
c.100	Hopewell tribe of Ohio start to build huge burial mounds, some with bases larger than the Egyptian pyramids

AD	
c.300-c.900	Mayan civilization in Central America
c.900	First Maoris arrive in New Zealand
c.1000	Greenland Vikings reach America
c.1325-1520	Aztec civilization in Mexico

HISTORY

AFRICA	
1250	Mamelukes seize power in Egypt
1300s	Mali Empire in west Africa
1400s-1500s	European settlements on west coast
1500s	Songhai Empire replaced Mali Empire
1652	Dutch found Cape Colony
1869	Suez Canal opened
1880s	'Scramble for Africa'
1899-1902	Boer War
1914	All Africa except Liberia and Ethiopia colonized by European nations
1952-80	African states win independence
1981	President Anwar Sadat of Egypt is assassinated
1984-86	Severe famine in East Africa, millions face starvation
1985-86	Renewed unrest in South Africa results in international pressure for reform of apartheid
1986	US air raid on Libya strikes Tripoli and Benghazi
1990	Namibia becomes independent. In South Africa, African National Congress leader Nelson Mandela is freed from prison after 27 years
1994	The ANC are elected to power in South Africa; Nelson Mandela becomes president. Half a million people are killed during a civil war in Rwanda; more than 2 million refugees leave the country
1997	President Mobutu is overthrown after a civil war in Zaire; the country is renamed the Democratic Republic of Congo

ASIA	
1192	Yoritomo first shogun in Japan
1206-80	Mongols conquer empire in central Asia
1368-1644	Ming dynasty in China
1486-98	Voyages of Bartolomeu Dias and Vasco da Gama
c.1500-1870	African slave trade
1522-1680	Mughal expansion in India
c.1550-c.1650	Russians colonize Siberia
1630s	Japan isolates itself from rest of world
1644-1911	Manchu dynasty in China
1757	Battle of Plassey; British defeat French in India
1805	Beginning of East India Company's dominance in India
1839-42	Opium War; Britain takes Hong Kong
1857-59	Indian Mutiny
1867	Shoguns lose power in Japan
1900	Boxer Rebellion in China
1911	Republic established in China under Sun Yat-sen
1937	Japan invades China
1941	Japanese attack Pearl Harbor
1945	USA drops atomic bombs on Japan
1947	Indian independence
1948	State of Israel founded
1949	Communist victory in China
1957-73	Vietnam War
1980-88	Iran-Iraq War
1982	Israel invades Lebanon
1988	In Pakistan Benazir Bhutto becomes first woman Muslim prime minister
1989	Anti-government demonstrations in Tiananmen Square, Beijing, violently crushed
1990	Iraq invades its neighbour Kuwait
1991	A US-led 29-country coalition attacks Iraq; Iraq surrenders and relinquishes Kuwait
1997	Hong Kong is handed back to China by the British

HISTORY

EUROPE

1337	Beginning of Hundred Years' War in France
1347-50	Black Death
c.1450	Gutenberg starts printing
1450-53	English driven out of France
1453	Constantinople falls to Ottoman Turks
1455-85	Wars of the Roses
1521	Martin Luther leads Protestant split from Roman Church
1618-48	Thirty Years' War
1642-48	English Civil War
1643-1715	Reign of Louis XIV
1750	Start of Industrial Revolution
1756-63	Seven Years' War
1789	French Revolution begins
1799	Napoleon seizes power in France
1815	Battle of Waterloo; Congress of Vienna
1821-29	Greek War of Liberation
1848	Year of revolutions throughout Europe
1854-6	Crimean War
1870-71	Franco-Prussian War
1885-95	Daimler and Benz work on automobile; Marconi's wireless
1914-18	World War I
1917	Bolshevik revolution in Russia begins
1933	Hitler becomes German Chancellor
1936-39	Spanish Civil War
1939-45	World War II
1941	Germany invades USSR
1945	Defeat of Germany. Cold War begins
1957	USSR launches first space satellite. Treaty of Rome: formation of European Economic Community
1989	Communism starts to decline rapidly in Eastern Europe
1990	East and West Germany are united
1991	USSR breaks up as its republics start declaring their independence
1991-92	Break up of Yugoslavia
1995	The US-brokered Dayton peace accord ends war in Bosnia
1997	Diana, Princess of Wales dies

AMERICA AND AUSTRALASIA

c.1400-1525	Inca civilization in Andes
1492	Columbus reaches America
1519	Cortes begins conquest of Aztec Empire
1532	Pizarro begins conquest of Inca Empire
1608	French colonists found Quebec
1620	*Mayflower* puritans (Pilgrim Fathers) settle in New England
1642	Tasman discovers New Zealand
1770	James Cook claims Australia for Britain
1776	American Declaration of Independence
1788	British colony founded at Botany Bay, Australia
1840	Britain annexes New Zealand
1846-48	USA-Mexico War
1861-65	American Civil War
1898	Spanish-American War
1911	Mexican Revolution
1914	Panama Canal opened
1917	USA enters World War I
1929	Wall Street Crash begins Great Depression
1941	USA enters World War II
1945	United Nations set up
1959	Cuban Revolution
1963	President Kennedy assassinated
1969	Neil Armstrong lands on the Moon
1981	First Space Shuttle flight
1983	US troops invade Grenada after Marxist takeover
1985	Earthquake in Mexico City claims 5,000 lives
1986	Space shuttle *Challenger* explodes after take-off. Jean Claude Duvalier's regime in Haiti is overthrown
1990	US troops overthrow President Manuel Noriega of Panama
1992	Earth Summit held in Rio de Janeiro to discuss environmental protection
1994	USA lifts 30-year-old trade embargo on Vietnam

Hitler

Horse: *The overall shape and appearance of a horse or pony is called its conformation. The parts of the horse's body are called the points.*

Labels: Forelock, Mane, Withers, Flank, Chest, Elbow, Hock, Knee, Stifle, Fetlock, Heel

Hitler, Adolf (1889-1945)
Hitler became 'Führer' (leader) of Germany in 1933. He was an evil dictator whose Nazi party led Germany into World War II. German armies conquered most of Europe and millions of Jews were murdered on Hitler's orders. But Britain, the United States, the former USSR and their allies defeated the Nazis. To avoid capture, Hitler killed himself.

Hockey
Field hockey is one of the most popular games in the world. It can be played on any smooth, level surface. It is played by two teams of 11 players a side. The object of the game is to hit a small, hard ball with a curved stick into the other team's goal.

Ice hockey was first played as an organised sport in Canada in the late 1800s. It is played on ice with six players, on skates, in each team. Instead of a ball they have a hard rubber disc called a 'puck'.

Holocaust
Holocaust means a great destruction of life by fire. In recent times the word has been used to refer to the murder of six million Jews and thousands of others by the Nazis in Germany

and German-occupied countries before and during World War II. Many of these victims were sent to concentration camps to be tortured, starved, and made to work under horrific conditions before being executed.

HOMER

Two very famous poems called the *Iliad* and the *Odyssey* are said to have been the work of Homer. The poems were written in Greece about 800BC. Both poems are about the Trojan War. The *Iliad* tells the story of how the Greeks captured the city of Troy. The *Odyssey* describes the homeward journey of the Greek hero Odysseus.

HORSE

The first horse was an animal no larger than a small dog. It is known as *Hyracotherium*. It had four toes on its front feet and three on its back feet. Gradually over millions of years, the horse evolved, losing all its toes except one, the hoof.

No one knows when horses were first tamed. Their first use was to pull war chariots, and cavalry played an important part in wars until early in this century. Horses were the fastest form of transport until the 1800s when the steam locomotive and motor car replaced them. Also, their strength made horses invaluable on farms where they were used to pull wagons and ploughs.

Many different types of horses have been bred. Among the largest are the Shire and Clydesdale breeds. The Shetland pony is one of the smallest.

HOVERCRAFT

A hovercraft is often called an air-cushion vehicle because it glides above the ground or water on a cushion of air. The cushion of air is created by a huge fan, which forces air beneath the craft. The air is held there by flaps or skirts around the sides.

Backward-facing propellers on top of the craft propel it forwards and steer the craft. The propellers are powered by engines like those of an aircraft.

***Hovercraft:** The hovercraft hovers just above the waves, held up by a cushion of air.*

HUMAN BEINGS

People exactly like us have lived for only a few thousand years. We belong to a group of mammals called the primates. Our scientific name is *Homo sapiens*, which means 'thinking man'.

Fossil remains of our ancestors have been found in Africa and Asia. These early human-like creatures walked on two legs, and their skulls and teeth were quite like our own. But their brains were much smaller, about the same size as an ape's. After these 'ape-men' came creatures much more like modern humans. They had bigger brains and they could use tools. Having a bigger brain made it possible for primitive people to develop until *Homo sapiens* appeared perhaps about 100,000 years ago.

The human brain gave human beings the power to hunt, kill, capture and tame other animals. Human beings developed skills far greater than those of any other creature. They learned to make

Human Body: *The skeleton (left) provides the body with a strong framework, consisting of around 206 bones. Muscles (right) are responsible for movement and are attached to the bones.*

and use fire, to grow food and to make metal tools. They settled in villages and towns, and used language and writing to store and pass on the knowledge they had gained. In this way, civilization gradually developed.

Human Body

Our bodies are made of millions of tiny cells which are grouped together into separate tissues and organs. Skin protects us from heat, cold, injury and germs. Our bones give us our shape and allow us, with the help of our muscles, to move about.

Our bodies need oxygen and food. We get the oxygen from the air when we breathe. The blood carries the oxygen to every cell of the body. It also carries digested food, which is burnt by the oxygen to give us energy.

The body produces lots of waste. Some of this is excreted through the skin when we sweat, some (carbon dioxide) when we breathe out. Other waste is removed via the bowels and the bladder.

The only organs which are different in a man and a woman are the reproductive organs. A woman has a vagina and ovaries which contain ova (eggs). A man has a penis and testes which contain sperm. The fertilization of a female egg cell by a male sperm cell produces one new cell which has all the makings of a complete new human body.

See also BLOOD; BRAIN; BREATHING; CELL; EAR; EYE; HEART; REPRODUCTION; SKIN.

Hummingbird

Hummingbirds are the smallest birds in the world. Most kinds live in the great forests of South America. Hummingbirds are marvellous fliers. They can hover in mid-air and even fly backwards. Their wings beat so fast they make a humming noise.

Hummingbird:
A hummingbird rolls its tongue into a tube to suck nectar from a flower.

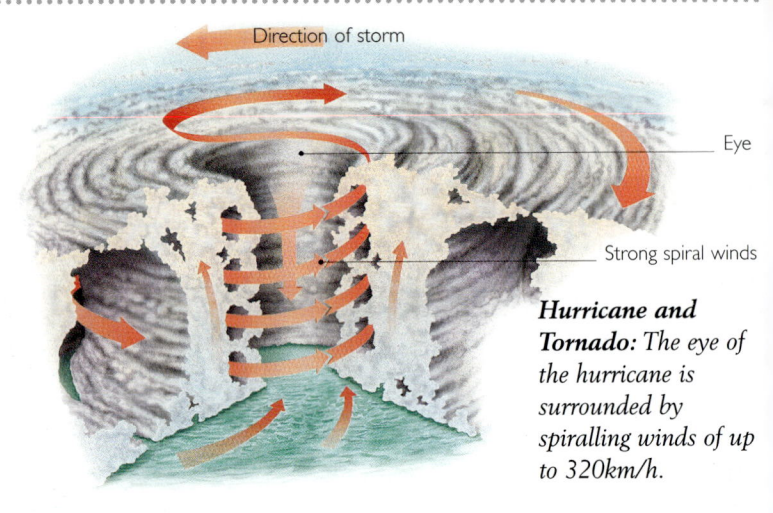

Hurricane and Tornado: The eye of the hurricane is surrounded by spiralling winds of up to 320km/h.

HURRICANE AND TORNADO

A hurricane is a storm in which the wind circles or spirals inward about a low-pressure area. The winds can be very strong – sometimes more than 300km/h – and there is torrential rain, causing floods. Yet the centre or 'eye' of the storm is quite calm. In the seas off China and Japan, storms like these are called typhoons. In the southern Pacific and Indian oceans, they are called cyclones.

A tornado is a funnel of cloud that sometimes forms on the bottom of a thundercloud, spiralling downward towards the ground. Many tornadoes never reach the ground. But some spin faster, until the winds inside them are going round at about 480km/h. They hit the ground and leave a trail of destruction.

HYDROFOIL

The hydrofoil is a type of watercraft that has large, winglike structures attached to the hull. As the craft gains speed, the hull rises out of the water on these ski-like projections. Because the hull no longer has to push against the water, the craft can travel much faster than an ordinary boat.

HYDROGEN

Hydrogen is an element. It is a colourless gas and has no smell and no taste. It is very light – more than 14 times as light as air.

Atoms of deuterium and tritium, isotopes of hydrogen, can be made to join together or *fuse* at a very high temperature to release huge quantities of energy. This is the principle of the massively destructive hydrogen, or 'H', bomb.

Ice Age

The Ice Ages were times of intense cold. Sheets of ice spread southwards from the North Pole, covering much of Europe, North America and Asia. The most recent Ice Age ended about 11,000 years ago. Glaciers (rivers of ice) carried soil and rocks along with them like huge bulldozers. They scraped the land clear of soil and smoothed hills and valleys.

During the recent Ice Age, many plants and animals were killed by the cold. Human beings had to find ways of keeping warm. They took to the shelter of caves and made clothes from the skins of animals. In time the ice sheets melted and the weather grew warm again. But it is not certain that in the future there will never be another Ice Age.

See also GLACIER.

Iceberg

Icebergs are islands of ice which drift in the cold polar seas. They are formed from masses of ice which break off the end of a glacier or ice sheet and float off into the sea. An iceberg can weigh

Iceberg: More than 80 percent of an iceberg is submerged beneath the surface of the sea. The tip may rise up to 100m above the sea.

millions of tonnes. But only the tip of the iceberg shows above water. Five times as much is hidden beneath the surface.

See also GLACIER.

Ice Hockey
See HOCKEY.

Ice-Skating
Ice-skating is the sport of gliding across ice on skates, which are metal blades attached to the soles

of boots. People in Scandinavia about 2,000 years ago were probably the first ice-skaters. Nowadays most people skate in indoor 'rinks' where the ice is specially formed by refrigeration. The sport of ice-skating has three main branches: figure skating, ice dancing and speed skating. In figure skating, the skaters make circles, figures-of-eight and other patterns as they glide across the ice. In ice dancing they dance on the ice, and in speed skating they race one another on ice.

IMMUNE SYSTEM

The immune system is the body's way of defending itself against infectious diseases. The bacteria or viruses causing diseases are like invaders. The body fights them off by producing substances known as antibodies, which attack the invaders and gradually overcome them. This is how we 'get over' infectious diseases. Sometimes doctors give this process a helping hand through what is known as vaccination. They inject a patient with a vaccine, a very mild form of an infection. The body produces antibodies. After that it will be better able to fight off more serious forms of the disease.

See also BACTERIA; DISEASE.

INCAS

Hundreds of years ago the Incas ruled an empire in the Andes Mountains. Its heart lay in the South American country we now call Peru. All the people living in the mountain valleys had to work for the Incas. In return, the Incas made sure that everyone had a home and enough to eat.

The Incas became very rich. In

Incas: An Inca chief (or curaca) holds high a special ceremonial vessel during festivities in honour of the Sun god. These were held each year in June.

1532 Spanish explorers came seeking gold. They had horses and guns and they captured the Inca king, Atahualpa. They made themselves rulers of Peru.

INDIA

India is a large country (about 3.28 million sq km). More than 900 million people live in India. The north is cut off from the rest of Asia by the Himalaya Mountains. Great rivers, such as the Brahmaputra and Ganges, flow across the plains that lie south of these mountains.

Parts of India are dry and hot. It is cooler in the mountains, but most people live in the fertile river valleys. India gets most of its rain during the monsoon season. Many Indians are poor farmers, who live in small villages. Others live in crowded cities like Calcutta. Industry is developing in India. There are steelworks, mines, textile and engineering factories.

Most Indians follow the Hindu religion. But there are also Buddhists, Sikhs, Muslims and Christians. Civilization began 4,500 years ago in the area that includes India. From the late 1700s until 1947 most of India was ruled by Britain. Then it became independent, although it still remains part of the British Commonwealth.

See also GANDHI; PAGE 62.

INDIAN OCEAN

The world's third largest ocean covers more than 74,000,000 sq km. The Indian Ocean's biggest island is Madagascar off the coast of Africa. Other islands include Mauritius and the Seychelles. The ocean includes the Bay of Bengal, the Red Sea and The Gulf, known sometimes as the Arabian Gulf, sometimes as the Persian Gulf. In the Indian Ocean's northwestern corner, near Arabia, its waters are shallow and very warm. In the far south, near Antarctica, they are sometimes close to freezing point.

INDUSTRIAL REVOLUTION

This is the name given to the great change that took place in Europe and America when goods began to be produced in factories. Before that time, many things were made by hand by craftworkers in their own homes. When James Watt harnessed the power of steam in the mid-1700s, all this changed. England's textile industry was revolutionized by the invention of machines that would spin thread and weave cloth. Cities grew as more and more people left farming areas to seek jobs in the factories.

The Industrial Revolution soon spread to the United States. The new factories created wealth. Railroads and canals were built; coal was mined to fuel steam

INSECTS

Industrial Revolution:
Smoke billows from the factory chimneys, and wafts above the terraced houses clustered around the workplace.

engines and to make steel. The new wealth was not for everybody, however. Workers often lived in crowded conditions in the towns that grew up around the factories. They worked long hours, often for little pay. These bad conditions eventually led to the formation of labour unions, which fought hard for better pay and conditions.

INSECTS

Insects are found in every part of the world. There are hundreds of thousands of different kinds of insects – including more than 750,000 different kinds of flies – but they are all built on a similar plan. The body is divided into three sections. An insect's head has eyes, jaws and antennae, or feelers. The middle part, or thorax, carries three pairs of jointed legs and sometimes two pairs of wings as well. The end part is called the abdomen. Some insects get around by flying; others are astonishing jumpers. A grasshopper can jump as much as 75cm.

Most insects reproduce by laying eggs. Instead of bones, they have a hard case covering the outside of their bodies. As the insect grows, it has to shed this case and grow another.

Some young insects develop into adults without changing shape. They are called *nymphs*. But many kinds of insects go through two big changes in shape. At each stage, the insect looks different and has a different way

INSECTS

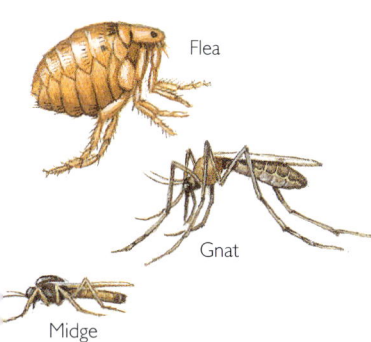

Ladybird • Harlequin Longhorn • Great Diving Beetle • Stag Beetle • Brazilian Rhinoceros

Flea • Gnat • Midge

Insects: *About 80 percent of all known animals are insects, including beetles (above), parasites (left) and flies (below).*

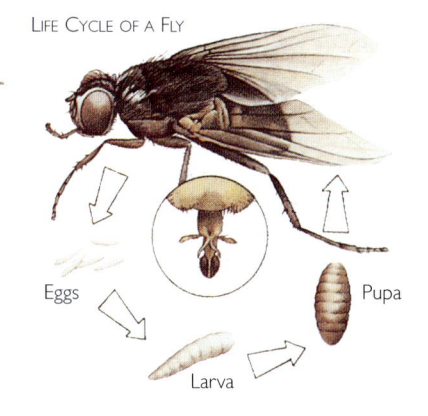

LIFE CYCLE OF A FLY

Eggs • Larva • Pupa

of life. Butterflies lay eggs. They hatch into larvae called caterpillars. A caterpillar grows and turns into a pupa, or chrysalis. Finally, the adult butterfly emerges from the pupa. This process of biological change is known as *metamorphosis*.

Some insects are harmful. Insects such as the mosquito and the tsetse fly carry diseases. The Colorado beetle attacks potato crops. But many insects are useful.

Bees and other insects pollinate flowers. The silkworm makes silk. Ladybirds, a kind of beetle, eat greenfly, a garden pest.

See also ANT; BEES AND WASPS; BUTTERFLIES AND MOTHS; PARASITE.

INTERNATIONAL DATE LINE

Geographers have divided the globe into sections with lines that run from pole to pole. These lines are called meridians. Each section is in a different time zone, because as the Earth rotates, the Sun faces different parts of the Earth at different times. The world's nations have agreed that the date changes at the 180th meridian. This imaginary line is called the International Date Line. Each date begins on the west side of the line and ends on the east side.

INTERNET

The Internet is a huge network in which computers all over the world are linked to each other by telephone lines. Using the Internet people can pass information, including pictures, sounds and video material, from a computer on one side of the world to a computer on the other. With the right equipment, anyone anywhere can link up to it. A popular Internet service is the World Wide Web which is a convenient way of steering information around the Internet. Another is e-mail (electronic mail), a way of sending messages to other people linked up to the Internet.

INUIT PEOPLES

The Inuit (or Eskimos) live in the cold Arctic regions. All Inuit once hunted for their food. They travelled in skin canoes, called

***International Date Line:** In each of the world's 24 time zones, time differs by one hour from the next. West of Greenwich it is earlier, east of Greenwich it is later. A traveller crossing the International Date Line in the Pacific Ocean gains or loses a day.*

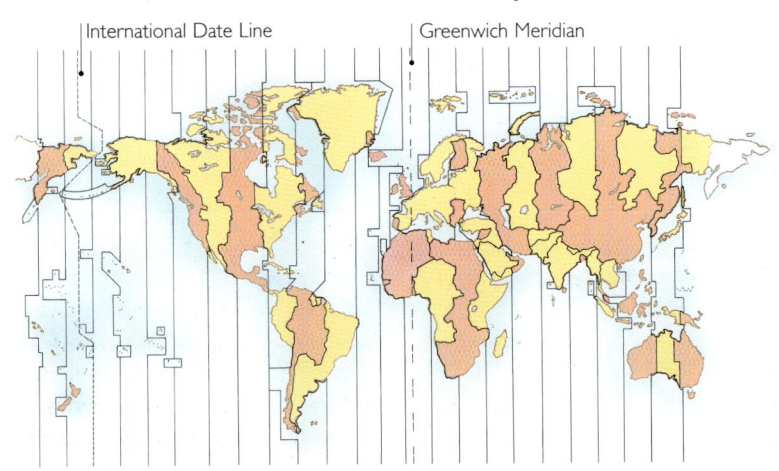

International Date Line | Greenwich Meridian

Iron and Steel:
Molten iron and scrap steel is poured into a furnace, where oxygen is blown into it to raise the temperature and to remove impurities.

kayaks, and on sledges. In summer they lived in skin tents and in winter they built igloos. Most Inuit now live in modern settlements.

IRELAND
See BRITISH ISLES.

IRON AGE
This is the name given to a period when people began to use iron to make knives, axes and swords. Iron was first used about 2300BC in Asia Minor. It reached Britain in about 500BC. The Iron Age followed the Bronze Age.

Iron ores are found in many places in the world and can be smelted (made into iron) fairly simply on charcoal fires.

See also BRONZE AGE.

IRON AND STEEL
Steel is our most important metal. No other metal that is so strong is so cheap. Steel is not a pure metal. It is an alloy made up mainly of iron, together with small amounts of carbon and one or two metals. Iron by itself is quite soft and weak,

but adding the other ingredients makes it hard and strong.

Steel is like iron in other ways. It is magnetic, and it rusts easily. But by adding metals, such as chromium and nickel, we can make a steel that does not rust. It is called stainless steel.

Iron is found in the form of a mineral, or ore, in the ground. Crude iron is made in a blast furnace by heating iron ore with coke and limestone. Steel is made by purifying the crude iron in other furnaces.

See also ALLOY.

IRRIGATION

Irrigation waters the land to help crops to grow. In many places of the world not enough rain falls each year, or it rains only at certain times of the year. Farmers therefore have to get their water from rivers, wells or lakes.

The ancient civilizations of Egypt, India, China, Assyria and Babylon depended on irrigation. Today, engineers build dams to make artificial lakes. The water can then be released into pipes, earth channels or river systems as it is needed.

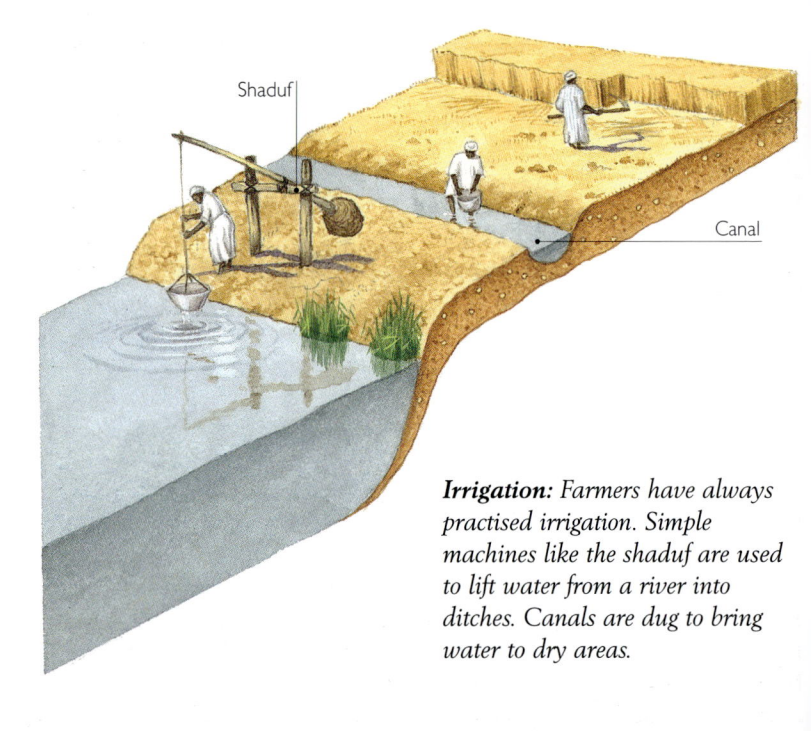

Irrigation: Farmers have always practised irrigation. Simple machines like the shaduf are used to lift water from a river into ditches. Canals are dug to bring water to dry areas.

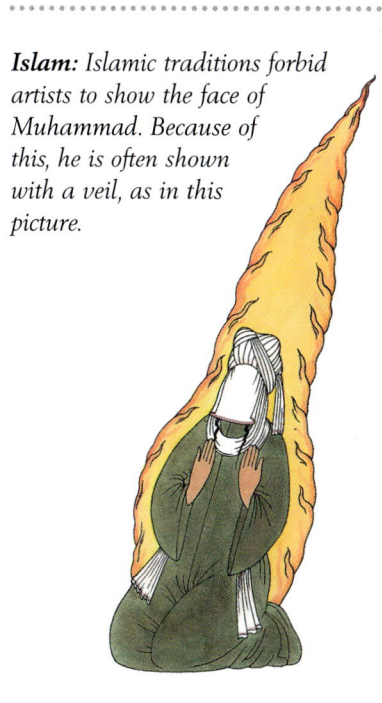

Islam: *Islamic traditions forbid artists to show the face of Muhammad. Because of this, he is often shown with a veil, as in this picture.*

ISLAM

Islam is one of the world's great religions. It was begun in AD622 in Arabia by Muhammad, and today has more followers than any other religion except Christianity. Its followers are called Muslims, and its holy book is the *Koran*. Muslims believe in one god (Allah) and in Muhammad as his prophet. Islam is widespread in North Africa and southwest Asia.

See also MUHAMMAD.

ISRAEL

Israel is a country bordering the Mediterranean Sea in southwest Asia. Most Israelis are Jews, and the main language is Hebrew. Many Arabs also live in Israel. Much of the country is hot desert, but farmers grow oranges, cotton, and grain on fertile plains and in fields watered by irrigation. Israel maintains an uneasy peace with its Arab neighbours after conflicts in the 1960s and 1970s.

See also PAGE 62.

ITALY

On the map Italy looks like a boot sticking out into the Mediterranean Sea. The islands of Sardinia and Sicily are also part of Italy. In the north the Alps form a mountain wall between Italy and the rest of Europe.

Southern Italy is warm and fairly dry. In the north it is cooler, with more rain. Both agriculture and industry are important. Most of the factories are in northern Italy. Italy is famous for its wine and for 'pasta' – foods such as spaghetti, macaroni and ravioli.

Most Italians are Roman Catholics. The centre of the Catholic Church is the Vatican, a tiny independent state in the middle of Rome. Italy has many old and beautiful buildings. A lot of them are in Rome, because 2,000 years ago the Romans ruled Italy. Later, separate city states grew up. The greatest were Genoa, Florence and Venice.

See also PAGE 60.

J

JAPAN

The islands which make up the country of Japan lie off the northeast coast of Asia. The largest islands are Honshu, Hokkaido, Kyushu and Shikoku. Earthquakes are common and there are volcanoes and hot springs. Japan has heavy rainfall and a cool, temperate climate.

Most Japanese live in cities. Rice, fish and vegetables are the main foods. There are many factories making all kinds of goods from cars and ships to radios and zip fasteners.

The Japanese came from mainland Asia perhaps 3,000 years ago. Ancient Japan was ruled by warrior lords. Until the 1850s Japan had little contact with the world outside. But then its rulers decided to allow trade with European countries.

Japan became powerful, and its rulers became warlike. In World War II Japan joined Germany and Italy, and Japanese forces conquered much of Asia. But in 1945 Japan surrendered. Today Japan's emperor no longer has any power. There is an elected parliament and a government led by a prime minister.

See also PAGE 62.

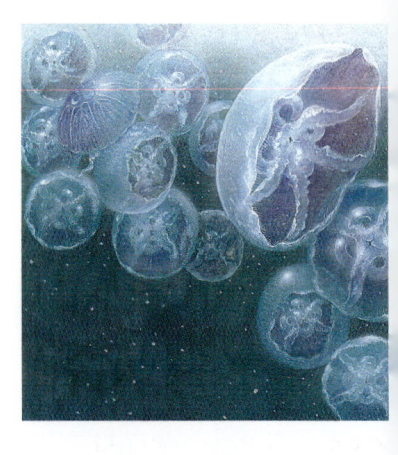

Jellyfish: *A very common jellyfish called* Aurelia *is often washed up on the shore. Up to about 50cm across, it is easily recognized by the four purplish rings on top. It can sting but it is not dangerous.*

JEFFERSON, THOMAS (1743-1826)

Thomas Jefferson, the third president of the United States, was a scholar and thinker as well as a politician. His father was a rich Virginia farmer who gave his son the best possible education. In 1776 it was Thomas Jefferson who wrote most of the Declaration of Independence. He was governor of Virginia from 1779 to 1781. Then he lived for many years in France before returning to America. He was president for two terms from 1801 to 1809. Under him, the United States bought Louisiana from France. After retiring in

1809, he went back to his home, Monticello, where he spent his last years studying and helping to set up the University of Virginia.

JELLYFISH

A jellyfish looks like a transparent umbrella floating in the sea. The body of this sea animal is mostly water. If it is stranded on the beach, a jellyfish dies.

Jellyfish swim by squirting out water from their 'umbrellas'. They catch small sea animals with stinging tentacles which hang beneath their bodies.

JESUS CHRIST

Jesus Christ was the founder of Christianity. Christians believe that he was the son of God. He taught people to trust in God and lead good peaceful lives, and he promised eternal life in heaven. He performed miracles, healing the sick and making blind men see again. Jesus' followers said he was the Messiah. But others feared he was just a troublemaker. The Romans, who were the harsh rulers of the Jews, thought so too. Jesus was arrested and executed on the Cross. But his followers went on teaching others what he had taught them, even though the Romans at first tried to stop them. Many of these early Christians were killed, or martyred, for their belief in Jesus.

JET ENGINE

The jet engine was developed by both Britain and Germany. In 1930, Frank Whittle, a British engineer, patented the first gas turbine for jet propulsion. Germany flew the first successful

Jet Engine: The ramjet is the simplest jet engine. It has neither compressor nor turbine, and is used in missiles. The turbojet is the most common type of engine on commercial airliners.

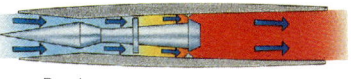

Ramjet

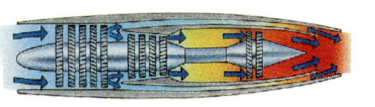

Turbojet

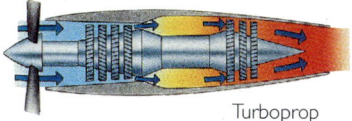

Turbofan

Turboprop

jet aircraft, the Heinkel 178, in August 1939.

The aircraft gas turbine consists of a rotating shaft with a compressor at the front and a turbine wheel at the back. When the shaft turns, air is drawn into the engine and compressed. It enters combustion chambers, where it mixes with liquid fuel such as paraffin. This mixture burns. The hot gases produced are allowed to escape from the back of the combustion chamber. As the fast jet of gas moves backwards out of the exhaust, it thrusts the engine forward.

The jet engine is smaller and lighter than the piston engine which it has largely replaced. It works efficiently at high speeds and produces great power.

JOAN OF ARC (1412-1431)

In 1429, France was at war with England. Joan was a French girl who believed God told her to save France. She persuaded France's King Charles VII to let her lead his army and, aged just 17, won five battles. But she was captured by the English and burned at the stake as a witch. In 1920 she was made a saint.

JUDAISM

Judaism is one of the world's oldest religions. Its followers are called Jews. They believe in one god, and the Hebrew Bible is their holy book. Christians include the Hebrew Bible in their Bible, calling it the Old Testament. Today, though Israel is their spiritual home, Jews live all over the world.

Joan of Arc: *Memorials, such as this stained-glass window, to France's heroine, Joan of Arc, can be seen in churches all over France.*

K

KANGAROO
Kangaroos live in Australia. They are the largest of the marsupials, the animals which carry their young in pouches.

Kangaroos eat grass and leaves. They travel about in groups called mobs, led by an old male known as a boomer. With their powerful hind legs and using their long tails to balance them, kangaroos can leap long distances.

KENNEDY, JOHN F. (1917-1963)
John F. Kennedy was the 35th president of the United States. In 1961, he became the first Roman Catholic to be elected to this office. He tried to help the poor and underprivileged. He was assassinated in Dallas, Texas.

KENYA
Kenya is one of the most beautiful countries in Africa. It has grassland, tropical forests, desert and the cliffs and ancient volcanoes of the Great Rift Valley. It is a hot, dry country.

Kenya's main exports are tea and coffee, and also fruit, vegetables, sugar, cement and petroleum products.

Some of the most ancient fossil remains of human beings have been discovered in Kenya. From the earliest days of seafaring, traders were attracted there – the Greeks, Portuguese, Romans and Arabs all built settlements. The influence of Britain spread in the late 19th century, until Britain granted Kenya independence in 1963. The capital city is Nairobi.

KING, MARTIN LUTHER (1929-1968)
Martin Luther King was a black American clergyman and leader in the struggle for racial equality in the United States. Because he admired the teachings of Gandhi, he advised people not to use violence when they demonstrated against the segregation of black

Kangaroo: A kangaroo carries its young, called a joey, in its pouch for almost nine months.

people. He won the Nobel Peace Prize in 1964. He was assassinated in 1968 in Memphis, Tennessee.

Kings and Queens

In the past, most countries were ruled by 'monarchs': kings or queens. Usually the king's eldest son succeeded him, which meant that the same royal family might reign for hundreds of years.

English kings ruled with the help of their barons. In 1215 the barons forced King John to sign the Magna Carta, which said that the king should not misuse his powers. Later, English monarchs had to take the advice of parliament. Britain is now a 'constitutional monarchy'. The Queen is the head of state, but her powers are limited by law. She reigns (holds office), but she does not rule (govern).

Kings and Queens: *Henry VIII was King of England from 1509 to 1547; he had six wives.*

KINGS AND QUEENS OF ENGLAND SINCE THE NORMAN CONQUEST (1066)

William I	1066-1087*
William II	1087-1100
Henry I	1100-1135
Stephen	1135-1154
Henry II	1154-1189
Richard I	1189-1199
John	1199-1216
Henry III	1216-1272
Edward I	1272-1307
Edward II	1307-1327
Edward III	1327-1377
Richard II	1377-1399
Henry IV	1399-1413
Henry V	1413-1422
Henry VI	1422-1461
Edward IV	1461-1483
Edward V	1483
Richard III	1483-1485
Henry VII	1485-1509
Henry VIII	1509-1547
Edward VI	1547-1553
Mary I	1553-1558
Elizabeth I	1558-1603

KINGS AND QUEENS OF GREAT BRITAIN FROM 1603

James I (VI of Scotland)	1603-1625
Charles I	1625-1649
Commonwealth	1649-1660
Charles II	1660-1685
James II	1685-1688
William III and (to 1694) Mary II	1689-1702
Anne	1702-1714
George I	1714-1727
George II	1727-1760
George III	1760-1820
George IV	1820-1830
William IV	1830-1837
Victoria	1837-1901
Edward VII	1901-1910
George V	1910-1936
Edward VIII	1936
George VI	1936-1952
Elizabeth II	1952-

*Dates refer to length of reign.

KIWI

The kiwi is the national bird of New Zealand. It cannot fly, but it waddles about the forest, particularly at night, searching for worms and insects to eat. The kiwi has hair-like feathers, no tail, strong claws and a long bill. It is the only bird that has nostrils at the tip of its bill.

KNIGHT

A knight in medieval times was a warrior who had vowed to be courageous yet gentle. This code of behaviour was called chivalry. A knight gave military service to a lord or an organization such as the Church. In return, he was granted land to farm.

The training to become a knight was long and severe. A boy of

Knight: Heavily armoured medieval knights on horseback try to unseat each other, in a contest known as a tournament.

noble birth began as a page in the household of another noble family at the age of seven. At 14, he became a squire and began to learn the skills of a knight, such as fighting on horseback. He took vows of knighthood at about 21.

KNOT

A knot is a way of tying rope, string, or thread. We all use knots to tie packages, but many special knots were first developed by sailors to perform different jobs on a sailing ship. A bend is used to tie ends of rope together; a hitch is used to tie a rope to a post.

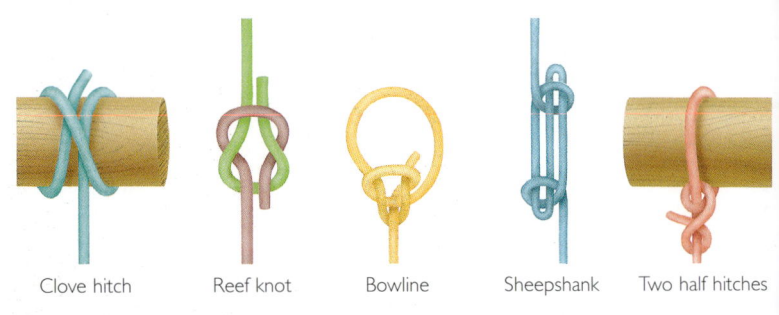

Clove hitch | Reef knot | Bowline | Sheepshank | Two half hitches

Knots: *Choosing the right knot is half the skill of knot tying.*

Common knots are the reef knot, bowline, clove hitch, half hitch, slipknot, and sheet bend.

KOALA
Although it looks like a small bear, the koala is a marsupial. It lives in Australia. Koalas are good climbers. They live in eucalyptus trees, feeding on the leaves.

KORAN
The Koran is the holy book of Muslims. It is believed to have been dictated to Muhammad, the great prophet of Islam, by the archangel Gabriel. It was written down between AD 610 and 632.

KREMLIN
The Kremlin is the oldest part of Moscow. It was once the fortress home of the kings, or tsars, of Russia. A high wall surrounds the palaces and gold-domed cathedrals of the Kremlin, still the seat of the Russian government.

KU KLUX KLAN
The Ku Klux Klan was an organization set up in 1866 by white southerners in the United States to prevent newly freed blacks from voting and exercising other rights. Members, dressed in white sheets and hoods, beat up and murdered blacks and public officials. The KKK used violence against both black and white civil rights workers in the South in the 1960s, but now has little support.

Koala: *A young koala rides on its mother's back after leaving the pouch.*

LAKE

Many lakes were formed during the Ice Ages by glaciers scooping out hollows in the land. When the ice melted, the hollows filled with water. Some lakes are artificial – created when dams are built across rivers.

Other lakes are so big that they are called seas. The Caspian Sea in Asia is the largest lake in the world. Its water is salty because the lake has no outlets. The lake gets smaller because of evaporation. The largest freshwater lake in the world is Lake Superior in North America.

See also ICE AGE.

Lake: Lakes form in large hollows in the land. The rivers which flow in and out of most lakes bring mud and sand from other places, so some of them clog up and disappear.

LANGUAGE

When we speak, we are using language. Language is a collection of 'sound signs' or words. We use it to communicate with one another. There are more than 2,800 different languages in the world and many more dialects or local variations. Chinese is the language spoken by the largest number of people. English is spoken in more countries than any other language.

All languages change. People make up new words and often 'borrow' foreign words.

LASER

A laser is an instrument that produces a thin beam of very pure light. The beam from some lasers is so powerful that it can blast a hole through metal. Other lasers can be used in surgery to remove or repair diseased body tissues.

An exciting new use of lasers is in communications. Laser beams can carry television signals and telephone messages along glass fibre tubes. Sending telephone calls by laser is replacing our present telephone system, in which we use copper wires.

LATITUDE AND LONGITUDE

Because we know that the world is round, we can show it on a globe and divide it into sections with accurately drawn lines.

The lines that run east and west and are parallel to the equator are called *parallels* of latitude. Those that run north and south and pass through the poles are called *meridians* of longitude.

These lines are measured in degrees. By using these lines we can give the position of any place in the world. London is latitude 51° 30' N, longitude 00° 05' W.

LAW

All countries have rules which tell people how to behave and which must be obeyed. They make up the law of a country.

Law is made and works differently in different societies. In many countries groups of men and women are chosen by other people to make the laws. These people are called legislators and the law they make is *statute law*. Some law is made by judges. It is called *case law*. The law that comes from the customs of the people is called *common law*.

Lawyers are people who have trained especially to understand the law. The job of the police and the courts is to arrest and punish people who break the law.

LEAD

Lead is one of the heaviest metals. It is soft and easy to shape and does not rust. Lead is mixed with other metals to make useful alloys, such as pewter, which contains lead and tin. The metal that used to be used for printer's type contains lead. Solder used to join electrical wires and pipes also contains lead. And lead is also used in car batteries.

See also ALLOY.

LEAF

All a plant's food is manufactured in its green leaves. Light, water and carbon dioxide are used to make a form of sugar. From the

Leaf: Leaves, including needles, are the easiest part of the tree to identify. Simple leaves may be rounded, oval, triangular or long (like sweet chestnut). They may have toothed or smooth edges, or they may be lobed (like oak).

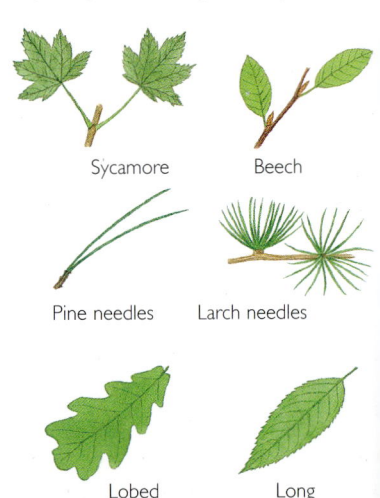

Sycamore

Beech

Pine needles

Larch needles

Lobed

Long

Lens: Convex lenses (left) make things look bigger, while concave lenses (right) make things look a bit smaller.

sugar the plant makes starch and other kinds of food that it needs.

The process that makes the food is called *photosynthesis*. It relies on the green colouring inside a leaf called *chlorophyll*. The carbon dioxide comes from the air. The water comes from the soil through tiny tubes called veins, and the carbon dioxide enters the leaf through little holes called *stomata*. The energy for photosynthesis comes from sunlight.

Leaves of most plants growing in mild climates wither and fall off in the autumn. Lack of sunlight in winter makes them unnecessary. First the water supply to the leaves is cut off. This destroys the green colour and gives the leaves red, orange and brown tints.

LENIN, VLADIMIR (1870-1924)

Lenin is remembered as the man who made Russia a Communist country. When he was 17, Lenin decided to work against the Tsar (emperor) of Russia, because he thought the Tsar's rule was harsh and unjust. He became a Bolshevik (Communist) and in 1917 was the leader of the Communist Revolution.

LENS

A lens is a specially shaped piece of a transparent glass or plastic that refracts or bends rays of light. It makes an object look bigger or smaller. A lens which is thicker in the middle is called *convex*. It makes objects seen through it look bigger. A lens which is thicker at the edge is called *concave*. Objects seen through it look smaller.

LEONARDO DA VINCI
(1452-1519)

Leonardo was a great Italian artist, scientist and inventor. He was fascinated by the way in which the human body, machines, and the universe work. He designed war engines, a sort of helicopter, a parachute and diving gear. His *Last Supper* and *Mona Lisa* are among the most famous paintings in the world.

LEOPARD AND CHEETAH

The leopard lives in Africa and Asia. It is an expert tree climber and sometimes lies in wait for its prey in a tree. It can drag a half-eaten antelope into the branches out of reach of hyenas.

The cheetah of Africa is the fastest land animal. It hunts by stalking its prey and then chasing it at great speed. Not even the swift antelope can escape, for the cheetah can run at speeds of over 110km/h, though it can only do so in short bursts.

Leopards and cheetahs both belong to the cat family.

LICHEN

You often see a grey crust on rocks and tree trunks. It is made of tiny plants called lichens. A lichen is really two plants in one. One part is a fungus. The other part is a green plant called an alga. The fungus cannot make its own food. Instead, it takes in water and minerals for the alga. The alga uses the water and sunlight to make food for itself and the fungus.

Leopard

Cheetah

Leopard and Cheetah: *A leopard, with a golden coat covered in black spots, waits for its prey. Cheetahs live in the open country.*

Parmelia caperata

Sea Ivory

Cladonia floerkeana

Lichen: *Lichens can survive in some of the hottest and coldest places on Earth. But they particularly favour the clean air of the Arctic and the moist woodlands along Europe's western coast.*

LIGHT

The Sun is a huge furnace that gives out vast amounts of energy as heat and light. Its light is one of the most important things to us on Earth. It enables us to see by day. We see things because objects reflect light into our eyes. Sunlight also gives green plants the energy to make their food. And all animals, including ourselves, rely on plant food in order to live.

Light travels in straight lines – you cannot shine a torch round a corner. But you can reflect the torch beam round a corner with a mirror. Light also bends when it passes from air into glass or water. This is called *refraction*. The bending of light by curved pieces of glass, or lenses, makes it possible to magnify objects, as in the microscope and telescope. When white light is bent by a wedge of glass (a prism), it splits up into bands of colour. A laser is a powerful beam of very pure light.

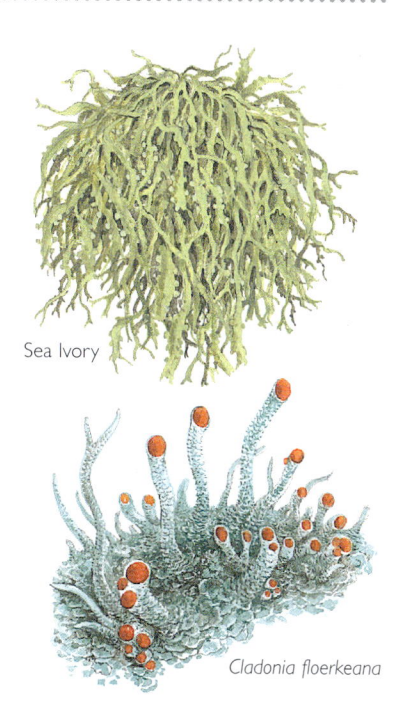

See also COLOUR; LASER; SUN.

LIGHTNING AND THUNDER

About 44,000 thunderstorms occur each day, mainly in the tropics. Lightning is a gigantic electric spark that zig-zags between the clouds during a

Lightning and Thunder: *Lightning and thunder happen at the same time, but we see lightning before we hear the thunder clap.*

thunderstorm. It can also travel down to the ground, where it can cause great damage. It can split trees and set fire to buildings. Tall buildings have to be protected from lightning by a lightning conductor. Lightning may flash in sheets, in balls or sometimes in forked streaks.

The thunder is produced by the sudden expansion of air that has been heated by the lightning flash. Thunder is heard after a flash because light travels faster than the speed of sound.

LINCOLN, ABRAHAM (1809-1865)

Lincoln began life poor, but became one of the most famous presidents of the United States. He hated slavery, and led the North to victory against the South in the American Civil War. He was assassinated by John Wilkes Booth, a supporter of the South, in 1865.

See also CIVIL WAR.

LINDBERGH, CHARLES (1902-1974)

Lindbergh was an American pilot who performed a remarkable feat of daring and endurance. He flew

Lindbergh:
Charles Lindbergh made the first single-handed non-stop transatlantic flight in The Spirit of St Louis, *a plane he had designed himself.*

The flight took 33 1/2 hours and captured the imagination of the world.

LION
The lion is sometimes called 'the king of beasts'. With the tiger, it is the largest member of the cat family. Lions live in groups called *prides*. Only the males have manes. The females, called lionesses, do most of the hunting. Lions feed mainly on antelopes and zebras. They creep up on their prey and generally kill it after a short chase. Lions once lived in Europe. Nowadays, wild lions are found only in parts of Africa and in a special reserve in India.

non-stop in his single-engine plane, *The Spirit of St Louis*, from New York to Paris in May 1927.

LISTER, JOSEPH (1827–1912)
Lister was an English surgeon who did much to make operations safe. He used carbolic acid to clean instruments and to

Lion: *A lion and lioness doze in the African sun. They can sleep for more than 18 hours a day.*

139

Ocellated Lizard

Common Wall Lizard

Lizard: There are about 180 species of typical lizards worldwide, of which around 38 occur in Europe, mostly in the south.

kill germs. He was also the first person to use catgut in surgery for stitching wounds.

LIZARD

Lizards are reptiles. Most lizards have four legs, but some are legless. The slow worm is a legless lizard. Unlike snakes, lizards have movable eyelids and visible ears.

Lizards generally live in warm climates. Most kinds lay eggs, but some produce live young. Lizards feed on insects, small mammals or plants. They prefer dry land, but the marine iguana is a good swimmer.

See also REPTILE.

LLAMA

The llama looks like a small woolly camel without a hump. This hardy creature lives in the Andes Mountains of South America.

Llamas are useful because they can carry loads along narrow mountain tracks. They also provide people with meat, wool, skins for making leather, and fat for candles.

LUTHER, MARTIN (1483–1546)

Luther was a monk who thought the Roman Catholic Church had moved too far away from the teachings of the Bible. He also objected to the custom of selling people pardons for their sins. Many Christians agreed with Luther. They started a great religious movement – the Reformation – which resulted in the formation of the Protestant churches.

M

MACHINES, SIMPLE

Machines are devices that put energy to work. Most machines are complicated devices, but they are all based on six types of simple machine: the lever; the inclined plane; the wheel and axle; the pulley; the wedge; and the screw (see illustrations).

Starting from these simple machines, engineers have developed machines which can do a vast range of things. All machines, whether the simple lever or a giant crane, make it possible for people to do things more quickly and easily than they could by hand.

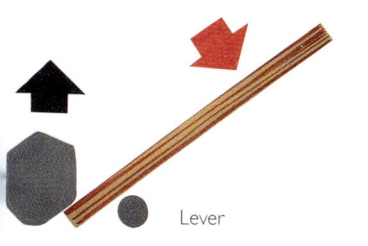

Pulley

Jackscrew

Inclined plane

Lever

Wedge

Block and tackle

Wheel and axle

Machines: *Six of the illustrations on this page show the simplest possible machines. You may not realise it but you see some of them every day. The seventh, the block and tackle, is used to lift heavy weights. The more wheels that are used, the easier the lifting is.*

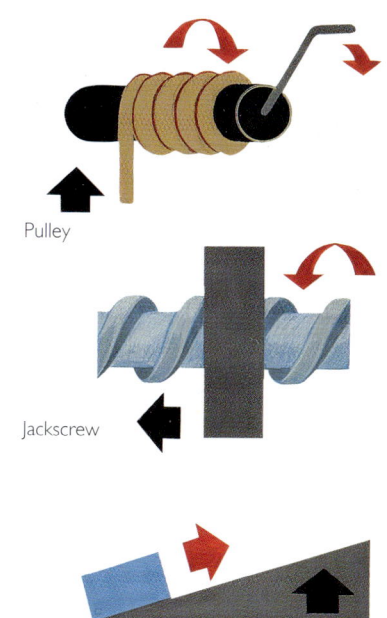

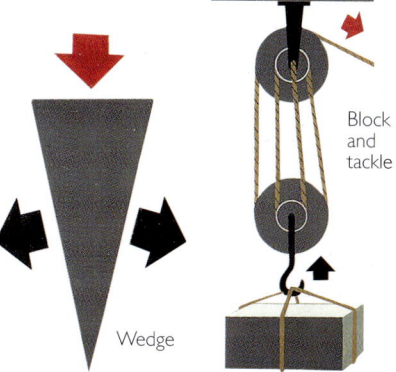

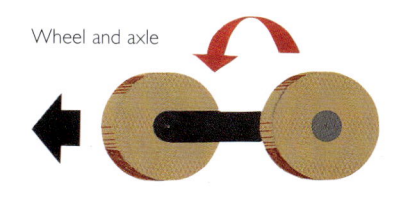

141

MAGELLAN, FERDINAND
(1480-1521)

Magellan was a Portuguese navigator in the service of Spain. He sought a sea route westwards to the Moluccas where spices were grown. He set out with four ships, found the route to the Pacific through what he named the Magellan Strait, and went on to the Philippines. There he was killed by natives. One of his ships completed the first voyage around the world in 1522.

MAGIC

Before people understood what caused such things as storms or disease, many thought that nature was controlled by good and evil spirits. They believed that magic gave them power over these spirits. Some magic was good, or 'white'; but other magic was bad, or 'black'. The clever tricks of stage magicians and conjurors today really have nothing to do with magic.

MAGNET

Magnets can pick up or attract pieces of metal, particularly iron and steel. This power is called magnetism. The magnetism is most powerful at the ends of the magnet. If you hang a bar magnet by a thread, it always points its ends towards the Earth's North and South magnetic poles. So we

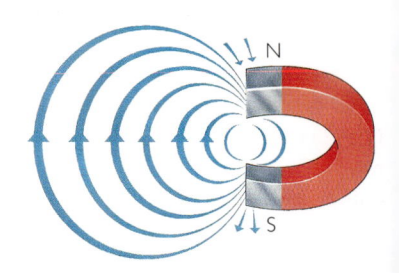

Magnet: Both the north and south poles of a horseshoe magnet can be used to pick up an object. The invisible lines of magnetic force stretch out between the two poles.

call the two ends its north and south poles. The magnet always points North-South because the Earth itself acts like a giant magnet. And one magnet affects another. The needle in a compass is a magnet.

MAMMAL

Mammals are the most advanced animals. They are vertebrates (animals with backbones) and they are warm-blooded. They can control the temperature of their bodies by sweating or panting when it is hot, and shivering when it is cold. Because of this, mammals can live in both hot and cold climates. They usually have hairy or furry skins.

Almost all mammals, including human beings, give birth to live young, rather than eggs. The female feeds the young with milk from her body, and cares for them until they can look after themselves unaided.

Mammals range in size from tiny shrews to huge whales. Most mammals are land animals, but dolphins and whales spend all their lives in the sea.

Mammoth

The mammoth was a hairy elephant. It lived during the Ice Age but is now extinct. Mammoths had long woolly hair and a thick layer of fat to keep out the cold. Prehistoric people hunted mammoths for food and sometimes drew pictures of them inside caves.

Mao Zedong (Mao Tsetung) (1893-1976)

Modern China was founded by a farmer's son, Mao Zedong. He led the peasants in a revolution which changed China's government and way of life. He became a Communist, and for many years the Communists fought against the government. Mao was their leader, and in 1949 he led his armies to victory. China became a Communist state.

See also COMMUNISM.

Mammoth: The now-extinct woolly mammoth, with its inward-curving tusks, was closely related to the modern elephant.

Maps and Globes

A map is a drawing which shows all or part of the Earth's surface. It can show how cities, roads, railways, rivers, mountains, forests and other features are arranged on the land.

A flat map cannot be really accurate because the Earth is round. Maps are drawn by various methods called *projections*. A globe is like a ball with a map of the world drawn on it. Globes are more accurate than flat maps, but less convenient.

Maps are drawn to scale. For example, a distance of one centimetre on the map may represent a kilometre on the ground itself.

Political maps show countries, and often cities, roads and railways as well. Physical maps show mountains, rivers and other land features.

MARCONI, GUGLIELMO (1874-1937)

Marconi, an Italian, worked with, and made important discoveries about, radio waves. He patented wireless telegraphy and, in 1901, he sent the first wireless message across the Atlantic.

MARCO POLO (c.1254-1324)

The book, *The Travels of Marco Polo*, recorded the adventures of this Venetian merchant. With his father and his uncle he journeyed to China in 1275. The emperor, Kublai Khan, favoured Marco and made him first a court attendant and later an official. He served the emperor for 17 years. They returned home in 1295 bringing with them great wealth.

MARX, KARL (1818-1883)

Marx was the founder of the modern Communist movement. His writings greatly changed the way many people thought about society. He helped write *The Communist Manifesto* in 1848 arguing that all old forms of government had to be overthrown. In *Das Kapital* he wrote that working people should rule and run the factories.

MATHEMATICS

Mathematics is a science that deals with numbers and shapes. Arithmetic is one branch of mathematics. The other main branches are algebra, geometry, trigonometry and calculus. Arithmetic deals with figures. Algebra deals with figures and symbols. Geometry deals with shapes. Trigonometry deals with the measurement of triangles and the problems associated with this. Calculus deals with changing quantities.

MATTER

All solids, liquids and gases are matter. Matter is anything that takes up space, responds to the force of gravity, and stays still

Marconi: *An early Marconi wireless set, with speaker and headphones. In a modern radio, the glass valves have been replaced by transistors.*

Maya: *The Maya of Central America built massive pyramids and were the only ancient American people to develop writing and an accurate calendar.*

unless acted upon by an outside force. We can see, hear, touch, taste or smell some kinds of matter, and measure it. These qualities distinguish matter from things that are mental, like ideas, or like love or hate.

MAXWELL, JAMES CLERK (1831-1879)

James Clerk Maxwell was a scientist who made important discoveries about electricity and magnetism. Born in Scotland, he was educated in Edinburgh but later moved to Cambridge University in England, where he became a professor. Long before the radio was invented, he was one of the first people to suggest that radio waves must exist. He was also interested in colour and light and produced one of the first colour photographs, using the three-colour process.

MAYA

The Maya Indians developed a civilization in Central America from the AD400s. They built great cities of stone, with palaces, temples, pyramids, and observatories. The Maya were astronomers and mathematicians, and they developed an advanced kind of writing. Like the other early civilizations in the Americas, they never developed the wheel. They did not have metal tools until late in their history, and most of their great engineering feats were accomplished using stone tools. Descendants of the Maya still live on and near the Yucatán Peninsula.

MAYFLOWER

The *Mayflower* was the ship that brought the Pilgrims from Plymouth to Massachusetts in America in 1620. Persecuted for their Puritan beliefs in England, this intrepid band planned to start a settlement in Virginia, but storms blew the *Mayflower* off course. After more than two months at sea the settlers reached what is now Cape Cod. They crossed Cape Cod Bay and founded the colony of Plymouth in December 1620. The *Mayflower* returned to England the following April.

Mayflower: *An elderly merchant ship called the* Mayflower *carried settlers to North America in 1620.*

MEASUREMENT

How long is your desk? How heavy are you? How much water is in the bottle? We find the answers to these questions by measurement. We measure by using devices or instruments marked with a scale of numbers. To measure length we use a rule. For weight, we use a pair of scales. For volume, we use a measuring jug.

Although the numbers on the scales may be the same, they mean different things. On the rule, 20 may mean 20cm; on the pair of scales, 20kg; and on the jug, 20ml. The centimetre, kilogram and litre are different units of measurement. They are units of length, weight and volume in the metric system of measurement.

The metric system is one in which the units go up in steps or multiples of ten. It was devised in France in the late 1700s and has been in use in most of Europe for most of this century.

MEDICI FAMILY

The Medicis ruled the city state of Florence in Italy for 300 years during and after the Renaissance. They made it into a prosperous and beautiful city and had magnificent palaces and churches built. Two of the most famous of the Medici rulers were Cosimo (1389-1464) and Lorenzo the Magnificent (1449-1492). The last of the Medicis to rule died in 1737.

MEDICINE

Since very early times people have searched for medicines to heal wounds and cure diseases. The first drugs came from berries and herbs which had healing powers.

The ancient Greeks and Romans knew what the inside of the human body looked like. But they did not know how the different parts worked, or what made them go wrong.

Medicine made little progress until the 1600s, when doctors began studying anatomy (the parts of the body). By cutting up dead bodies, they began to find out how the body works. But since no one knew about germs, doctors did not bother very much about cleanliness. Many patients died because hospitals were dirty places.

Over the next 200 years progress in medicine was slow. But in the 1700s vaccination was discovered as a way of preventing disease, and later antiseptics were developed to kill harmful germs. Anaesthetics came to be used to deaden pain during operations. In the 1900s the discovery of X-rays meant that doctors could examine the insides of their patients to find out what was wrong without cutting them open. Powerful new drugs called antibiotics were also discovered.

See also DISEASE; DRUGS; X-RAY.

ADVANCES IN MEDICINE

1590	Microscope	Zacharias Janssen
1593	Thermometer	Galileo
1628	Blood circulation	William Harvey
1796	Vaccination	Edward Jenner
1846	Anaesthetic	William Morton
1865	Antiseptic surgery	Joseph Lister
1877	Germs cause disease	Louis Pasteur
1895	Psychoanalysis	Sigmund Freud
1895	X-rays	William Roentgen
1898	Radium	Pierre and Marie Curie
1928	Penicillin	Alexander Fleming

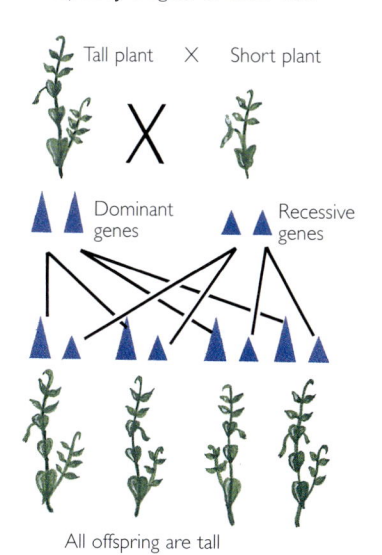

Mendel: By crossing tall plants with short ones, Mendel showed that tallness is dominant over shortness, because all the offspring were tall.

Tall plant X Short plant

Dominant genes

Recessive genes

All offspring are tall

MENDEL, GREGOR (1822–1884)

Mendel was an Austrian monk who studied the way in which physical characteristics are passed on from parent to child. He observed that

Meteor: *Meteors usually burn up about 50km above Earth. Anything larger than a stone will light up the sky as a fireball. It may explode or hit the ground as a meteorite.*

the colour and shape of peas were passed on from one generation to the next according to certain laws.

His discoveries went unnoticed until improved microscopes made it possible to see chromosomes, the minute thread-like bodies which carry these hereditary characteristics.

See also GENETICS.

METALS

There are over 60 different metals. They make up the most important group of elements. They are very different from the other elements. Metals pass on, or conduct, electricity and heat well. Most non-metals do not. Many metals have a silvery, shiny surface. They are tough and strong, but can be bent and hammered without breaking.

Most metals are found in the form of mineral ores. They must be separated out before they can be used. There are several different ways of taking, or extracting, a metal from its ore. Iron is extracted by smelting, aluminium by means of electricity.

Metal may be shaped by casting, hammering, rolling, forcing through holes and cutting.

See also ALUMINIUM; COPPER; GOLD; IRON AND STEEL; MINING.

METEOR

On some nights you may see bright streaks in the sky. Though they look like falling stars, these glowing trails are actually made by meteors, lumps of rock or metal. As they shoot through the upper part of the Earth's atmosphere they burn up in a flash of light.

MEXICO

Mexico is a republic and lies just south of the United States. Most of it consists of a broad, central plateau that is flanked on both sides by mountain ranges. On the west is the Pacific Ocean and on the east, the Gulf of Mexico and the Caribbean Sea. There are three main kinds of climate – cool, temperate and hot – and a huge variety of plant life.

Over a third of Mexico's 93,674,000 people work on the land, growing mostly maize, beans, coffee, cotton, sugar and vegetables.

MICROSCOPE

A microscope makes small objects look bigger, so that we can see things that are invisible to the naked eye.

Ordinary microscopes magnify by bending light rays with glass lenses. The bent rays make an image which is bigger than the original object. Electron microscopes are much more powerful than ordinary microscopes, and can magnify things hundreds of thousands of times. They magnify by bending beams of electrons, rather than light rays.

See also LENS; LIGHT.

Michelangelo: *This great Italian sculptor and painter carved a huge statue of Moses for the tomb of Pope Julius II.*

Mexico is rich in minerals. Its silver and gold originally attracted the Spanish. There is also oil. Mexico's factories produce a wide variety of goods.

MICHELANGELO (1475–1564)

Michelangelo was a sculptor, architect, painter and poet who lived in Italy at the time of the Renaissance. Among his most famous statues are the *Pieta* and *David*. He painted a scene on the ceiling of the Sistine Chapel in the Vatican depicting the creation of the world.

See also RENAISSANCE.

Microscope: *An optical microscope has a base, a tube containing the lenses, and a body, or upright, to hold the tube.*

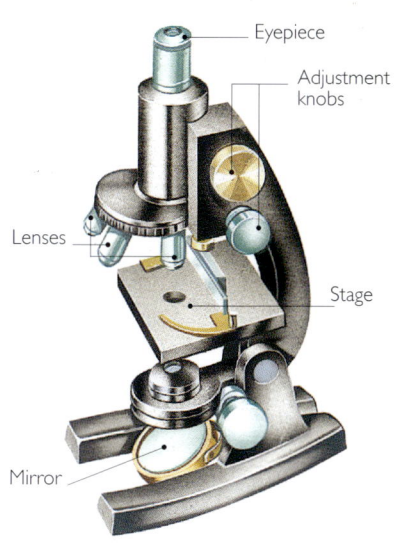

MIDDLE AGES

The Roman Empire fell in AD476 and it took 1,000 years for strong nations to grow out of the confusion that followed. In between lay the Middle Ages. In the early Middle Ages, Europe was overrun by barbarians. They sacked and burned towns, and soon the art and learning of Rome and the classical world was forgotten, except by monks.

To defend themselves, people banded together under the protection of strong leaders, or kings. The peasants became the vassals of rich nobles and knights. They traded crops and services for protection. The nobles became vassals of the king. In return for the king's protection, they promised to supply soldiers in war. This is known as the feudal system.

Life in the Middle Ages was often harsh and cruel. Anyone who broke the law was severely punished. And anyone who questioned the Church's teachings was punished harshly too. But slowly knowledge grew. Beautiful cathedrals were built.

Universities and schools were founded. Gradually government became more settled, and trade flourished. With the voyages of discovery in the 1400s and the Renaissance, the Middle Ages came to an end.

Middle Ages: *Many medieval towns held a market once or twice a week. The town square would be filled with bustling crowds and traders shouting their wares.*

MIDDLE EAST

The desert lands of southwest Asia and northeast Africa are often called the Middle East. This area stretches from Egypt to Iran. Most of the people are Muslim Arabs. Many are poor, but oilfields have made some Middle East countries rich.

In 1948 the Jews founded the independent state of Israel in what had been British-ruled Palestine. The Arabs would not accept this. As a result, there have been five wars between Israel and the Arab countries, in 1948, 1956, 1967, 1973 and 1982.

See also PAGE 62.

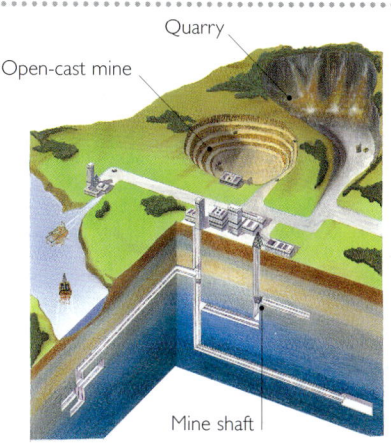

Mining: *Thousands of years ago, our ancestors began mining flint to shape into tools and weapon heads. Since then we have discovered many uses for the Earth's rock and mineral resources.*

MIGRATION, ANIMAL

Many swallows spend the summer in Europe. But in the autumn they fly south to the warmth of Africa. This journey is called migration.

Many animals migrate to find food or to breed. Caribou move south to escape the Arctic winter. African antelope migrate during the dry season to find water and fresh grass. Frogs, toads and newts spend most of their time on land. But they return to ponds and streams to lay their eggs.

MINERAL

A mineral is any substance that can be mined. There are nearly 3,000 kinds of minerals. Some, such as gold and silver, are pure elements. But most, such as salt and coal, are combinations of the 92 naturally occurring elements. Pure minerals are made up of atoms arranged in regular patterns known as crystals. This is what makes jewels like diamonds and emeralds sparkle.

See also GEMS; MINING.

MINING

Mining means taking minerals from the ground. It is one of our most important industries and supplies many other industries with their raw materials.

Sometimes mineral deposits can be dug out from the surface. Other deposits lie just below the surface.

The soil is first stripped off, then explosives break up the deposits.

Often the mineral deposits are buried deep in the ground. Miners have to travel by lift down shafts and in trains along tunnels to reach them.

MISSILE

A missile can be anything that is thrown or fired at a target. Today the word usually means a military weapon that has an automatic control system. Many are powered by a rocket engine and carry an explosive warhead. A guided missile is controlled by radio or radar and stays within the Earth's atmosphere. A ballistic missile goes beyond the atmosphere under rocket power, but returns to Earth in an unguided path called a ballistic trajectory.

MOLLUSC

Molluscs are animals with soft bodies. To protect themselves, many molluscs have shells.

Some molluscs, like the mussel, stay inside their shells and hardly ever move. Others, such as the cockle, use their single foot to move around.

Slugs and snails are molluscs but slugs have little or no shell. They crawl very slowly. Slugs and snails are garden pests, eating young and low-lying plants. The largest and most active molluscs

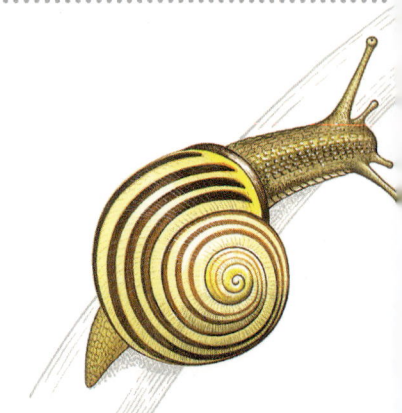

Mollusc: The brown-lipped snail is a land-dwelling mollusc, with eyes at the tips of its longer tentacle.

are the octopus, which has no shell, and the squid, which has its shell inside its body.

MONASTERY

A monastery is the home of a religious community. The monks who live in the monastery take vows promising not to marry, not to have possessions or money, and do whatever work they are asked to do. They spend the day working, studying or in prayer. Some monks work outside the monastery as missionaries and teachers. The long tunic many monks wear is known as a habit.

The first Christian monasteries were started about 200 years after the death of Christ. By the Middle Ages there were several important 'orders' of monks and friars (friar means brother).

Money

Originally, people did not use money. They bartered or traded. When people settled in towns, trade became more complicated. The barter system was too clumsy. So token goods, such as cattle or shells, were used. This was the beginning of the money system.

Later small pieces of metal, or coins, came into use. The first were made just before 600BC in Asia Minor. Governments issued coins, using gold, silver, bronze, copper and other alloys. They made them in a place called a mint.

Merchants in the Middle Ages began to exchange pieces of paper, promising payment for goods bought. They set up banks, in which to keep their gold safe. The banks began to issue paper money, or bank notes, and people gradually accepted that these had the same value as gold.

Today, the government controls how much money is made by minting coins and printing notes. The money we use is token money: that is, modern coins are made of cheap metals and have little value in themselves. The real value of money is the amount of goods it will buy.

Monkey: *The colobus and mandrill are both Old World monkeys living in Africa. New World monkeys include the spider and woolly monkeys.*

Monkey

Monkeys belong to the group of animals called primates. Old World monkeys live in Africa and Asia. New World monkeys live in Central and South America. New World monkeys have prehensile tails, which can grasp a branch like an extra hand. Old World monkeys cannot do this.

Monkeys are lively, intelligent animals. They use their hands and feet to hold things. Most monkeys live in groups. They eat fruit and other parts of plants, insects, small mammals and birds' eggs.

MOON

The Moon is a ball of rock, about a quarter the diameter (width) of the Earth. It has no atmosphere. Because there is no air there is no weather on the Moon, and no sound. There is no water and no life at all. It is very hot in the sunlight, but icy cold when in the shade.

The Moon's surface is not smooth. There are great, flat plains and jagged peaks and mountain ranges. Everywhere on the Moon there are pits, or craters. The whole surface is covered with loose rocks and a thick layer of fine dust.

The Moon travels around the Earth once a month. The shape of the Moon appears to change during the month. What changes is the area we can see which is lit by the Sun. This area changes because of the Moon's movement around the Earth.

See also ECLIPSE.

Moon: *The Earth-turned face of the Moon (top) has many lava plains or maria; the far side (below) is cratered.*

MOSES

Moses was one of the most important leaders of the ancient people of Israel, living more than 3,000 years ago. According to the Bible, the Israelites had become slaves of the Egyptians. The Old Testament tells how God appeared to Moses in a burning bush and told him to bring his people to freedom. Moses led them through the Red Sea whose waters parted to let them pass, then rolled back down again to drown the pursuing Egyptians. Later, God gave Moses the Ten Commandments, the laws that are still the basis of much Jewish and Christian teaching.

Mosque

Mosques are the buildings in which the services of the Islamic religion take place. Most mosques have a dome, a minaret, from which the faithful are called to prayer five times a day, and a prayer niche showing the direction of Mecca.

Moss

Mosses are simple plants. They do not have flowers, but reproduce by sending out tiny offshoots. Spores, or cells, grow on these shoots. When the spores are ripe, they are blown away by the wind. New moss plants develop from them.

Motion Picture
See Film.

Motorcycle

A motorcycle is a vehicle which has two and sometimes three wheels. The first motorcycles were built at the end of the 1800s when men such as Edward Butler, an Englishman, and Gottlieb Daimler, a German, began making powered bicycles and tricycles. The first motorcycle races in 1907 encouraged improvements in design which soon brought the motorcycle to something like its present form with electric ignition, variable gears, and the engine mounted low down between the two wheels.

Mountain

Mountains are masses of rock which rise at least 600m above the surrounding land.

Mountains are usually grouped together in ranges, chains or massifs. Some mountains are the cones of volcanoes. But most are formed by folding and sideways movements of the crust, or outer skin, of the Earth. These movements push up the rocks to build mountains. Mountain-building takes millions of years. It is still going on today in parts of the Earth. The rocks are worn away by rain, wind, ice and snow.

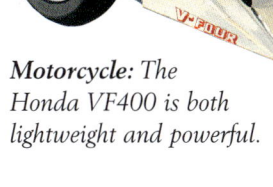

Motorcycle: The Honda VF400 is both lightweight and powerful.

HIGHEST MOUNTAINS	
Asia	**Metres**
Everest	8,846
Godwin Austen	8,611
Kanchenjunga	8,597
Makalu	8,470
Dhaulagiri	8,172
Nanga Parbat	8,126
Annapurna	8,075
Gasherbrum	8,068
Gosainthan	8,013
Nanda Devi	7,817
South America	
Aconcagua	6,960
North America	
McKinley	6,194
Africa	
Kilimanjaro	5,895
Europe	
Elbruz	5,633
Mont Blanc	4,810
Antarctica	
Vinson Massif	5,139
Oceania	
Wilhelm	4,694

The height of a mountain is always measured in height above sea level. The world's highest mountains are in the Himalayas in Asia. Mount Everest (8,846m) is the highest.

MOZART, WOLFGANG AMADEUS (1756-1791)

The Austrian composer Mozart was a musical genius. He began writing music at the age of five. Two years later his father took him to play at concerts in the great cities of Europe. Mozart wrote church music, opera and nearly 50 symphonies. He worked hard but earned little money and died very poor at the age of 35.

MUHAMMAD (AD570-632)

The Arab prophet Muhammad founded the religion of Islam. He taught people to stop worshipping idols and follow the 'true God', called Allah. In 622 Muhammad's enemies drove him out of his birthplace, Mecca. He fled to the city of Medina, and converted many people to the new religion. By the time Muhammad died, Islam had spread throughout the Arab world.

MUSHROOMS AND TOADSTOOLS

These plants belong to the fungus group. Fungi are not green. They contain no chlorophyll, so they cannot use sunlight to make their food like other plants. Instead they feed on dead and decaying plant and animal matter. Some are parasites. Fungi have no flowers or seeds and reproduce by means of cells called spores which are carried by the wind.

See also PHOTOSYNTHESIS.

MUSIC

Music is a set of sounds arranged in a way that is pleasant to hear. It has rhythm (the beat), harmony (the total sound when several notes are

MUSIC

Death cap

Chanterelle

Ugly milk cap

Lawyer's wig

Mushrooms and Toadstools: Some of these fungi are extremely good to eat; others are deadly poisonous.

Mozart, Beethoven and Brahms. They wrote symphonies (long pieces of music for orchestras) and chamber music (for smaller groups of instruments). They also wrote music for choirs. Some composers have written operas – musical plays in which all the words are sung.

played together) and usually melody (the tune). Music is made up of notes that may be long or short, loud or soft, high or low.

At first music had a simple melody and rhythm. But it gradually grew more complicated. Two or three tunes were played together. This rich sound was called counterpoint.

People who make up music and write it down are called composers. Two great composers of counterpoint were Bach and Handel. Much great music has been written for orchestras by composers such as Haydn,

FAMOUS COMPOSERS

Antonio Vivaldi	Italian (1678?-1741)
Johann Sebastian Bach	German (1685-1750)
Wolfgang Amadeus Mozart	Austrian (1756-1791)
Ludwig van Beethoven	German (1770-1827)
Franz Schubert	Austrian (1797-1828)
Hector Berlioz	French (1803-1869)
Frédéric Chopin	Polish (1810-1849)
Robert Schumann	German (1810-1856)
Franz Liszt	Hungarian (1811-1886)
Giuseppe Verdi	Italian (1813-1901)
Richard Wagner	German (1813-1883)
Johannes Brahms	German (1833-1897)
Peter Ilyich Tchaikovsky	Russian (1840-1893)
Antonin Dvorak	Czech (1841-1904)
Edvard Grieg	Norwegian (1843-1907)
Edward Elgar	British (1857-1934)
Giacomo Puccini	Italian (1858-1924)
Gustav Mahler	Austrian (1860-1911)
Claude Debussy	French (1862-1918)
Jean Sibelius	Finnish (1865-1957)
Sergei Rachmaninov	Russian (1873-1943)
Igor Stravinsky	Russian (1882-1971)
Dmitri Shostakovich	Russian (1906-1975)
Benjamin Britten	British (1913-1976)

Musical Instruments

People often call this kind of music 'classical' music. There are many other kinds of music, including folk songs, jazz and pop music. Modern music is very different from the music of the 1800s. It has difficult rhythms

Musical Instruments: *In the Western orchestra, instruments are arranged into families of strings, woodwind, brass and percussion.*

Flute

Trumpet

Clarinet

Violin

French horn

Kettle drum

Harp

Tubular bells

Cymbals

and sounds, and sometimes requires electronic instruments as well as wind, stringed and percussion instruments.

See also BACH; BEETHOVEN; MOZART; OPERA.

MUSICAL INSTRUMENTS

Musical instruments have been made for thousands of years. There are three main groups of instruments. Wind instruments are played by blowing down a hollow wooden or metal tube with holes cut in it. By covering some holes with the fingers, different notes are produced. Wind instruments include flutes, clarinets, trumpets and horns.

The stringed instruments have strings stretched across a hollow box. The strings are bowed, as in a violin, or plucked, as in a guitar, to make different notes. Short strings make high notes and long strings make low notes. Stringed instruments include violins, guitars, banjos and lutes.

Instruments such as drums, cymbals and bells, which are hit with hammers or sticks, are called percussion instruments.

See also ORCHESTRA.

Mythology: *In one of the great ancient Greek myths, Perseus turned the court of King Polydectes to stone by holding up the hideous head of Medusa.*

MYTHOLOGY

Mythology is the study of the myths, or stories, that ancient peoples told about their creation and origins, their gods and goddesses. The most familiar to us are the myths the ancient Greeks and Romans created. Myths were a part of their religion, for they believed that many gods and goddesses inhabited the Earth – gods of the Sun and Moon, gods of war, of the sea and forests, of rain and thunder. The Greek gods lived on Mount Olympus, and the stories told about them were full of heroic adventures and amazing feats. The Greek poets Hesiod and Homer recorded many of these myths in writing. The Romans adopted many of the Greek myths and told dramatic stories about their own gods and heroes that were similar to the Greek myths.

The Norse people of Scandinavia also developed a rich mythology.

N

Napoleon Bonaparte (1769-1821)

After the French Revolution in 1789, Napoleon conquered much of Europe. In 1804 he made himself Emperor of France. But in 1812 his army had to retreat from Russia, and in 1815 the British and Prussians beat the French at the Battle of Waterloo. He was exiled, and died on the island of St Helena.

Nasser, Gamal Abdul (1918-1970)

Nasser was an Egyptian revolutionary and army officer. He helped to depose King Farouk in 1952 and became president in 1956. He tried to modernize Egypt. In 1956 he nationalized, or took over, the Suez Canal.

Nelson, Horatio (1758-1805)

Nelson was a great British admiral whose statue stands above Trafalgar Square, London.

He fought and defeated the French fleet led by Napoleon near Alexandria in 1798 (the Battle of the Nile). His most famous battle was at Trafalgar in 1805; he was shot and killed during this battle.

Native American

Native Americans were the first peoples in North America. Scientists believe that they came from Asia between 15,000 and 35,000 years ago. They crossed the land that then connected Asia with Alaska, and moved southwards.

There were hundreds of tribes, each with its own customs and way of life. Some tribes lived by hunting and food-gathering, others were farmers and fishermen.

When the first Europeans came

Napoleon: Napoleon's greatest victory was at the Battle of Austerlitz, where he defeated a combined force of Austrians and Russians in 1805.

Native American: The tepee, the traditional home of Plains tribes, is a cone-shaped tent made from skins and bark and supported by poles.

to North America, relations with Native Americans were friendly. But as Europeans settled the continent, the Native Americans were threatened by new diseases and the loss of tribal lands. Wars broke out, and during the 1800s, the U.S. Army forced the few remaining tribes to live on government reservations. Today, many Native Americans are reviving old traditions and teaching others about tribal art, religions and medicine.

Nervous System

The nervous system consists of the brain and the nerves, the bundles of fibre that connect the brain to the different parts of the body. It controls functions, such as breathing and the beating of the heart, that the body carries out automatically. It also enables the body to respond to outside events. A two-way traffic flows along the nerves. Some, known as sensory nerves, carry signals to the brain telling it about sensations such as heat, cold and pain. Others, known as motor nerves, carry instructions from the brain to the body telling it how to react. If you touch something hot, for example, the sensory nerves carry pain signals to the brain, and the motor nerves carry back the instructions to jerk your hand away.

Nest

Many animals build nests for their young. Usually they are well hidden and out of reach of enemies. Some are simple, just scrapes in the ground or untidy piles of twigs. But many are elaborately built of mud, grass, moss, feathers and wax. Birds, fish, insects, reptiles and mammals build nests.

Nest: Weaver birds build their nests with the entrance facing downwards to deter predators.

NETHERLANDS, BELGIUM AND LUXEMBOURG

These three countries form the area of Europe known as the Low Countries. In 1948 they forged an economic union known as Benelux, and in 1957 they were founder members of the European Union.

The Netherlands is largely flat and much of it lies below sea level. It is well-known for its dikes and canals. Dairy farming, greenhouse vegetables and horticulture are very important but other industries are growing rapidly. The Dutch have a long and successful seafaring history and Rotterdam is the busiest port in Europe.

Belgium's population is divided into the Dutch-speaking Flemings in the north and the French-speaking Walloons in the south. Its capital, Brussels, is home to the European Parliament. Belgium is heavily industrialized and steel manufacturing is its most important industry.

Luxembourg is one of the smallest countries in Europe. It is an international centre of banking and finance.

NEWTON, ISAAC (1642-1727)

Newton was one of the greatest scientists and mathematicians the world has known. He was the first person to explain the force of gravity, which holds the universe together. Newton carried out many experiments with light and split up light into a spectrum, or band of colour. He built the first reflecting telescope and he invented calculus.

See also COLOUR; GRAVITY; LIGHT; TELESCOPE.

NEW ZEALAND

Two long and narrow islands, the North Island and South Island, and a few smaller islands make up the country of New Zealand. It lies in the south Pacific Ocean.

New Zealand has mountains, volcanoes, hot springs, fast-flowing rivers and glaciers. Most of the towns and cities are on the coast.

The grasslands are ideal for sheep and cattle farming. New Zealand is famous for its butter, cheese and meat, and for fruit.

The native Maoris settled in New Zealand about 1000 years ago. Although the Dutch explorer Abel Tasman discovered and named New Zealand in 1642, the country was mainly settled by people from Britain.

See also PAGE 63.

NIGERIA

Nigeria is named after the river Niger which flows through the country to the Atlantic Ocean. Its landscape ranges from swampy plains and rainforests to grasslands and rock. It is one of the world's major oil producers, exports large quantities of cacao, peanuts and

Nobel Prize: Alfred Nobel (1833-1896) left much of the fortune he had made from dynamite to fund six Nobel prizes.

palm oil, and has a growing tin and coal mining industry.

Nigeria's 120 million people are from a great number of different ethnic groups and speak many languages. Nigeria was a British colony from 1914 to 1960. Recent decades have been dominated by military rule, although there have been attempts at democracy.

NOBEL PRIZE

Every year six Nobel prizes may be awarded, for outstanding work in chemistry, physics, medicine, literature, economics and the cause of peace. Two or three people may share a prize, and the winners may come from any part of the world. To win a Nobel prize is a very great honour. The money for the prizes was given by Alfred Nobel, a Swedish chemist, who invented the explosive dynamite.

NOMADS

Nomads are groups of people who wander from place to place with their animals and possessions. They do not build permanent houses. Some nomads keep flocks and herds, and move to find fresh grazing land for their animals.

NORTH AMERICA

This is the third largest of the Earth's continents. It stretches from the cold wastes of Alaska in the north to the hot deserts of Mexico and the tropical forests of Central America in the south. Canada and the United States of America cover most of North America.

Down the western side of North America run the rugged Rocky Mountains. In the centre of the continent are wide grasslands called prairies. The Canadian Shield, a wild region of lakes and forests in northern Canada, has valuable minerals, such as coal and oil. In the south of the continent are coastal plains, swampy in places. The longest river in North America is the Mississippi. The Great Lakes are the largest freshwater lakes in the world.

Crops grown in North America include wheat, fruit, vegetables and cotton. Canada and the United States are great industrial countries, with plentiful raw materials.

North America is a continent of great contrasts. It has some of the world's largest cities, such as Mexico City and New York. But there are huge areas with hardly any people at all. The United States is one of the richest countries in the world. But in Central America the countries are small and poor.

The first people in North America came from Asia. They were the ancestors of the American Indians and the Inuit (or Eskimos). Much later Europeans came, bringing with them Negro slaves from Africa.

See also PAGE 62-63.

Nuclear Energy

Under certain conditions atoms of uranium can be made to split. When they do so, large amounts of energy are released as heat and light. The splitting of the atom, or rather of its nucleus, is called nuclear fission.

Scientists can now control the fission of uranium and use the energy it releases to produce nuclear power. In furnaces, called reactors, great heat is produced when the nucleus of the atom splits. This heat is used to drive turbines and generate electricity. Nuclear power is also used to drive some ships.

In atomic bombs, the nuclear reaction is uncontrolled and all the energy is released, causing devastation over a huge area.

Nut

Some trees bear fruits called nuts. Inside the tough shell of the nut is a seed. Ripe nuts fall to earth in autumn. The seed sends a new shoot pushing through the shell; and a new tree begins its life.

Hazelnut

Brazil nut

Walnut

Peanut

Horse chestnut

Sweet chestnut

Nut: *The hard shell of the nut protects the seed inside it.*

O

Oasis

An oasis is a fertile area in a desert. Sometimes water comes to the surface naturally. Sometimes wells are sunk to tap it. Some oases cover many square kilometres and may support a city. Others have only a few huts.

Ocean

About 70 percent of the Earth's surface is covered by water. The large areas of salty water which separate the continents from each other are called oceans.

There are five oceans. The biggest and deepest is the Pacific Ocean, which separates America and Asia. Next come the Atlantic Ocean and the Indian Ocean. The Antarctic and Arctic Oceans surround the Poles.

Around most coasts a shelf of land runs out under the sea. This is the continental shelf. It lies up to 180m deep, and may stretch for hundreds of kilometres. Beyond the continental shelf, the ocean floor drops away steeply. It flattens out again at a depth of about 3,650m. The bottom of the ocean is called the abyss. It is a flat plain, crossed by ridges, high mountains and deep trenches.

Life abounds in the oceans. Today, sea creatures range in size from enormous whales to tiny drifting animals, too small to be seen without a microscope. There are many marine plants, including huge seaweeds.

The oceans are never still. The rise and fall of the tides, which takes place roughly every twelve hours, is caused by the gravitational pull of the Earth and the Moon. The surface of the water is moved by waves, caused by the wind.

See also TIDES; WIND.

Octopus and Squid

The octopus and squid are soft-bodied molluscs that live in the sea. Octopus means 'eight feet', though we usually call its tentacles 'arms'. A squid has ten tentacles. Suckers on the tentacles

Octopus: *The octopus moves by jet propulsion like the squid, but can also crawl slowly on its eight arms.*

seize and hold prey, which the animals eat with a sharp, horny 'beak' in the centre of their bodies. If danger threatens, an octopus can squirt an inky liquid that forms a cloud in the water, behind which the octopus can escape. A giant squid can be up to 10m long, including the tentacles.

Oil

Oil is a greasy substance that does not mix with water. There are three kinds of oil: mineral, fatty and 'essential'.

Mineral oil is distilled from petroleum. It comes from the Earth's crust and is used for fuels and lubricants.

Oil: Undersea oil deposits can be reached from a platform perched on long legs. Engineers bore down through the rock to reach the oil.

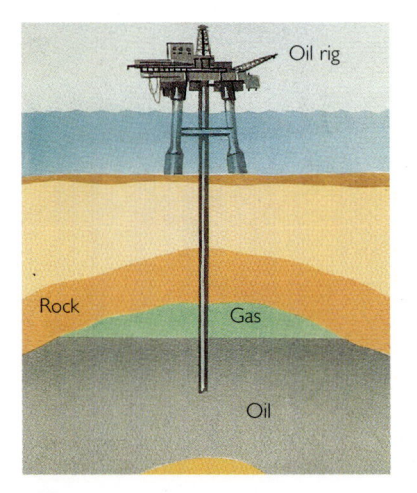

Fatty oils come from both animals and vegetables. Linseed oil, lard, butter and margarine are fatty oils.

Essential oils give scents and flavours to flowers and fruits. Lemon oil from lemon rind and cinnamon from bark are kinds of essential oils.

Olympic Games

Between 776BC and AD393, the ancient Greeks held athletic contests on the plain of Olympia every four years in honour of the god Zeus. The idea was taken up again in 1896, when the first modern Olympics were held at Athens. The Games are now held every four years, each time in a different country, and many nations take part in the different sports. The winners receive gold, silver and bronze medals. The most recent Olympic games were held in 1996 in Atlanta, Georgia.

Opera

An opera is a play in which the actors sing the words of the story. The first operas were written in Italy in the 1600s. The actors recited the story to music. Later, complete songs called arias were added. Many operas tell sad stories, but some are gay and have happy endings. Famous composers of operas include Monteverdi, Mozart, Verdi, Puccini and Wagner.

ORCHESTRA

The word orchestra is used to describe any group of musicians, large or small, which plays together under a conductor. There are various types: large symphony orchestras of about a hundred musicians, small chamber orchestras, orchestras with stringed instruments only, and theatre orchestras for musicals, ballets and opera.

The conductor directs and interprets the music, giving it its life and character. He indicates the speed, rhythm, expression and loudness of the music.

Orchestra: A typical orchestra is made up of about twenty different kinds of instrument, which are divided into four main sections – strings, woodwind, brass and percussion.

OTTER

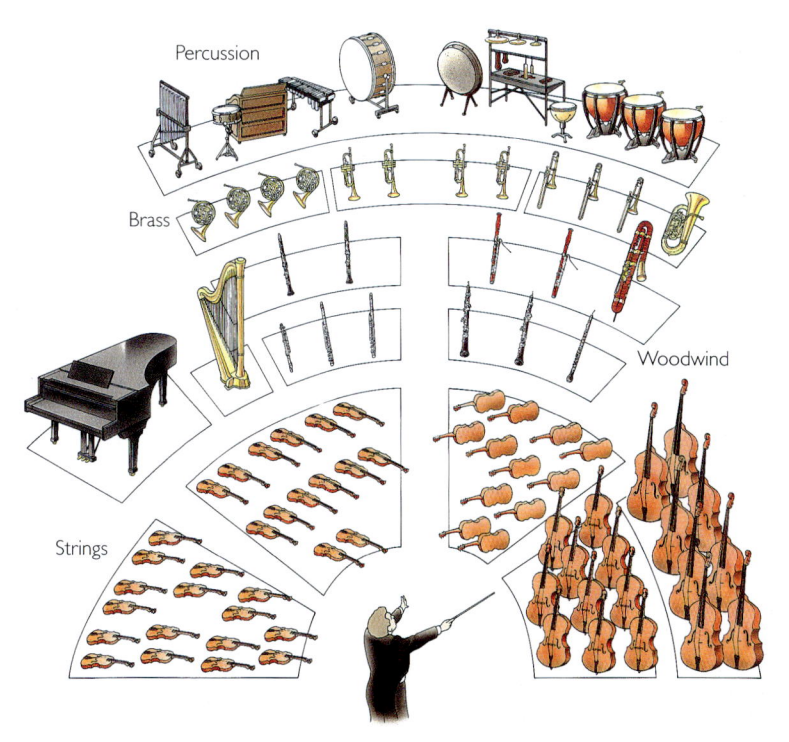

Otters belong to the weasel family. They are wonderful swimmers. They paddle the water with their webbed toes and use their strong tails as rudders. Their thick fur keeps out the wet and cold. The river otter eats mostly fish and frogs. Its home is a hole in the river bank called a holt. The sea otter is larger and rarely comes on land.

OTTOMAN EMPIRE

With its centre in present-day Turkey, the Ottoman Empire was once huge, including a large part of southeastern Europe and most of the Middle East and North Africa. Its rulers, known as sultans, were Muslims, followers of the Islamic faith.

The first Ottoman ruler was Osman I (1258-c.1326). The greatest was Suleiman the Magnificent (c.1494-1566). During his reign the Ottoman Empire reached the peak of its power, threatening to spread into Western Europe. It then declined slowly until it finally fell apart after World War I. The last sultan, Muhammad VI gave up his throne in 1922.

OWL

Owls are birds of prey. Their large eyes see well in the dark and they fly noiselessly on their broad wings. Hunting by night, they swoop down on small animals such as mice and voles, and carry them off in their strong claws. The

Owl: *The Barn Owl favours heaths, woods, fields and hedges.*

owl rips flesh with its hooked beak but it cannot digest fur, skin and bones. It spits them out in the form of a pellet.

OXYGEN

Oxygen, a colourless, odourless gas, is the commonest element on Earth. It combines easily with minerals and other substances. Oxygen is found in air, water and many different rocks.

All living things need oxygen. Animals need extra oxygen to move around and fire needs oxygen in order to burn.

See also BREATHING; PHOTOSYNTHESIS.

P

Pacific Ocean

The Pacific Ocean is the largest and the deepest of all the world's oceans. Its deepest part is deep enough to cover the world's highest mountain. The Pacific washes the shores of western North and South America, eastern Asia, and Australia, and stretches from the Arctic to the Antarctic. Thousands of islands in the Pacific were formed from volcanoes. Movements in the Earth's crust around the fringes of the Pacific often cause earthquakes and sometimes tidal waves.

Many of the tiny islands sprinkled over the Pacific are inhabited, including the islands of Melanesia (meaning 'black islands'), Micronesia ('small islands') and Polynesia ('many islands'). Some of the world's tiniest nations are here, countries like Tuvalu and Kiribati. Tuvalu, for example, is part of Polynesia. It consists of nine coral islands. Put together they cover only 26sq km, yet they are spread out in a chain about 600km long. A little over 9,000 people live on them – that equals the population of a smallish European market town.

The ocean provides half of the world's fish and shellfish.

Painting

The oldest known paintings were made by Stone Age people in caves thousands of years ago. Much later, people started to decorate their homes and temples with paintings. Egyptians, Greeks, Romans and Chinese painted vases, pottery and walls.

During the Middle Ages in Europe most paintings were done for churches. So painters mostly painted stories from the Bible. Later, Italian painters began to paint Bible characters who looked like real people.

During the Renaissance, painters often took scenes from history and

FAMOUS PAINTERS

Painter	Nationality and Dates
Giotto	Italian (c.1266-1337)
Jan van Eyck	Flemish (c.1387-1440)
Sandro Botticelli	Italian (c.1444-1510)
Leonardo da Vinci	Italian (1452-1519)
Albrecht Dürer	German (1471-1528)
Michelangelo	Italian (1475-1564)
Titian	Italian (1477-1576)
Raphael	Italian (1483-1520)
El Greco	Spanish (c.1541-1614)
Rubens	Flemish (1577-1640)
Velázquez	Spanish (c.1599-1666)
Rembrandt van Rijn	Dutch (1606-1669)
Goya	Spanish (1746-1828)
J. M. W. Turner	English (1775-1851)
Edouard Manet	French (1832-1883)
Paul Cézanne	French (1839-1906)
Henri Rousseau	French (1844-1910)
Vincent van Gogh	Dutch (1853-1890)
Vassily Kandinsky	Russian (1866-1944)
Henri Matisse	French (1869-1954)
Pablo Picasso	Spanish (1881-1973)
Jackson Pollock	USA (1912-1956)

Greek and Roman legends as their subjects. They also painted portraits of people from life, and realistic scenes from nature. During the 1700s many painters worked for fashionable society. They painted people in family groups, often against a background of a garden or a fine house.

Artists have always experimented with new ideas. 'Impressionist' painters, for instance, loved to paint light and shadow, and ignore the details, which could be captured perfectly in a photograph. By the early 1900s some were making pictures as designs and shapes, rather than as copies of objects. This is called abstract painting.

See also LEONARDO DA VINCI; MICHELANGELO; PICASSO.

PANDA

One of the world's rarest animals is the giant panda. It looks like a furry black and white bear.

Pandas live in bamboo forests in the mountains of China. They eat mostly bamboo shoots and leaves. Pandas do not breed easily in captivity, so few have been seen in zoos outside China.

PAPER

The word paper comes from papyrus, the reed the Egyptians used to make paper. The type of paper we use today was invented by the Chinese about AD 105. It was made of mulberry bark. Small pieces of bark were soaked to separate the fibres, then dried into flat sheets.

With the invention of the printing press in the 1400s the demand for paper grew. In 1799

Paper: Paper is made by crushing or chemically treating logs to make wood pulp, which is made into a thin slurry with water. The slurry passes onto a loop of wire mesh, and as the water is sucked out, the wood fibres form a web of paper. The web is squeezed between rollers, dried and usually coated with substances to make it smooth and white.

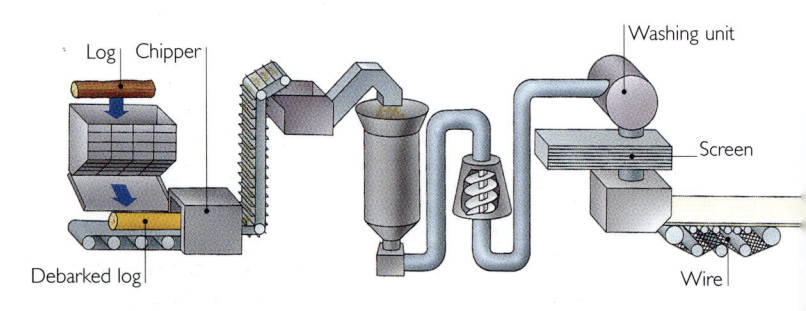

Louis Robert invented a machine to produce a continuous reel of paper. Today, most paper is made on machines from wood pulp obtained from tree fibres.

PARASITE

A parasite lives in or on some larger living thing and feeds on it. It is an uninvited guest. The animal or plant on which it lives is called a host. Parasites often harm their hosts by taking too much food, or by causing diseases. Mistletoe (a plant), tapeworms, fleas, lice and mosquitoes (animals) are examples of parasites.

PASTEUR, LOUIS (1822-1895)

Pasteur was a French scientist. He proved that bacteria and other germs cause diseases. Pasteur injected weakened germs into animals and people to stop them catching the diseases those germs usually caused.

He invented pasteurization: a method of heating milk and cooling it quickly to make it safe to drink. Pasteur also found out how tiny yeast cells turn sugar into alcohol.

PEARL HARBOR

Pearl Harbor in Hawaii was the site of the surprise Japanese air attack on the US Pacific Fleet on December 7, 1941. In less than two hours, five battleships and 188 planes were destroyed. More than 2,000 Americans lay dead and 1,200 were wounded. The United States declared war on Japan as a result and entered World War II on the side of the Allies.

See also WORLD WAR II.

PENGUIN

Penguins are sea birds that live on coasts around the Antarctic. Unable to fly, penguins use their wings as paddles and are excellent swimmers. They have a layer of thick fat to keep out the cold. Some kinds of penguins lay their eggs in rough nests on the rocks.

PERFUME

Perfume is a fragrant essence in which more than a hundred natural aromatic (sweet-smelling or spicy) materials may be blended. The materials come from about 60,000 different flowers, leaves, fruits, seeds, woods, barks, resins and roots.

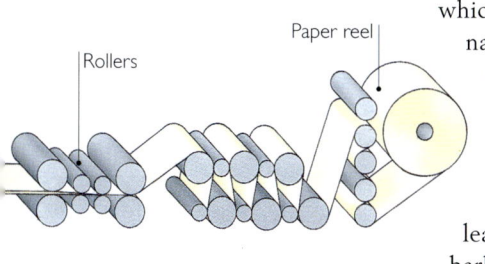

Paper reel

Rollers

PETER THE GREAT
(1672-1725)

As king, or tsar, of Russia, Peter the Great turned his country into one of Europe's most powerful nations. One of his ambitions was to build Russian ports on the shores of the Baltic Sea and the Black Sea. These would give Russia better contact with Western Europe. In 1695-1696 he fought a war with Turkey and won a firm foothold on the Black Sea. He also wanted to modernize his country, and in 1697-1698 he toured Western Europe to find out about the most up-to-date ways of doing things. Later he built a new Russian capital, St Petersburg, on the Baltic coast. He fought a long war against Sweden, winning a great victory at the Battle of Poltava in 1709.

PHILIPPINES

The Philippines is a nation made up of over 7,000 islands in the western Pacific. It is a producer of chromite, nickel and copper, as well as sugar cane, fruits and Manila hemp. Governed first by Spain and then by the United States, it became independent in 1946. In 1986 its virtual dictator, Ferdinand Marcos, was ousted, and in democratic elections Corazón Aquino came to power. She was replaced in 1992 by Fidel Ramos.

See also PAGE 62.

PHOTOGRAPHY

Photography was invented in 1839 by Louis Daguerre in France and William Fox Talbot in England.

Today there are cheap cameras

Photosynthesis: *Respiration is almost the reverse process of photosynthesis: carbon dioxide and water vapour are released from the leaves into the air.*

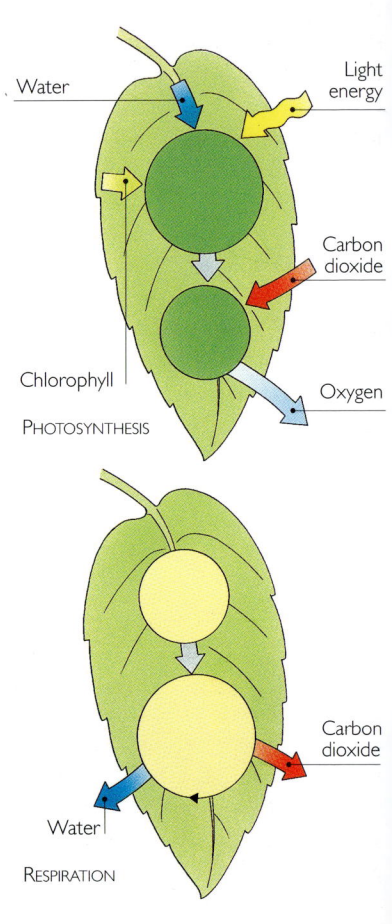

PHOTOSYNTHESIS

RESPIRATION

which work automatically as well as the complex equipment, processes and techniques used by television and the cinema and in medical and scientific research.

See also CAMERA.

PHOTOSYNTHESIS

This is the process by which plants make food. Water from the soil and carbon dioxide gas from the air are combined to form sugars. This process can take place only in living plant cells which contain the green colouring matter, chlorophyll. The energy comes from sunlight.

See also LEAF.

PHYSICS

Physics is the branch of science practised by physicists. They study matter and energy and how they relate to one another. This includes subjects such as electricity, magnetism and mechanics. An important branch of modern physics is the study of the atom and the minute particles that make it up.

PICASSO, PABLO (1881-1973)

Picasso was a Spanish artist who greatly influenced art in this century. His painting changed from a realistic style to abstract styles like Cubism which uses shapes such as cubes, triangles and geometrical shapes.

Picasso: Pablo Picasso was one of the most influential figures in 20th-century art.

PIG

The pig is a very useful, intelligent animal. We eat its meat as pork, sausages, bacon and ham, its skin can be made into leather, and its bristles go into brushes. Male pigs are called boars, and females sows. Pigs are unjustly accused of being dirty. They wallow in mud to keep themselves clean as well as cool.

PIRATE

Until about 150 years ago, sea voyagers had more to fear than sudden storms. They faced the added danger of pirates. These fierce bands of sea-robbers sailed the seas in fast, well-armed ships. When they saw a merchant ship, they chased and captured it. They stole its cargo and robbed the passengers of their belongings.

Some pirates became rich. Most were caught and hanged. By the 1800s ships could sail most seas without fear of pirates.

PIZARRO, FRANCISCO (c1475-1541)

The illegitimate son of a Spanish soldier, Pizarro became one of the most famous of the conquistadores, the men who conquered large parts of the Americas for Spain. In 1530 he landed with 180 followers on the coast of Peru. Two years later, he and his tiny army had captured the ruler of the vast Inca Empire. In 1533, they captured the Inca capital, Cuzco, high in the Andes Mountains. They had done all this using clever trickery. They also had guns and horses which gave them an advantage over the Incas, who had neither.

PLANET

See SOLAR SYSTEM.

PLANKTON

This is the drifting life of the sea. It is made up of tiny and microscopic plants and animals which float at or near the surface. Every sea animal depends in some way on plankton, because small fish feed on it and are eaten in turn by larger fish.

Bacteria

Fungi

Mosses

Horsetails

Cycads

Ginkgoes

Monocotyledon

Algae

Liverwort

Clubmosses

Ferns

Conifers

Dicotyledon

Plants: Botanists have classed plants into groups, mainly by the way they are built and the way they reproduce.

PLANTS

There are more than 335,000 kinds of plant. Most plants are green. The green colour is caused by a substance called *chlorophyll*. This is used by the plant to make its food. The way it does this is called photosynthesis.

The plant kingdom includes several groups. The simplest plants are algae. Some algae are simply a single cell, which reproduces itself by splitting in two. Others, such as seaweeds, are much bigger.

Fungi are plants which have no chlorophyll, so they are not green and cannot make their own food. Instead they feed on rotting or dead matter.

Mosses and liverworts are another group. They live on land. But, like fungi, they have no proper roots, and no flowers. Ferns are more advanced. They have stems, leaves and roots, but they cannot make flowers and seeds.

There are two sorts of flowering plants. Monocotyledons, such as lilies, daffodils and grasses, have long straight leaves. Dicotyledons, such as peas, roses and broad-leaved trees, have broad leaves.

Seed-bearing plants produce male and female cells. The cells join to form a fertile seed which grows into a new plant.

See also ALGAE; FERN; FLOWER; GRASS; LEAF; LICHEN; MUSHROOMS AND TOADSTOOLS; MOSS; PHOTOSYNTHESIS; SEED; TREE.

PLASTICS

Plastics are man-made materials that have a wide variety of uses. They can be made into furniture, car bodies, clothing and crockery. There are many different kinds of plastics, all of which can be shaped easily. Many of them are shaped by blowing, squirting or pressing into moulds.

Important plastics include nylon, polyethylene, PVC and polystyrene. All are made with chemicals obtained from oil. Some plastics are made from wood.

PLATO (c.428-347BC)

Plato was one of the world's most important thinkers. He came from the ancient Greek city of Athens and was a pupil and friend of Socrates. In about 386BC he set up a school at Athens called the Academy. In his most famous book, *The Republic*, he described a system for educating a 'philosopher king', his idea of the perfect ruler.

PLATYPUS

The curious duck-billed platypus is a mammal that lays eggs. It lives in Australia. It has webbed feet, a tail like a beaver, thick fur and a duck-like bill. The platypus lives in a burrow in a river bank, and feeds under water on insects, worms and shellfish.

PLAY

Plays were first performed in ancient Greece. Some were tragedies, plays that tell a serious story and often have sad endings. Others were comedies, plays with happy endings.

In the Middle Ages people performed miracle and mystery plays – stories from the Bible – or morality plays, in which the hero (main character) met a number of good and bad characters.

Some of the first indoor theatres were built in England in the 1500s. Companies of actors performed the plays of Shakespeare, Marlowe and Jonson. There was little scenery, and actors wore the clothes of their own day. Boys took women's parts, as women were not allowed to act.

Since the 1700s and 1800s plays have become closer to real life. They are written in simple, everyday language, and the plots (the stories) are usually about the lives of ordinary people.

FAMOUS PLAYWRIGHTS	
Aeschylus	Greek (c.525-456BC)
Sophocles	Greek (496-406BC)
Euripedes	Greek (480-406BC)
Aristophanes	Greek (c.450-406BC)
William Shakespeare	English (1564-1616)
Ben Jonson	English (1572-1637)
Jean Baptiste Racine	French (1639-1699)
Richard Brinsley Sheridan	Irish (1751-1816)
Henrik Ibsen	Norwegian (1828-1906)
Oscar Wilde	Irish (1854-1900)
George Bernard Shaw	Irish (1856-1950)
Anton Chekhov	Russian (1860-1904)
Jean Cocteau	French (1889-1963)
Bertolt Brecht	German (1898-1956)
Samuel Becket	Irish (1906-1990)
Tennessee Williams	American (1911-1983)
Eugene Ionesco	French (1912-1994)
Harold Pinter	English (born 1930)

POETRY

The oldest stories we know were first told as poetry. In a poem the words are often arranged to a musical beat or rhythm. Poetry which is written in a metre, or rhythm, is known as verse. But the rhythm does not have to be regular all the time. This would be dull. Blank verse has a rhythm, but it does not rhyme. Shakespeare used blank verse in his plays. Modern poets often prefer free verse, which does not rhyme or have a strict rhythm.

There are different styles and forms of poetry. Story poems with short verses and, often, with exciting stories are called ballads. Long story-poems are called epics.

The greatest of the ancient epic poems, full of the deeds of brave heroes, are the *Iliad* and *Odyssey* written by Homer, a Greek, and the *Aeneid* of the Roman poet Virgil.

Expressions of poets' feelings are called lyrics. They include such forms as the song, sonnet, ode, elegy and pastoral. Plays are sometimes written in poetry and these are called dramatic poems.

POISON

A poison is a substance which attacks the body, and can cause sickness or death. Some poisons are dangerous when swallowed. Others damage the lungs, the skin, and the nervous system. Chemicals, drugs, gases, acids and bad food can all be poisonous. Some medicines are poisonous if used wrongly. So it is important always to follow the directions carefully.

POLLUTION

Pollution is the contamination of soil, water or the atmosphere by harmful substances. Chemicals used to kill insects and weeds can build up and damage the soil. Sewage, waste from factories and oil from tankers pollute rivers and oceans. Smoke from chimneys and fumes from cars pollute the air.

Pollution can threaten our health, and even make it impossible for plants and animals to live. People are trying to find ways of preventing pollution.

Pollution: The gases that produce acid rain are released by power stations, factories and transport.

POPE

The Pope is the head of the Roman Catholic Church and bishop of Rome. St Peter was the first bishop of Rome. The Pope lives in the Vatican, a tiny independent state in Rome. His chief advisers are the cardinals. They elect a new pope.

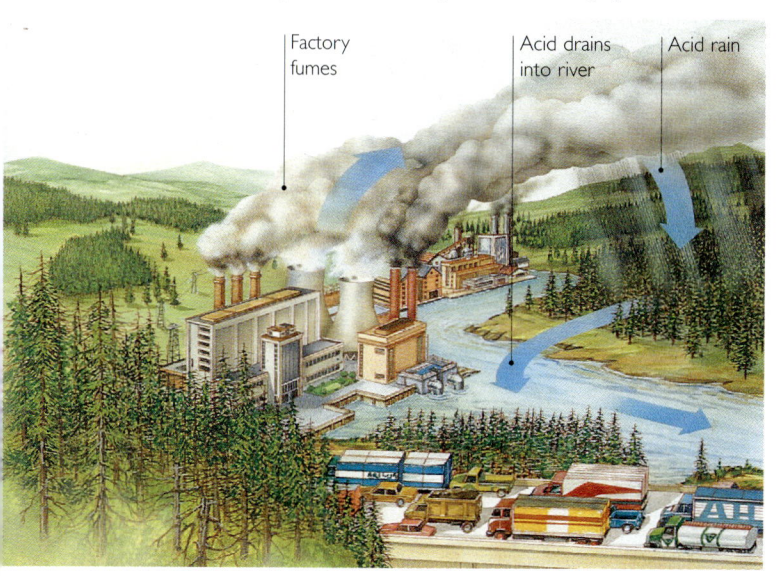

PORCUPINE
Porcupines are rodents. They live in forests and eat twigs, leaves and fruit. The porcupines of Africa and Asia live on the ground, but American porcupines are good climbers.

PORTUGAL
See SPAIN AND PORTUGAL.

POST OFFICE
In early times messages were carried by runners or by riders on horseback. Fresh messengers and horses waited at 'posts' along the road. Later, post coaches were used. The cost of delivering a letter was usually very expensive. In 1840 a cheap postal system was started in Britain by Rowland Hill. For a standard charge of one penny (which bought a postage stamp) a letter was delivered anywhere in the country.

See also STAMP.

POTATO
Potatoes are important food plants. The part you eat is a tuber, a swollen underground stem, in which the plant stores food. New plants grow from the 'eyes' in the starchy tubers.

The potato plant grows wild in the Andes of South America. Explorers brought potatoes to Europe in the 1500s.

Porcupine: Sharp quills, or spines, cover the body of the North American porcupine.

PRAIRIE
Prairies are large areas of flat or rolling grasslands, found particularly in central North America. Once they were home to prairie grasses and animals such as bison and wolves, but now their fertile soil is farmed for maize and wheat, or they are grazed by cattle. Only small, protected areas of native prairie are now left.

PREHISTORIC ANIMALS
The first animals appeared in the sea more than 700 million years ago. They may have been shaped as tiny blobs of jelly. Later some kinds developed protective shells.

PREHISTORIC ANIMALS

One common group, trilobites, looked like woodlice. All of these early animals were invertebrates.

The first vertebrate animals (animals with backbones) were the fishes, which appeared about 450 million years ago. At this time the land was almost empty. There were plants and insect-like creatures but no vertebrates. About 400 million years ago, some fishes crawled out of the water on to the land. They slowly developed legs instead of fins, and lungs with which they could breathe. They were the first amphibians.

Then came the reptiles. They adapted to different ways of life. Many were plant-eaters, but some were hunters, preying on other reptiles. About 200 million years ago some reptiles gave rise to dinosaurs. For millions of years dinosaurs ruled the Earth. The word dinosaur means 'the terrible lizard'. Some dinosaurs were quite small, but others were huge, the largest land animals that have ever lived. The last dinosaurs died out about 65 million years ago, but we know something of what they looked like from their fossil remains.

There were plant-eating and flesh-eating dinosaurs. Among the plant-eaters were the biggest dinosaurs, such as *Brachiosaurus* and *Diplodocus*. They walked on four thick legs, and had long necks and tails. Some giant dinosaurs were nearly 30m long. Others weighed 80 tonnes.

Flesh-eating dinosaurs were smaller and most of them ran on their hind legs. The largest and fiercest was *Tyrannosaurus*, the 'tyrant lizard'. It stood 5 1/2m high and weighed 7 tonnes. It had huge sharp claws and long sharp teeth.

Despite their size, dinosaurs had tiny brains. Scientists are not sure

Prehistoric Animals: *This parade of prehistoric animals includes the tallest, the longest, the fiercest and the most stupid dinosaur.*

why they became extinct. Perhaps the climate became cooler, and the vegetation changed, so that the dinosaurs could not keep warm or get enough food.

The first true birds may have evolved from dinosaurs which lived in trees and could just manage to glide from branch to branch.

The first mammals were small, insect-eating animals. For a long time they remained unimportant, while the dinosaurs ruled supreme. But when the dinosaurs died out, the little mammals took over and many different kinds developed. But many became extinct during the Ice Ages, when they were killed by a new mammal – man the hunter.

See also EVOLUTION; FOSSIL; ICE AGE; MAMMOTH.

PREHISTORIC PEOPLE

Prehistoric people lived before the beginning of written history. The first humans appeared some 200,000 years ago. The first written records appeared in the Middle East around 3300BC, but not on some South Pacific islands until about 200 years ago.

Prehistoric people hunted and fished, made tools, implements and pottery, farmed and made dwellings. We know about them through the study of archaeology, as archaeologists investigate the places where they lived and study the bones and objects that they find there.

PRESIDENT

France, Italy, the United States and many other countries all have a president. He or she is the head of state. In the United States the president is also head of government, like a prime minister.

PRIME MINISTER

A prime minister is a head of government. The prime minister usually leads the political party which has been voted the most seats in parliament. He or she chooses people called ministers to help run the government.

Prehistoric People: *Homo erectus, an early type of man, searches for roots, shoots and grubs in the soil.*

Printing

Before the 1400s, the usual way of producing books was to copy them by hand, so they were rare and expensive. Then, about 1450, Johannes Gutenberg made copies of the Bible on a printing press.

Gutenberg's method of printing was to build up his words from separate pieces of type, ink the type, then press paper against it. Printing by inking metal type (called letterpress) is still used. Many books are now printed by a photographic process (called lithography). The words are made up on a piece of film, and flat printing plates are made from the film. The plates are treated so that they pick up the ink only where the words are.

Protein

Proteins are the 'building blocks' of life. They are substances in foods that build body tissue and repair cells. They contain carbon, hydrogen, oxygen and nitrogen. Proteins also provide heat and energy. Most of our proteins come from meat, fish and cheese. Plants such as peanuts, beans and peas also contain quantities of protein.

Pyramid

The ancient Egyptians buried their pharaohs (kings) in tombs called pyramids. They had four triangular sides meeting at the pointed top. Some are made of more than two million blocks of stone. Thousands of people dragged the huge stones slowly into place. Inside was a tomb where the mummy (preserved body) of the pharaoh was laid, surrounded by treasure. The best known pyramids are a group of three built at Giza about 2680-2565BC.

Pythagoras (c580-500BC)

Pythagoras was an ancient Greek astronomer, mathematician and philosopher. He was one of the first to teach that the Earth and the other planets revolved around the sun. Perhaps his best-known contribution to geometry is the Pythagorean theorem.

Pythagoras: Pythagoras' theorem states that the square of the hypotenuse of a right-angled triangle is equal to the sum of the squares of the other two sides.

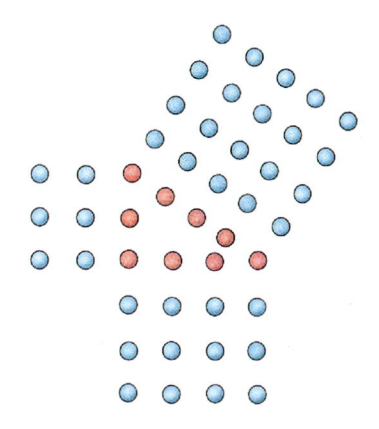

R

Rabbits and Hares
Rabbits are burrowing animals. They live in colonies called warrens. Rabbits breed rapidly.

Hares look like rabbits. But they are bigger, with longer ears and legs. Hares are swift runners. Unlike rabbits, they live alone in hollows called forms.

Raccoon
The raccoon has long grey fur, a short pointed nose and a bushy tail tinged with black. Raccoons live in the Americas.

Radar
Radar stands for 'radio detection and ranging'. It is a device that can 'see' far away objects by bouncing radio waves off them. The waves travel like echoes back to the radar. They are picked up by the radar antennae and show up as small dots of light on a screen. From the position of the dot, the location of the object can be worked out. Ships and planes rely on radar for safety.

Radio
Radio depends on radio waves. These invisible waves travel as fast as light waves. Radio works because radio waves can be made to carry signals which represent sound.

In a radio broadcasting studio sounds go into a microphone, where they are changed to electrical signals. These signals are combined with a 'carrier' wave, and transmitted by an aerial.

The aerial of a radio receiver picks up the carrier wave. Circuits in the receiver remove the carrier wave and leave only the electrical signals carrying the sound. These are fed to a loudspeaker which gives out the same sounds as went into the studio microphone.

Radioactivity
The atoms of most chemical elements do not change. But the atoms of some elements

Radar: Radar can detect the direction, speed and distance of an aircraft by bouncing radio waves off it.

Reflected waves
Transmitted waves
Radar screen

are unstable and emit (give out) atomic particles or radiation. We call this process radioactivity. Uranium and radium are radioactive elements.

See also ATOM; NUCLEAR ENERGY.

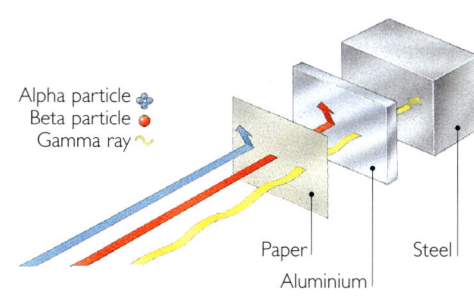

Radioactivity: The three forms of radioactivity, alpha, beta and gamma radiation, have different penetrating abilities.

RAILWAY

The first public railway to use steam locomotives was the Stockton and Darlington line in the north of England. It was opened in 1825. George Stephenson, an engineer, built the ten-mile track and its first engine, called *Locomotion*.

Steam locomotives, belching smoke, hauled passenger trains and goods wagons for over one hundred years. But there are few left today. They have been replaced by diesel and electric locomotives which are cleaner, quieter and cheaper to run.

Until the beginning of this century the railways had no rivals. Then the motor car and the aeroplane were invented. Railways were used less and less, and some lines closed. Now, new trains can travel twice as fast as a car.

RAIN AND HAIL

Rain comes from the water in seas, lakes, rivers and soil. The Sun's heat turns some of this water into water vapour which rises in the air. As the rising air cools, some of the water vapour 'condenses' or turns back to water droplets and becomes visible as clouds. As the air rises higher, more and more vapour turns back to water and the clouds grow bigger and darker. Finally, water droplets from the clouds fall to the ground as rain.

Sometimes the water droplets inside a thundercloud are carried so high and become so cold that they freeze into ice pellets. These may eventually fall to the ground as hailstones.

See also CLOUD.

RECORDING

Modern records are discs of plastic which 'store' sound in their grooves. Another way of recording sound is on tape. Here, the sound is recorded in the form of a magnetic pattern. Cassettes carry reels of tape which can then be played back on a home or car cassette player.

Television programmes can now be recorded on disc and tape. The sound track on films is often recorded as an image on the film.

See also VIDEOTAPE.

RED CROSS

The Red Cross organization helps the victims of wars and disasters. In 1859 the armies of France and Austria fought a terrible battle in Italy. A Swiss traveller, Jean Henri Dunant, saw thousands of wounded soldiers who had been abandoned. He tried to help them, and wrote a book describing what he had seen. As a result, the Red Cross was formed at Geneva in Switzerland (a country which never takes part in war). Its flag is a red cross on a white background.

REFORMATION

This movement in the 1500s ended the religious unity of western Europe and led to the establishment of the various Protestant Churches.

Until 1500 all Christians were Roman Catholics, with the pope as their spiritual head. Martin Luther, a German monk, disagreed with many of its teachings and protested in 1517. Many people agreed with him and a split developed. But not all Protestants believed the same things and so the movement itself split into many types of Protestantism.

REFRIGERATION

Foods last longer when they are kept cool in a refrigerator. Cooling slows down the processes which

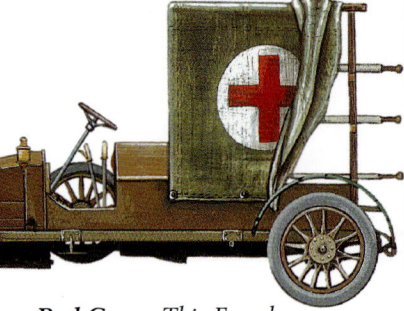

Red Cross: *This French Renault Red Cross ambulance dates from World War I.*

make food go bad. Deep-freezers keep foods fresh by freezing them.

Refrigerators are worked by electricity or gas. They have a pump that turns a vapour into liquid. The liquid is turned into vapour again inside the freezing compartment. As it does so, it takes up heat from the food. In another part of the refrigerator, the vapour is changed back into a liquid and recirculated.

Refugee

People who are forced to flee from their homes and take refuge in another area or country are called refugees. Mostly, refugees are escaping from invasion or war, but some flee to avoid ill-treatment or poverty in their own country. Some eventually return home, others settle in a new place.

Religion

A religion is a belief, a way of living, or both. It may mean belief in a god or gods with powers greater than our own, and in another life after this one. It may involve prayer and worship.

All the world's great religions began in Asia. The oldest religion to teach that there is only one god is Judaism, the religion of the Jews.

The followers of Islam are called Muslims. Muslims believe in Allah, the one god. Their holy book is called the *Koran*.

Hinduism is the chief religion of India. Hindus believe people's souls are reborn many times.

Buddhism is another important Eastern religion. Its founder, Buddha ('The Enlightened One'), taught people how to escape from suffering and find peace.

Renaissance: The Tempietto in Rome marked a return in European architecture to the classical lines used by the ancient Greeks.

People who follow the teachings of Jesus Christ are Christians.

Other important world religions are Confucianism, Taoism, Shintoism and Sikhism.

See also BIBLE; BUDDHA AND BUDDHISM; HINDUISM; JESUS CHRIST; KORAN; MAGIC; MUHAMMAD.

Rembrandt VAN RIJN (1606-1669)

Rembrandt was a Dutch artist who has become one of the most famous painters in the world. He was a master in the use of light, colour and mood.

Renaissance

In the 1300s there began a rebirth of learning in Europe. Scholars rediscovered and studied the

REPRODUCTION

Fertilized egg | Divides into two

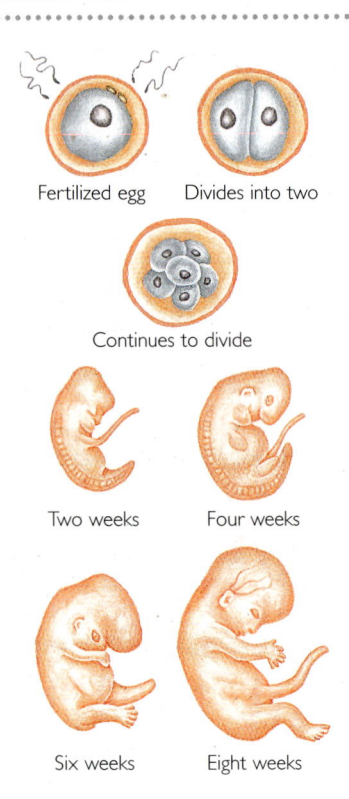

Continues to divide

Two weeks | Four weeks

Six weeks | Eight weeks

Reproduction: Once a human egg has been fertilized, it starts to divide to make countless new cells.

ancient writings of Greece and Rome. Artists such as Leonardo da Vinci and Michelangelo recaptured the beauty of 'classical' Greek architecture and sculpture. Scientists such as Copernicus and Galileo questioned the old ideas about the universe. 'Humanist' thinkers taught that human beings were not just weak creatures ruled by God.

REPRODUCTION

All animals and plants can reproduce. Simple animals and plants can reproduce on their own. They either divide in two (like the amoeba) or make special cells which grow into new plants (like the fungi).

More advanced forms of life reproduce sexually by producing special sex cells. When a male cell joins with and fertilizes a female cell, this grows into a new individual. In flowering plants a male sex cell stored in a pollen grain joins a female sex cell in the carpel. In animals, the male cells are called sperms, and the female cells, eggs.

See also ANIMAL; CELL; FLOWER; GENETICS; HUMAN BODY.

REPTILE

Reptiles are cold-blooded animals – their body temperature is the same as the temperature of their surroundings. Because of this reptiles cannot live in very cold lands. In places where there are cold winters, they hibernate.

Reptiles have tough, scaly skins and most lay leathery-shelled eggs. Baby reptiles hatch fully developed and are not cared for by their parents.

There are four main groups of reptiles: alligators and crocodiles, snakes and lizards, tortoises and turtles, and the very rare tuatara.

Most eat insects and small animals, but some eat plants.

See also CROCODILES AND ALLIGATORS; LIZARD; SNAKE; TURTLE AND TORTOISE.

RESPIRATION
See BREATHING.

REVOLUTION
The word revolution means 'turn around' or 'complete change'. If a country has a revolution, its government and laws are overthrown, often by war and bloodshed.

The most famous revolutions in history happened in America, France and Russia. In 1776 the American colonies broke away from Britain and became an independent republic. The French Revolution, in 1789, overthrew the king and the nobles who ruled France. In 1917 the rule of the Russian Tsar was ended, and the world's first Communist government was established.

RHINOCEROS
The rhinoceros is the second largest land animal, after the elephant. The black rhinoceros and the white rhinoceros live on the African plains. Actually, both are grey. The rhinoceroses of India, Java and Sumatra live in dense forests. Rhinoceroses eat grass, shoots and twigs.

RICE
Rice is a member of the grass family. Its grains are one of the most important cereals grown. It is a staple food for many people in Asia, though it is grown and eaten in many other parts of the world. Rice is planted in flooded fields called paddies. The young shoots are grown in 7-10cm of water. Rice has long, narrow leaves and clusters of flowers that turn into the rice grains.

RIVER
Rivers begin their lives as small streams in hills or mountains. Some begin as trickles of water from melting glaciers. Others bubble up through the ground as springs.
Gravity makes water flow downhill. At first the river

Rhinoceros: *Tick birds keep the rhinoceros' skin clean by eating the ticks and insects that settle there.*

River: *As the river moves farther away from its source, its valley becomes shallower and smoother.*

rushes along, fed by rain and melting snow. When it reaches flatter country, the river flows more slowly. Other streams, called tributaries, may join it.

Finally, the river flows into the sea, sometimes through a fan-shaped network of channels known as a delta. The fresh water of many a river meets the salt water of the sea in a river mouth, or estuary.

See also WATER.

ROAD

Roads are made up of layers. Tarmac roads have layers of tar and stones on top of well-rammed soil. Concrete roads are made up of layers of concrete.

John McAdam was a pioneer roadmaker in the 1800s, and Italians built the first motorway in the 1920s. Two thousand years before, their ancestors, the Romans, were building fine roads throughout Europe, North Africa and the Middle East.

ROBOT

Robots are programmable machines with arms that can move in several directions. Robots can be instructed to carry out different tasks. The instructions or programs are stored in the robot's computer brain.

Most robots work in industry and do jobs such as paint spraying, welding, and heavy lifting and loading. Some robots work in places which are dangerous for humans such as nuclear power stations and outer space.

See also COMPUTER.

ROCK

The inside of the Earth is a hot, molten mass. But the outer skin, or crust, is made up of solid rock. All rocks belong to three great groups: the igneous, the sedimentary and the metamorphic. All igneous rocks were once molten (melted) and came from deep in the Earth. Sedimentary rocks are formed of layers of materials such as sand and clay which have been cemented together under pressure. Metamorphic rocks have been changed from their original form to another by heat and pressure.

ROCKET

A rocket is a kind of engine. It works by shooting out a stream of gases backwards. As the gases go backwards the rocket goes forward. The rocket works rather like a jet engine. Both burn fuel to make hot gases, which shoot out in a stream. But the rocket carries its own oxygen to burn the fuel. The jet engine gets its oxygen from the air.

See also JET ENGINE.

RODENT

Rodents are mammals that have chisel-like front teeth which are specially adapted for gnawing. There are more than 6,000 species of rodent. Beavers, squirrels, gerbils, hamsters and porcupines are all rodents.

They are found everywhere. Some are good swimmers, like beavers with their webbed feet and paddle-like tails. Others, like most squirrels, live in trees. Guinea pigs were originally mountain-dwellers – they were tamed long ago by the people of the Andes in South America and raised for their meat.

Rats often live in cities, towns and other places where humans live. They may eat and spoil our food, and also spread disease. The smallest rodent is the mouse. The largest is the capybara which is the shape and size of a pig.

Rodents have many enemies. They are preyed on by hawks, owls, snakes, foxes and other animals.

Rocket: *The rocket Saturn launched Apollo 11 to the Moon on July 16, 1969.*

Rome, Ancient

According to legend, Rome was founded by twin brothers called Romulus and Remus. At first the Romans were ruled by foreign kings. But in 509BC the people set up a republic and elected their own rulers. They fought against their neighbours and built a powerful army. In 217BC the first emperor took power.

Without their army, the Romans would never have conquered and ruled their empire, which stretched from Britain to the Middle East.

The capital of the empire was originally the city of Rome, built on seven hills. In AD395 the empire was divided into two. One half was ruled from Rome, the other from Byzantium (Constantinople).

Rome was no longer strong. Its government was dishonest, and the army could no longer fight off the barbarian raids. Around AD476 the western empire fell, and Rome was destroyed. In the east, the Byzantine Empire lasted until 1453 when Constantinople was captured by the Turks.

See also BYZANTINE EMPIRE; CAESAR; HANNIBAL.

Roosevelt, Franklin Delano
(1882-1945)

Franklin D. Roosevelt became president of the United States in 1933 and remained in office until he died. He had wanted to keep America out of World War II, but once in the war he created an alliance with Britain and the USSR, and eventually they won.

Rubber

Rubber trees grow in tropical countries such as Malaysia and Indonesia. To make rubber, cuts are made in the bark of the tree and a milky sap (latex) oozes out, which is treated with acid to produce crude rubber. Rubber is used to make the soles of shoes, tyres, tubes and many other things. Much of the rubber used now is made by the plastics industry.

Rugby Football
See FOOTBALL.

Russia

With an area of 17,075,400sq km, Russia is the largest of the ex-USSR republics. A train journey from its western border to the Pacific coast in the east takes over a week. The population of Russia is about 147 million and its capital is Moscow.

Rutherford, Ernest
(1871-1937)

Rutherford was a New Zealand-born British physicist. He was a pioneer of atomic science and his main research was in the field of radioactivity. Rutherford was the first to 'split' the atom. He won the Nobel chemistry prize in 1908.

S

Saint

A saint is a holy person whom Christians believe came close to being perfect. Some saints, like St Francis of Assisi, are remembered for their good lives. Others, such as St Bernadette of Lourdes, are believed to perform miracles of healing.

To become a saint a person must be canonized with the approval of the Roman Catholic Church. A commission is set up by the Church to examine carefully everything known about the person's life.

Salt

Salts make up a class of chemicals. There are many different salts, but the one we know best is the salt we eat – common salt. It is made up of the two elements sodium and chlorine. Our bodies need salt. There is salt in blood, sweat and in tears.

Satellite

A satellite is a small body which circles around a larger one. The Moon is the Earth's satellite. It circles the Earth once a month.

Satellite: Communications satellites pick up and transmit TV and telephone signals.

Most planets have satellites. We often just call them moons.

The Earth now has many man-made satellites circling around it. The first artificial satellite, called *Sputnik I*, was launched by the Russians in 1957. To resist Earth's gravity, a satellite must speed round at 28,000km/h. Satellites can be very useful. Some help in weather forecasting. Some relay telephone and television all over the world.

Scandinavia and Finland

Scandinavia (Sweden, Norway, Denmark and Iceland) and Finland, in northern Europe, are among the northernmost inhabited areas of the world. Northern Scandinavia – populated by the Lapps – lies inside the Arctic Circle and has an Arctic climate, while the south is kept mild by the Gulf Stream, a warm ocean current.

The scenery is the legacy of the Ice Age, with ice caps, glaciers, mountains, lakes and sea inlets called fjords. Iceland also has active volcanoes, including a new one, Surtsey, which emerged in 1963.

The area is rich in natural resources such as timber, iron ore, and offshore oil and gas from the North Sea. Fishing, shipbuilding, forestry and farming are all important industries.

Sculpture: The art of making attractive models and statues is very ancient, as some of the earlier examples show.

c.5750BC

c.2300BC

c.AD700

19th century

SCIENCE

The word 'science' just means knowledge. In science, people try to find out about the world around them by observing things and carrying out experiments. Scientists try to classify new facts, and fit them in with what they know already.

Chemistry, physics and biology are the main branches of science. Chemistry studies the way matter is made up. Physics studies the properties of matter and energy, and biology studies living things.

See also CHEMISTRY; ZOOLOGY.

SCOTT, ROBERT (1868-1912)

Robert Falcon Scott was a British naval commander and explorer. In 1911 he led an expedition to the South Pole, but reached it on January 18, 1912, to find that the Norwegian Roald Amundsen had got there first. Scott and the other members of his expedition died on the return journey.

SCULPTURE

Making models and figures, or statues, is a form of art called sculpture. Sculpture is done in two ways: by carving and moulding. In carving, the sculptor cuts into a block of wood or stone with sharp tools. In moulding, he makes a model in soft clay, then bakes the clay to harden it. From the hard model he makes a mould, and pours into it wet concrete or hot, liquid metal (such as bronze). When this hardens, a perfect 'casting' of the model is left.

Today sculptors also use materials such as pieces of glass, metal and cloth, as well as wood and stone.

Sea

Some large areas of water around the edges of oceans are partly or completely surrounded by land, forming seas. The largest of them all is the South China Sea, part of the Pacific Ocean that lies between mainland China and Southeast Asia and the islands of Malaysia and the Philippines. Some seas, like the Mediterranean, are almost completely cut off from the oceans they were once part of.

Large areas of water like the Sea of Galilee, which were formed inland and were never part of an ocean, are also called seas.

Sea Horse

The sea horse is actually a small sea fish. It gets its name from its horse-like head. The sea horse swims in a curious upright position, fanning its dorsal (back) fin. It can cling on to seaweed, using its coiled tail.

Seals and Sea Lions: Seals and sea lions glide through the water steering with their tails. Their bodies are streamlined to reduce water resistance.

Seals and Sea Lions

These mammals spend most of their time in the sea. Their legs have become flippers, and they are expert swimmers, but they have to come to the surface to breathe. Seals and sea lions catch fish under water. Seals swim by moving their bodies from side to side. Sea lions use their front flippers like oars.

These animals come ashore to breed. They gather in large colonies on rocky coasts. Seals are slow and clumsy on land. But sea lions can turn their back flippers forwards and move quite quickly.

Seasons

The different times of the year are called seasons. They are caused by the way the Earth orbits, or travels around, the Sun. When the North Pole leans towards the Sun, northern lands have their summer

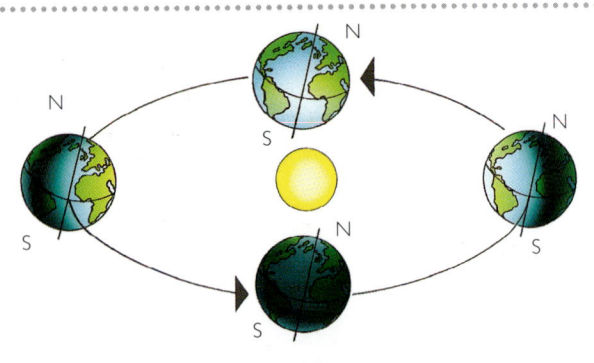

Seasons: *Seasons happen because the Earth is tilted as it orbits the Sun during the course of the year.*

and southern lands their winter. At the opposite point of the orbit, when the North Pole leans away from the Sun, northern lands have their winter and southern lands their summer. Spring and autumn are the points in the orbit when the equator faces the Sun, so northern and southern lands have roughly the same amount of warmth.

Seed: *Seeds are scattered in many different ways. Some, such as the maple, are carried by the wind.*

SEAWEED
See ALGAE.

SEED
Most plants reproduce themselves by means of seeds. They are formed in the plant's ovary. A seed contains an embryo – the plant in its earliest form. Seeds lie dormant or asleep until conditions are right for them to germinate. To germinate they need moisture, warmth, air and darkness.

SENSES
Senses tell us what is happening around us and inside us. We have external senses of hearing, taste, touch, sight and smell. Each sense comes from nerve endings or sense organs which send signals to our brain along the nervous system. For example, nerve endings on our tongue, called taste buds, tell us whether food is salty, sour, sweet or bitter. Internal senses tell us

when we are hungry, tired or thirsty. Muscle sense tells us the position of different parts of our body.

Seven Wonders of the World

Travellers in ancient times marvelled at the Seven Wonders of the World. Of these, only the Pyramids can still be seen. The Lighthouse at Alexandria, the Colossus of Rhodes, the Statue of Zeus at Olympia, the Hanging Gardens of Babylon, the Temple of Artemis, and the Museum at Halicarnassus have all been destroyed.

Shakespeare, William (1564-1616)

Shakespeare is often called the world's greatest writer. He was born in Stratford-on-Avon. His plays are written in some of the most beautiful poetry in the English language. Some like *Richard II* and *Richard III* are about history. Others, like *A Midsummer Night's Dream*, are comedies. *Hamlet*, *Macbeth* and *King Lear* are great tragedies.

Shark

Sharks are the most feared hunters of the sea. Drawn by the smell of blood, they will kill fish, seals, porpoises and even whales.

Shark: The mako shark is a fast streamlined swimmer whose speed allows it to attack large swordfish.

Some sharks are man-eaters, but most kinds are harmless to people.

Sharks are strong, fast-swimming fish. Their gaping jaws are full of sharp teeth. Instead of bones, sharks have gristly skeletons.

Sheep

Sheep are important farm animals. We make their wool into cloth, eat their meat and wear their skins. Sheep feed on rough pasture, and their thick coats keep out bad weather. Wild sheep live in the mountains in parts of America, Europe and Asia.

Ship

For at least 4,000 years ships have been sailing across seas. They still transport most of the world's cargo between the continents, but few carry passengers.

SILICON CHIP

- Viking longship
- Galleon
- Clipper
- Aircraft carrier
- Steamship
- Supertanker
- Cruise liner
- Catamaran

Ship: *When the steam engine was invented, ships no longer relied on the wind.*

Until about a hundred years ago, most ships were propelled by sails. For many years ships had only one square sail on a single mast. They could only sail well with the wind and relied on oars to propel them at other times. The Viking longships were an example of this.

By the 1400s ships were built with several masts, one of which carried a triangular fore and aft sail which made sailing easier in all winds. Soon came the three-masted caravels and galleons. Last of the sailing ships were the graceful and speedy clippers, which were used to carry goods such as wool or tea from Australia or the Far East.

See also SUBMARINE.

SILICON CHIP

Silicon is the most common element after oxygen in the Earth's crust. Silicon chips are tiny pieces of silicon – as small as 1sq mm – made to carry minute electrical circuits which are used in digital watches, electronic calculators, and computers and transistor radios.

See also COMPUTER.

SILK

The beautiful smooth cloth called silk is made from threads spun by the silkworm. This is actually the caterpillar of a moth. When the caterpillar is fully grown, it wraps itself in a cocoon of fine silk, stuck together with gum. The ancient Chinese were the first to discover how to wash away the gum and unwind the silk on to reels. It was then dyed and woven into cloth.

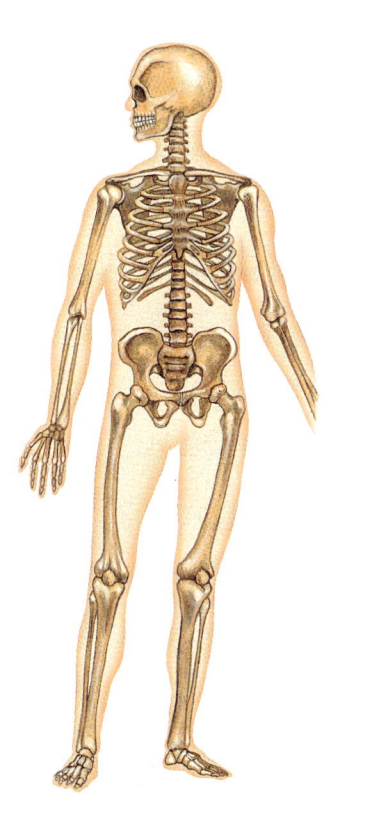

SILVER

Silver is a beautiful shiny metal which is used to make jewellery and expensive tableware. It can be shaped by bending and hammering.

Silver conducts (passes on) heat and electricity better than any other substance. It also forms compounds that are sensitive to light. These compounds are used in photography.

SKELETON

All the bones of your body make up your skeleton. The skeleton supports the soft parts of the body and is an anchor for the muscles. In vertebrates (animals with backbones), the skeleton is inside the body. Many invertebrates (animals without backbones) have an exoskeleton, which is like a hard crust on the outside of the body. Insects and spiders have exoskeletons. There are more than 200 bones in the human skeleton.

SKIING

Skiing has been the main way of getting about on deep snow for thousands of years. Skis from

Skeleton: *Adults have about 206 bones in their bodies.*

Skunk: *The best-known skunk is the striped skunk, which is black with white markings on its back.*

about 3000BC have been found in Sweden. It is only during the last hundred years that skiing has been enjoyed as a sport. Ski racing and ski jumping were developed in Scandinavia about 1860. Downhill and slalom races are also international competitions.

SKIN

Skin is more than just the covering of the body. It helps prevent us getting too hot or too cold. It helps keep out harmful germs. And it helps the body get rid of waste.

The skin is in two layers. The outer layer is the epidermis. It grows all the time, to replace dead skin cells which are rubbed off. Underneath the epidermis is a thicker layer called the dermis. It contains nerves and blood vessels. Hair grows out of it. The sweat glands are here too.

SKUNK

Skunks live in North America. They are relatives of badgers and weasels, and live in woodlands. They eat insects, birds' eggs and small mammals. If attacked, the skunk raises its bushy tail, and squirts out a foul-smelling spray of liquid from a special gland.

SLAVERY

Slavery means owning people. Slaves can be bought and sold as workers. Many of them died because their owners treated them so badly. In ancient Egypt, Greece and Rome there were a great many slaves.

When Europeans began settling in America, they took Negro slaves from Africa to work on the plantations. This slave trade was not stopped until the 1800s. All the Negro slaves in the southern United States were freed in 1865 after the American Civil War.

SLEEP AND DREAMS

We spend about a third of our lives asleep. Our minds and bodies do not stop working while we sleep, but they do slow down. Without sleep, we feel tired and cross, and we cannot concentrate.

Part of the brain is active during sleep. Though our eyelids are closed, our eyes move rapidly. When this happens, scientists know we are dreaming.

Sloth

In the South American forest lives the slow-moving sloth. This strange mammal spends its life hanging upside down in trees. It eats leaves and fruit. The sloth's hooked claws are good for climbing, but useless for walking on the ground. The hair of the sloth hangs downwards, so rainwater runs off easily. Sometimes algae grow on the hair, helping to hide the sloth from enemies such as the jaguar.

Snake

Snakes are legless reptiles. Unlike lizards, snakes have no eyelids. Most snakes lay eggs, but some give birth to live young.

All snakes prey on other animals, such as insects, birds, frogs and small mammals. Poisonous snakes kill their prey by biting it with their fangs and injecting poison, or 'venom', into its body. Many snakes have no poison but grab their prey with their sharp teeth. Some large snakes, like the python, coil their long bodies around their prey and crush it until it suffocates.

There are some 2,500 different kinds of snakes, of which about 150 are dangerous to humans.

See also REPTILE.

Snow and Sleet

Inside a cloud are millions of tiny water droplets. At the top, where the air is coldest, the water freezes to ice. Sometimes the drops of ice melt as they pass into warmer air and they fall as rain. But if the air is cold enough, they fall as snowflakes.

Snowflakes are tiny crystals. Each one has a beautiful pattern and always has six sides. A large snowflake is made of thousands of crystals stuck together.

Sleet is a mixture of snow and rain, falling when the air is not quite warm enough to melt all the ice drops falling from the clouds.

See also RAIN AND HAIL.

Snake: The poisonous coral snake is brightly coloured as a warning.

SOAP

Soap is a substance which helps wash away dirt and grease. The tiny soap particles are able to stick to and surround specks of dirt, and float them away in the water. Soap is made by boiling animal or vegetable fat with a chemical called an alkali.

Chemical cleaners called detergents are often used today instead of soap.

SOCCER
See FOOTBALL.

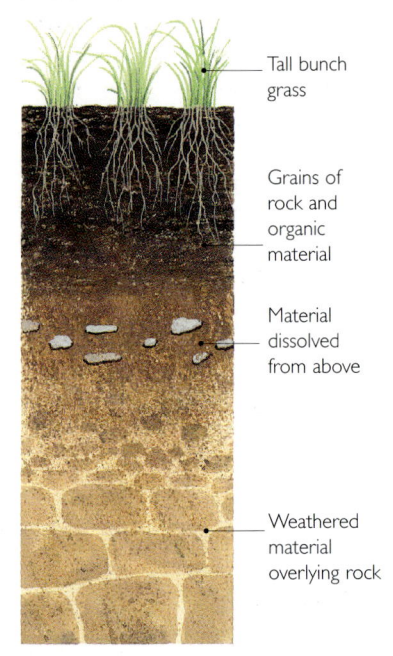

Soil: Soils have three distinct layers, or horizons, between the surface of the earth and the rock below.

- Tall bunch grass
- Grains of rock and organic material
- Material dissolved from above
- Weathered material overlying rock

SOCIALISM

Socialism is a system of economics in which the central government operates state-owned industries and important natural resources. Such industries may include railways, water, and gas companies. Unlike communists, socialists believe in a democratically elected government. Socialist ideals go back to the ancient Greek philosopher Plato. Today socialist ideas are applied by governments in many countries of the world.

SOCRATES (c.469-399BC)

Socrates was an ancient Greek thinker and teacher. He developed the Socratic method, by which he used questions to help his students discover the answers they were seeking. One of his most famous pupils was Plato.

SOIL

A handful of garden soil does not look very interesting. But it is alive with millions of tiny plants and animals which help to keep soil fertile. Soil is made from crumbled rocks. The process of wearing down rocks into small pieces takes millions of years. When plants and animals die, their remains are broken down by bacteria into 'humus'. Humus holds moisture in the soil and binds the soil together. Fertile soil holds a lot of water and air.

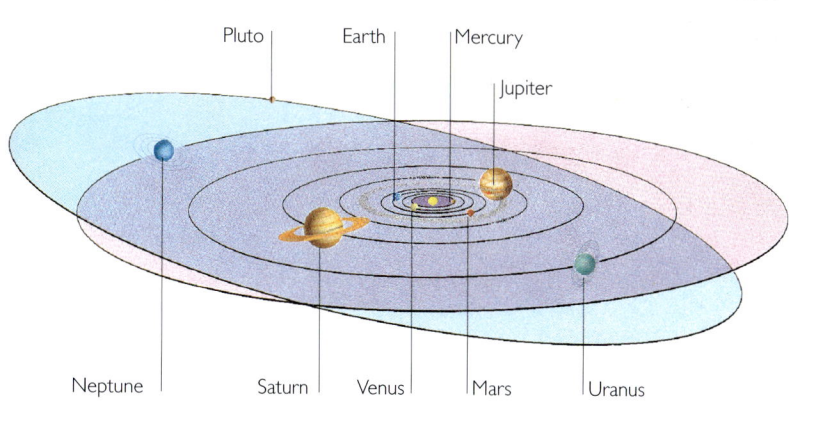

Planets labeled in diagram: Pluto, Earth, Mercury, Jupiter, Neptune, Saturn, Venus, Mars, Uranus

Solar System: *The planets go around the Sun in elliptical orbits, which means they follow a path like a flattened circle.*

SOLAR SYSTEM

The solar system is made up of the Sun and all the heavenly bodies in orbit around it. The Sun's great mass exerts a gravitational pull that keeps the planets, their satellites, comets and asteroids moving around it.

Planets are small bodies which circle around the Sun. Unlike stars, planets do not produce their own light. They shine because they reflect the Sun's light. There are nine planets circling the Sun, Mercury (the planet nearest the Sun), Venus, Earth, Mars, Jupiter, Saturn, Uranus, Neptune and Pluto. There may be other planets beyond Pluto which have yet to be discovered.

The planets can be divided into two groups, gaseous and rocky. The Earth is the biggest of the rocky planets, which also include Mercury, Venus, Mars and Pluto. The other planets are made up mainly of gases. Saturn, Jupiter, Uranus and Neptune are surrounded by rings of gas and dust.

The planets are not the only bodies orbiting around the Sun. There are also the asteroids, sometimes known as the 'minor planets'. They are much smaller than planets – the largest are a few hundred kilometres across. About 2,000 asteroids have already been recorded, and more are being discovered all the time.

All of the planets except Mercury and Venus have their own satellites orbiting around them – the Moon is Earth's only satellite.

The Earth is the only planet known on which life can exist. Mercury and Venus are too hot for life to exist. And the outer planets are too cold. It is just possible that some kind of life could exist on Mars. But there are other planets in the universe, circling around other suns.

Sound

Sound is produced by objects that are vibrating to and fro. If you pluck a violin string and touch it, you can feel it vibrating. A vibrating string gently nudges the molecules around it. These air molecules nudge other air molecules and a wave spreads from the string through the air, just as ripples spread on a pond.

When the sound wave strikes our ears, it causes our eardrums to vibrate and nerves send signals to the brain. This is how we hear. If there were no air, there would be nothing to carry the sound. That is why there is no sound in space.

Sounds are described in various ways. They can be loud or soft; high or low. High sounds, or, rather, high-pitched sounds, are made by things that vibrate rapidly. Low-pitched sounds are made by slow vibrations.

Some things produce sound waves pitched too high for us to hear. We call these waves ultrasonic.

South Africa

The Republic of South Africa lies at the southern end of Africa. It is a warm, sunny land and many wild animals roam in its huge national parks. But there are also large cities, such as Johannesburg, Cape Town and Durban. South Africa is a rich country. Farming and mining (for gold, diamonds and uranium) are the chief activities.

Although most South Africans are black, coloured (of mixed race) or Asian, the races lived separately under the apartheid system for many years. This was abolished by the government in 1991.

See also PAGE 61.

South America

There are 13 countries in South America. At 17,600,000sq km, it is the fourth largest continent in the world. It has dense rain forests, barren deserts, wide grasslands and high mountains.

The Andes Mountains, the highest in all South America, stretch for over 7,000km down the western side. In the centre of the continent are vast plains. They include the forests of the Amazon basin which cover an area the size of western Europe, and the grassy pampas of Argentina.

South America is rich in minerals, such as copper, tin, iron, bauxite, diamonds and emeralds. Mining is an important industry everywhere, and there are also large oilfields, particularly off the coast of Venezuela.

Today, South America is a

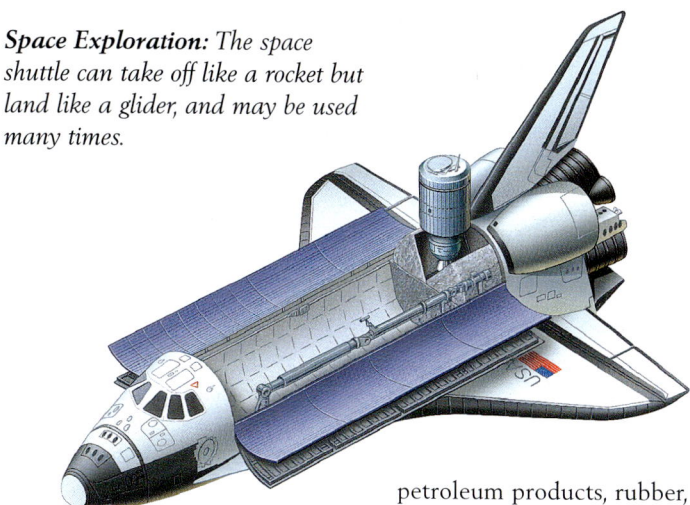

Space Exploration: *The space shuttle can take off like a rocket but land like a glider, and may be used many times.*

rapidly changing continent. Until recently many of its governments were controlled by military leaders, but more are democratic now.

See also ARGENTINA; BRAZIL; INCAS; PAGE 62.

SOUTHEAST ASIA

Southeast Asia includes Brunei, Myanmar, Singapore, the Philippines, Malaysia, Indonesia, Cambodia, Laos, Vietnam and Thailand. It has forested mountains, broad river valleys, volcanic regions, low plains and palm-fringed beaches. Its tropical climate with monsoon rains make it an ideal rice-growing area.

The main industries are agricultural, although manufacturing industries also thrive in the cities. The region's main exports include rice, oil and petroleum products, rubber, coconut and palm oil, electronic equipment, timber and tin.

All of the countries except Thailand were part of European empires but gained independence during the 20th century. Many countries fell under military rule, and oppression continues today. Vietnam, Cambodia and Laos were all involved in a major war in the 1960s and 1970s which greatly damaged their economies and environment. Much has been done since to repair the damage, and both tourism and trade are steadily developing.

SPACE EXPLORATION

The Russians launched the first spacecraft, *Sputnik I*, in October 1957. The first man went into space in April 1961 when the Russian Yuri Gagarin flew once around the Earth. The Americans put the first men on the Moon in July 1969.

Today, many spacecraft are being sent into space. Some, like satellites and probes, are unmanned. Satellites carry equipment such as measuring instruments, tape recorders, radios and cameras. Probes are sent to explore the Moon and planets. Probes have already photographed all the planets out to Neptune, and have landed on Venus and Mars.

The space shuttle is the first re-usable spacecraft. Launched into space by a rocket, the winged orbiter goes into its path around the Earth. When its mission is complete, the orbiter is slowed until it drops out of orbit. Once back inside Earth's atmosphere, the astronauts manoeuvre the shuttle like a glider, bringing it to a landing on a runway.

See also ASTRONAUT; SATELLITE.

SPAIN AND PORTUGAL

Spain and Portugal are in southwestern Europe. Much of the centre of Spain is a high plateau that is dry and dusty. The north is green and fertile, while the south is hot and dry. Portugal lies on the Atlantic coast to the west of Spain. It is rocky, mild and damp in the north, but flat and very hot in the south.

Many Spaniards work in industries such as car manufacturing, catering and tourism, and many others are farmers, producing goods such as olives, oranges and onions. One of Portugal's main exports is cork, and both countries are famed for their wines and ports.

In the 1400s Spain and Portugal built up a huge empire, mainly in South America, but they lost their power throughout the 1600s.

During the 1900s both countries were ruled by harsh dictators, but became democracies in the 1970s.

SPECTRUM

The band of colours that we see in a rainbow, from red to violet, is called the spectrum of colours. White light is made up of all the colours of the rainbow, which can

Spider: *The black widow is one of the few spiders that are poisonous to humans. There are about 30,000 different kinds of spider.*

be seen when we put a triangle-shaped block of glass called a prism in front of a beam of ordinary white light.

The spectrum of light in turn is just one section of the electromagnetic spectrum. This includes all forms of radiation, including radio waves, microwaves, infrared rays, light waves, ultraviolet rays, X-rays and gamma rays.

SPIDER

Spiders may look like insects but they are not. Their bodies are made up of two parts (not three) and they have eight legs (not six). They are related to scorpions.

All spiders make silk inside their bodies. Some spiders use the silk to make webs to trap insects for food. However, not all spiders build webs. Wolf spiders chase their prey on the ground. Crab spiders lurk inside flowers, while trapdoor spiders lie in wait in holes.

STALACTITE AND STALAGMITE

These are two types of mineral deposits found in caves. Stalactites grow downward from the roof. Stalagmites grow up from the floor of the cave and can be as much as 30m high.

Both are formed by water that seeps into the caves and drips from the limestone ceilings. The water is often saturated with

Stalactite and Stalagmite:
As water drips into a limestone cave, lime deposits may come out of solution to form a rocky 'icicle'.

dissolved minerals that are then deposited in icicle-like formations. Stalactites and stalagmites are sometimes called dripstones.

See also CAVE.

STALIN, JOSEPH (1879-1953)

Stalin was a revolutionary leader who worked to overthrow the Tsar of Russia in 1917. As leader of the Soviet Union from 1924 to his death, he helped to turn Russia into an industrialized state. But Stalin was responsible for millions of deaths, and in 1956 he was denounced as a dictator.

STAMP

Postage stamps were first used in Britain in 1840. They were the idea of a man called Rowland Hill. The first British stamps were a penny black and a twopenny blue. To stop stamps being used twice, the post office 'cancels' them with an ink postmark. This shows where and when the letter was posted.

See also POST OFFICE.

STAR

The stars we see in the night sky are balls of glowing gases. They are so far away that they seem very tiny, but if we could get closer, they would look like the Sun. Stars shine by nuclear power: heat and light produced when atoms of hydrogen gas fuse, or join together.

Astronomers are not sure how stars originated but many think that they are formed out of great clouds of cool dust and gases.

See also NUCLEAR ENERGY; SUN; UNIVERSE.

STEAM ENGINE

James Watt built the first really efficient steam engines in the late 1700s and made them suitable for driving machinery of all kinds.

In Watt's type of engine, steam pushes a piston back and forth in a cylinder. The piston is connected to whatever is to be driven – for example, the wheels of a locomotive. Steam is produced by burning coal or wood in a furnace beneath a boiler. The hot gases from the furnace pass through tubes in the boiler and heat the water. The steam which is produced drives the pistons.

STONE AGE

This is the name given to the period before people learned to obtain and use metal. Tools and weapons were made from flint and other rocks and wood. The Stone Age probably began about three million years ago.

There are three Stone Age periods: the Old (Palaeolithic), Middle (Mesolithic) and the New (Neolithic).

At the beginning of the Old Stone Age, hunters made clumsy

Steam Engine: James Watt designed this rotary steam engine in 1783.

stone axes. Thousands of years passed before they could chip flint into double-edged blades to make more effective implements: knives, scrapers and weapons.

Middle Stone Age people made more intricate tools and weapons. Many were set in wooden or bone hafts and handles, making them easier to use.

Farming replaced hunting in the New Stone Age. Tools became more refined and more specialized for a particular task.

See also BRONZE AGE; IRON AGE.

SUBMARINE

Ships that can travel under water are called submarines. A submarine dives by letting water into tanks around the hull (body). This makes it heavier than water. To surface, it blows the water out, making it lighter again.

Ordinary submarines are propelled under water by a propeller driven by electric batteries. They have to surface when their batteries run down. On the water they are propelled by diesel engines, which also charge the batteries. Nuclear submarines are powered by a

Submarine: At 170m long, the Russian Typhoons are the world's biggest submarines.

nuclear reactor. They can remain under water for months at a time.

The crew of a submarine use a periscope to see above the surface of the water. A periscope is an instrument that can also be used to see over walls and around corners.

SUGAR

Plants make sugar for their own food. The sugar that we use to sweeten food is called sucrose. It comes from sugar beet and sugar cane. Other sugars are fructose (from fruits), glucose (from fruits, vegetables and grain), and lactose (from milk).

Sugar is a very important food because it supplies energy and heat and helps to form fat.

SUN

The Sun is our nearest star. It is a great ball of very hot gases swirling in space. All the time it pours out heat and light, as atoms of hydrogen gas join together inside it to form atoms of another gas – helium. Life on Earth

Sun: Our Sun is a fiercely hot globe of burning gas, mostly hydrogen, measuring nearly 1.4 million km across.

depends on this heat and light. Without it, the Earth would be a dark, cold, dead lump of rock. All living things need warmth, and plants need sunlight to make food.

The Sun is like many other stars in the sky. It appears bigger and hotter only because it is nearer than the other stars. The Earth is part of the Sun's family, or solar system. It is one of nine planets circling around the Sun.

See also SOLAR SYSTEM; STAR.

SWITZERLAND AND AUSTRIA

Switzerland and Austria, in central Europe, are bordered by the Alps. They are both lands of mountains, forests, lakes and green pastures. Other than producing hydroelectric power from its rivers, Switzerland has few natural resources. It is a world centre of banking. Austria produces timber, iron ore, lead and copper, and also manufactures steel and paper. Both countries have thriving tourist industries, especially for winter sports.

Switzerland has remained a neutral country, keeping out of European wars since 1815. This has attracted the offices of many organizations that depend on international cooperation, such as the United Nations.

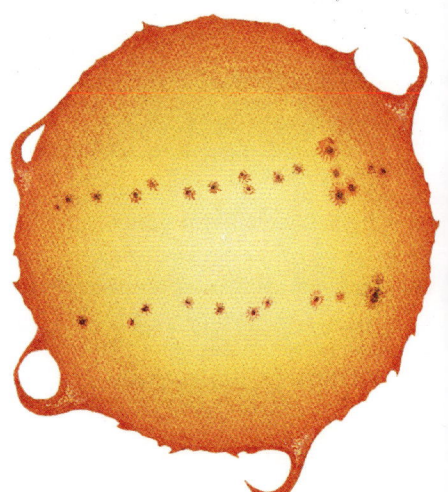

SYNAGOGUE

Synagogues are the centre of Jewish religious life, and are used for worship, meetings and study. Synagogues are built in many styles, but they all contain an ark, an ornately decorated chest where a copy of the Jewish Law is kept, with a light constantly burning in front of it.

They have a raised platform, the bimah, where people stand to conduct services and read the scriptures, and pews where the leaders of the community sit. Other people stand.

T

Talmud

The *Talmud* is one of the holy books of Judaism. It is a collection of ancient writings that includes many of the laws that govern everyday life for Jewish people and interprets these laws. The *Talmud* and the *Torah*, the other holy book of Judaism, together contain the religious and political laws of Jewish people, wherever they live.

Tank

A tank is a large, armoured military vehicle on a continuous 'caterpillar' track that allows it to travel over rough ground. It was first used by Britain during World War I. At the top of the tank is a rotating gun turret. The crew is protected inside the body of the tank. Tanks were used during World War II, both by the Germans in their *blitzkriegs* (lightning attacks), and in Allied landing operations in Europe and the Pacific.

See also War.

Tax

The government needs money to run the country. It gets this money mainly from the taxes we pay. Taxes pay for the roads, schools, hospitals and many other services a country needs.

There are several kinds of taxes. Most people pay tax on their income – the money they earn. Income tax is a direct tax. Indirect taxes are taxes on goods and services. A value added tax (VAT) is paid on goods we buy. Customs duties are paid when goods enter the country. Excise duties are put

Tank: *The American M-60 was developed after World War II.*

on goods such as
tobacco and alcohol.
Rates are local taxes paid
by householders to their
local councils.

TEA

Tea is made by pouring boiling
water on to tea leaves. The leaves
come from tea bushes, which are
grown mainly in India, Sri Lanka
and China. Tea first came to
Europe from China in the 1600s.
At first it was brewed and stored
in barrels, like beer.

TEETH

Teeth cut and chew food into
pieces small enough to be
swallowed. The kinds of teeth an
animal has depends on the kind of
food it eats.

Beasts of prey, such as wolves
and lions, have long sharp teeth.
They use them to kill their prey
and to tear the meat. Rodents,
such as squirrels, have gnawing
teeth. Grazing animals, such as
cattle, have flat grinding teeth.

Human beings have sharp
cutting teeth and flat grinding
teeth. This is because we eat both
meat and plant food.

Telescope: The way light passes through glass affects how we see objects, whether through a magnifying lens, a camera lens, or a telescope.

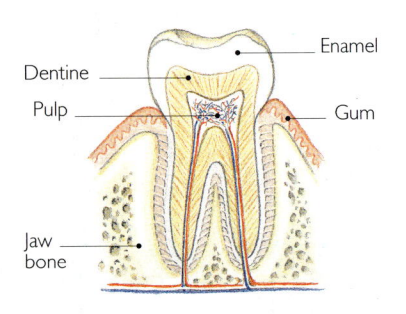

Teeth: Molar teeth (above) are sited at the back of the mouth and are used for grinding food.

TELEPHONE

The first telephone calls could only
be sent through wires. Now a
telephone call may travel by wire,
or by radio, sometimes bounced off
satellites. When you dial a number,
the telephone sends out electrical
pulses. They go to an exchange,
which automatically connects you
to the number you dialled.

When you talk, a microphone
changes your voice into electrical
signals. These travel down the
wires to the earpiece of the

person you are talking to. There they are changed back into the sound of your voice.

TELESCOPE

A telescope is an instrument that makes distant objects appear nearer and larger.

The simplest type, a refracting telescope, consists of a tube containing two lenses which bend the light rays from the distant object and make it appear nearer.

Most astronomers, however, use reflecting telescopes, which have a mirror to collect and bend the light. They are bigger and clearer than refracting telescopes.

Television: *The receiver's TV aerial picks up signals sent from the transmitter.*

Astronomers also use radio telescopes: large metal dishes which gather radio waves sent out by heavenly bodies.

TELEVISION

'Television' means 'pictures from a distance'. Television can show us live pictures of events on the other side of the world.

Two important pieces of television equipment are the camera and the receiver. The camera records an image of a scene on an electrically charged plate. A beam of electrons then sweeps back and forth across this plate. The result is electric signals which represent the brightness in different parts of the scene. These signals are combined with a radio wave and sent out by a transmitter.

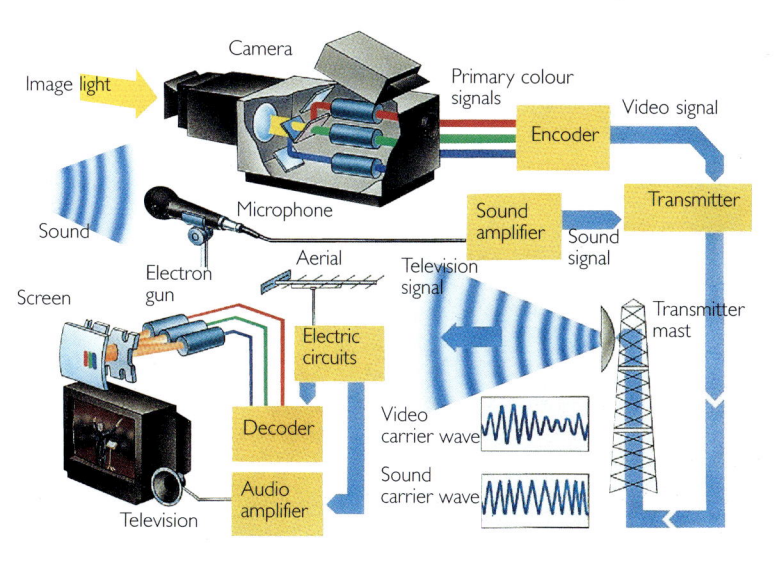

The aerial of the television set picks up the wave. Circuits in the set separate the signal from the wave. These signals then go to the picture tube where a 'gun' fires a beam of electrons at the screen causing a spot of light. The signals alter the strength of the beam and thereby the brightness of the spot. They also make the beam sweep back and forth in a series of lines of spots of varying brightness. The lines are very close together, and we see them as a complete picture.

TENNIS

When we use the word tennis we are usually referring to the game of lawn tennis. It is played on hard or grass courts. Two people play in a singles match; four people in a doubles match. Tennis today is a form of an old French game.

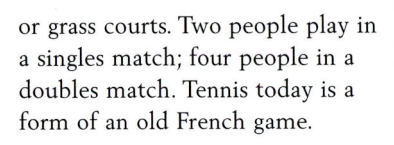

TERRORISM

Revolutionary groups, guerrilla fighters, and other extremist groups who cannot get what they want in peaceful ways sometimes use terrorism – acts of terror and violence carried out against the public, such as bombing, kidnapping, and hijacking aeroplanes and ships – to try to make governments give them what they want, or to overthrow a government altogether. Some terrorists are fighting for political or religious freedom at home, others use terrorism as a way of attacking foreign countries.

THEATRE

The first theatres were in ancient Greece. People sat in the open air on a hillside, while below actors and dancers performed on a space called the orchestra. Behind the actors was a changing room called the skene. This later became a stage, and it gives us the modern words 'scenery' and 'scene'. England's first theatres were built in the 1500s. Each had a jutting stage almost surrounded by the

Theatre: *William Shakespeare's Globe Theatre was built in London in 1599.*

Spring tides

Neap tides

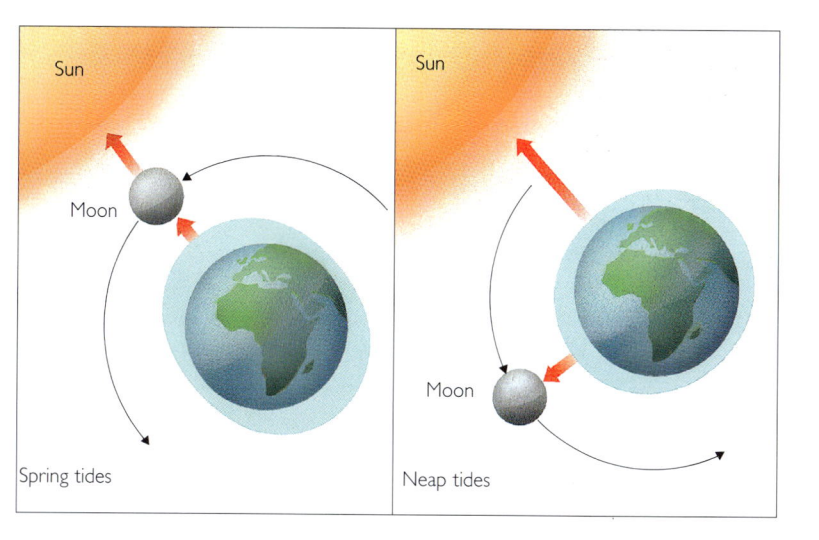

Tides: *Spring tides are high, because the Sun's gravitational pull is combined with the Moon's. Neap tides are the lowest.*

audience. Rich people sat under cover. Poor spectators stood in the uncovered 'pit'. But soon all theatres had roofs. Complicated scenery and stage machinery began to be used. And to hide the workings from the audience, a 'picture frame' was put round the stage. The audience now only sat in front of it. Some modern theatres have gone back to the old idea.

See also PLAY.

THERMOMETER

A thermometer measures temperature – how hot or cold it is. Most thermometers consist of a thin tube with a bulb of liquid. When liquids are heated, they expand, or grow bigger. So when the liquid in the bulb becomes hotter, it rises up the tube. The liquid used is generally mercury or coloured alcohol. A gas thermometer uses the effect of heat on gas.

Every thermometer has a scale marked on it. The most common scale is the Celsius, or centigrade scale. On this scale, the freezing point of water is 0 degrees, and the boiling point 100 degrees.

THUNDER
See LIGHTNING AND THUNDER.

TIDES
Tides are caused by the Moon and the Sun pulling the world's oceans towards them. This is the result of

gravity. Because the Moon is closer to Earth than the Sun is, its pull is stronger.

There are roughly two high tides and two low tides every 24 hours. When the Moon and Sun are on the same side of the Earth – at new and full Moon – their combined pull produces the biggest tides, called spring tides. When the Moon and Sun are pulling at right angles to each other, the smallest tides, called neap tides, occur.

Tiger: *A tigress watches over her two cubs as they play.*

TIGER

The tiger is the largest of the big cats. Its home is Asia. Most tigers live in hot forests. But the largest come from cold Siberia.

Tigers hunt alone and at night. They prey on deer, wild cattle and pigs. Only an old or sick tiger will attack people. The tiger's stripes camouflage it in long grass.

TIME

The day is a natural unit of time. It is the time the Earth takes to spin round once in space. Our other main natural unit of time is the year – the time it takes the Earth to travel once around the Sun. There are 365¼ days in a year.

The Moon circles the Earth about every 27 days. This gives us another unit of time – the month. Our calendar has 12 months in each year.

We measure time, or rather the passage of time, with clocks and watches. They help us split each day into 24 hours; each hour into 60 minutes; and each minute into 60 seconds. Day, hour, minute and second are units of time. We can say what time it is in two ways – by a 12-hour clock or a 24-hour clock.

See also CALENDAR; CLOCKS AND WATCHES.

TIN

Tin is a common but very important metal. It resists corrosion (being eaten away) by acids and is often used for protective coatings, such as on the inside of tins of food. Its most important use is in alloys like bronze and brass.

TOBACCO

Tobacco is made from the dried leaves of the tobacco plant. It originally grew wild in America.

The Spaniards brought tobacco to Europe in the 1500s, and today tobacco is grown in Asia, Africa and Europe as well as America.

Tobacco leaf can be made into pipe, cigar or cigarette tobacco, or snuff. Smoking is a harmful habit. It is especially bad for the lungs and heart.

TRADE UNION

Trade unions are organizations or associations of workers. By joining together in a union, workers are better able to negotiate, or bargain, with their employers for higher wages or better working conditions. Each craft or industry has its own union.

Trade unions began during the Industrial Revolution in the 1700s. Many workers were badly paid, and their work was often unhealthy or dangerous. The trade unions had a long struggle to improve conditions.

TRANSISTOR

A transistor is a small electronic device used to amplify or to strengthen signals in electronic equipment such as radios, computers and satellites. It is made from crystals of material such as germanium or silicon.

Transistors were invented in 1948. A large number of them can be put in a silicon chip a few millimetres square.

See also SILICON CHIP.

TREE

Trees are the largest of all plants. The world's biggest tree is the Californian redwood which can

Larch

Oak

Tree: *The leaves and fruit (cones) of the European larch, a conifer, are very different from those of the deciduous oak.*

reach a height of over 100m. Trees grow a little each year. The tips of their branches grow longer, and a ring of tissue in the main trunk and the older branches produces more cells to make them thicker.

Evergreen trees keep their leaves all year round. Conifers, such as spruce, pine and fir, are evergreens. They grow in colder climates. Their leaves are thin and hard, and look like needles. Conifers do not have flowers; instead, they have winged seeds hidden inside cones.

Many tropical trees are also evergreens. But they have broad leaves, and flowers. Broadleaved trees grow in cool countries too. Those that shed their leaves in autumn are called deciduous.

Tunnel

Ever since prehistoric people enlarged their caves, humans have invented ways of tunnelling out

Tunnel: The automatic tunnel digging machines used today are called moles. They have rotating cutters at the front and a conveyor belt to carry away the rock or soil.

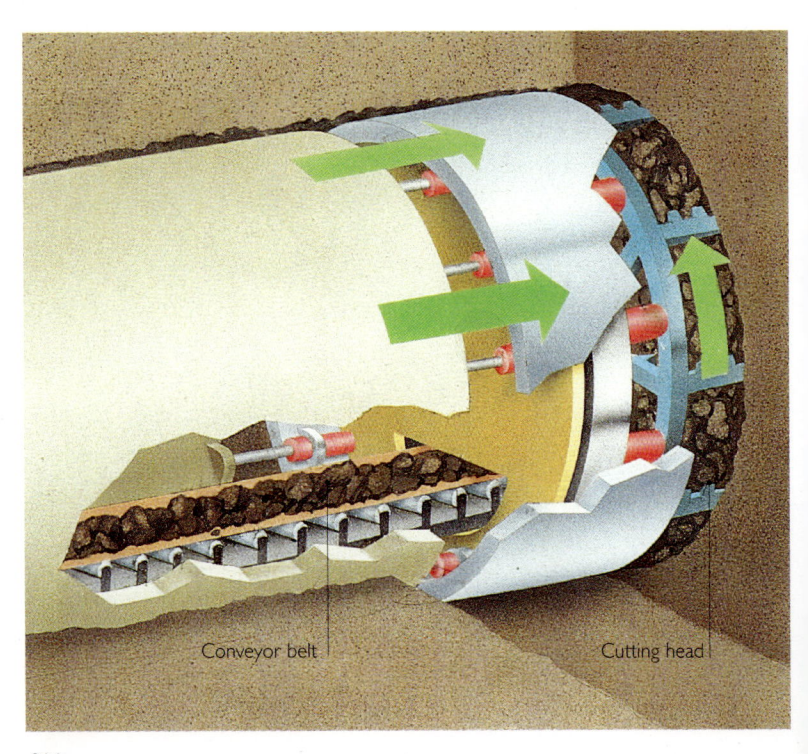

Conveyor belt — Cutting head

underground passageways. Today, tunnels are constructed under mountains, seas and cities, mainly for roads and railways and for providing services such as water and sewage.

Automatic tunnelling machines can be used on soft or hard rocks. They have a rotating drilling head and a conveyor belt to carry back the earth and rock. Some tunnels are dug out from ground level. Then the tunnel walls are built and the tunnel is covered over. Underwater tunnels are sometimes made from sections of tubing that are positioned in a trench, which is then filled in again around the tunnel.

TURKEY
See GREECE AND TURKEY.

TURTLE AND TORTOISE
Unlike other reptiles, turtles and tortoises have hard shells to protect their bodies.

Turtles live in the sea. They have flatter shells than tortoises,

Turtle and Tortoise: A snapping turtle can bite off a person's fingers with its powerful jaws.

and use their legs as paddles for swimming. On land they tend to be very clumsy.

Tortoises are land animals. They live in warm countries and eat plant food. A tortoise cannot run away from an enemy. Instead, it tucks its head and legs into its shell. Some tortoises can live to be much more than a hundred years old – which is older than any other animals.

See also REPTILE.

TWAIN, MARK (1835-1910)
The great American novelist and travel writer, Mark Twain, was born Samuel Langhorne Clemens. He grew up on the Mississippi River and later wrote about life on the Mississippi. His best known works include *The Adventures of Tom Sawyer* and *The Adventures of Huckleberry Finn*, both based on his experience as a boy.

U

Ultraviolet Rays

Light from the Sun can be split by a prism into a spectrum of colour. Red is at one end of the spectrum, violet at the other. Ultraviolet rays are found beyond the violet end of the spectrum.

These rays are very useful and important, although we cannot see them. They produce vitamin D in our bodies, which is necessary for growing bones. Ultraviolet rays can be used to kill bacteria.

United Kingdom

See British Isles.

United Nations

In the present century there have been two terrible world wars, and after each of them a special organization has been set up to try and prevent another such war from breaking out.

The League of Nations was formed after World War I. The United States never joined it and this weakened the League. Gradually other nations dropped out.

Despite the League's failure, it served as a model when the United Nations (UN) was founded after World War II in 1945. The UN still exists and tries to settle quarrels between countries peacefully. It helps refugees and children, and sends experts to fight hunger, disease and ignorance in poor countries. The headquarters of the UN are in New York. Here, the General Assembly and the Security Council meet to discuss world problems.

United States of America

Fifty states make up the United States of America – the USA. This huge country consists of the middle part of North America, Alaska in the far north, and Hawaii in the Pacific Ocean.

The climate varies from region to region. Some areas are hot in

United Nations: *The flag of the UN shows a map of the world surrounded by an olive wreath.*

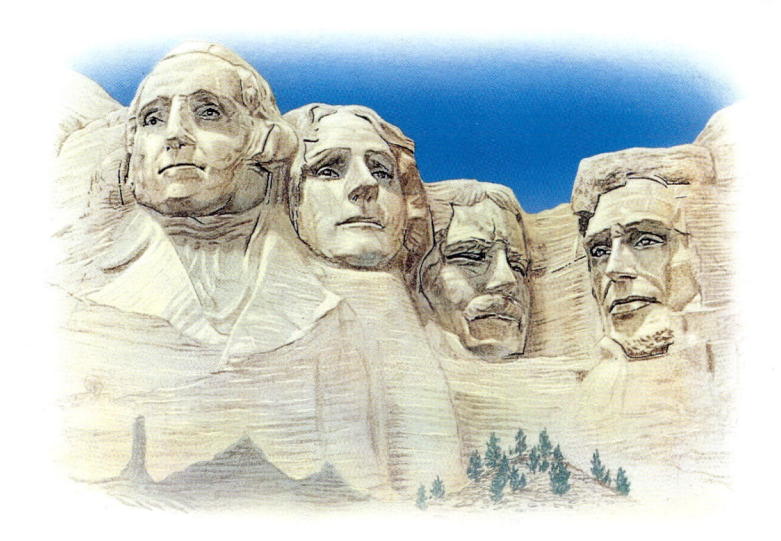

UNITED STATES OF AMERICA

United States of America: The faces of four US presidents are carved on a granite cliff at Mt Rushmore, South Dakota.

summer and cold in winter, but the south and west coasts have mild winters.

The United States has very great natural resources. Its farmland is fertile. Huge crops of wheat are grown on the prairies, and maize (corn), tobacco, cotton, fruit and vegetables are also grown. From the forests comes timber, while underground are valuable minerals, including coal, oil, natural gas, iron, gold, copper and uranium. Many rivers and lakes have been dammed to produce electricity.

More than half the people live in towns and cities, for the United States is the greatest industrial country in the world. Its factories make aircraft, cars, computers, machines, and many other kinds of goods.

The first Americans were the Indians, who lived by farming and hunting. But after Columbus's discovery of the 'New World', Europeans began settling in America. Beginning in the 1600s, the British set up 13 colonies on the east coast. But the colonists wanted to govern themselves, and in 1776 they declared themselves independent from Britain and became a republic, the United States of America. George Washington was the first president.

The republic grew into a union of 50 states. Many poor people from European countries came to

Universe: The universe is made up of all the galaxies, stars, planets, moons, asteroids and other bodies scattered through the emptiness of space.

the United States. Industry developed so quickly that the Americans soon enjoyed a higher standard of living than any other people in the world.

See also PAGE 63.

UNIVERSE

When we talk of the universe, we mean everything that exists. This includes the air, the sea, the Earth, the other planets, the Moon, the stars and space.

Years ago people thought that the Earth was the centre of the universe. They thought that all the other heavenly bodies circled around it. About 500 years ago people began to realize that the Earth was not the centre. Now we know that the Earth is only a tiny speck in the universe. It belongs to the Sun's family of stars called the Galaxy. The Galaxy belongs to a family of galaxies. And there are millions of such families in the universe. But most of the universe is just empty space.

URANIUM

This element is a rare whitish metal. It is radioactive, that is it gives off rays which cannot be seen but which will darken film.

Although it was discovered in 1789, uranium had very few uses until 1940. Then a method of obtaining energy from it was discovered. When uranium is bombarded with neutrons its atoms become unstable. They split and give off energy. This splitting process is called fission. Uranium is used for nuclear power and in atomic bombs.

See also NUCLEAR ENERGY.

V

VEGETABLE

Many of the plants we eat are called 'vegetables'. Vegetables are good food, supplying energy or body-building substances.

Various parts of vegetables are eaten. Potatoes, carrots and turnips are root vegetables; spinach is a leaf; brussel sprouts are leaf buds; and broccoli is a flower. Some fruits and seeds are eaten as vegetables. Tomatoes and cucumbers are fruits; peas and beans are seeds.

Vegetable: The part of the plant we eat may be its leaf, stem, root, seed or fruit.

Victoria: Queen Victoria presided over the British Empire.

VICTORIA (1819-1901)

Queen Victoria reigned for 64 years, longer than any other British monarch. She became queen when she was only 18. Victoria loved her husband, Prince

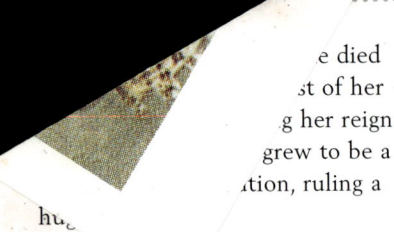

VIDEOTA...

Videotape is a means of recording sound and pictures on tape. Many television programmes are recorded on videotape to be sent across a network or for relaying at a later time.

Home videos are now very popular. Some of these are pre-recorded tapes of films or video games that can be played on a videocassette recorder (VCR) attached to a television set. Others are blank tapes that can be used to record television programmes.

VIKING

In the 8th century, fierce Vikings from Scandinavia began raiding the coasts of western Europe. They burned villages, robbed churches, stole cattle and carried off slaves. People were terrified of them, especially as Vikings often fought like madmen, as if eager to die in battle.

But the Vikings were not just pirates and robbers. They were also farmers and traders. Their craftsmen were highly skilled in using iron, gold and silver. And their sagas tell the story of their legendary exploits.

In their long ships (wooden boats with oars and square sails)

Vikings: *Olaf, King of Norway, was killed in a sea battle in AD 1000.*

they crossed the Atlantic Ocean to settle in Iceland and Greenland. They probably reached America around AD 1000. The Vikings also settled in Ireland, France, Russia and England.

VITAMIN

Vitamins are chemicals that our bodies need for healthy growth. We get vitamins from food. From lettuce, carrots, butter and eggs comes Vitamin A. It helps us grow. There are several kinds of Vitamin B. We eat them in cereals, milk, meat, vegetables and fruit. Vitamin C is found in fruit and prevents us getting a disease called scurvy. Vitamin D is important to babies. It prevents a bone disease called rickets. Egg yolks, fish oils, margarine and liver are rich in vitamin D. Sunlight has the same effect. Other vitamins are known as E and K. The body only uses vitamins in tiny quantities. A good varied diet gives it all the vitamins it needs.

VOLCANO

Volcanoes occur where the Earth's crust is being squeezed or stretched as new mountains are formed. The enormous pressures inside the Earth melt the solid rock to liquid magma. When the pressures become too great, gases and hot liquid rock, called lava, may burst through the centre of a volcano and out of a pit or crater at the top.

Volcanoes are usually cone-shaped with a crater at the top. Active volcanoes erupt for short periods and then remain dormant for long periods. If the lava remains bubbling in a lava lake, eruptions are just overflows. If, however, the lava solidifies and blocks the top of the volcano, the next eruption will explode.

Volcano: Hot lava and melted rock spout up from the central vent. The mountain is made from layers of cold ash and lava.

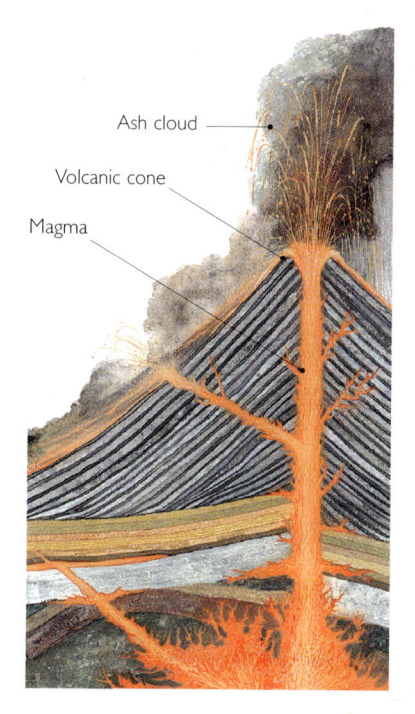

W X

WAR

People have always found it difficult to live in peace together. From prehistoric times, envy and greed have made one tribe attack another, in order to steal its land or animals. Later, great empires were founded by conquering armies.

In ancient Greece and Rome, soldiers were armed with swords, spears, slings and bows and arrows. Foot soldiers, or infantry, made up the largest part of an army.

Horsemen, or cavalry, played an important part in wars throughout the Middle Ages. Knights in armour, armed with lances, swords and clubs, battered their way through enemy ranks.

Gunpowder came into use in the 1300s. From then on wars were fought increasingly with guns. But it took many years before soldiers had guns light enough to carry easily.

By 1914 guns were so powerful that soldiers had to dig trenches for protection. During World War I whole armies were bogged down in trenches. The tank, first used in 1916, was a powerful new weapon.

World War II was fought in Europe, Africa and Asia. Most of the world's leading nations took part.

See also CIVIL WAR; WORLD WAR I; WORLD WAR II.

WASHINGTON, GEORGE (1732-1799)

George Washington, the first President of the USA, was a farmer from Virginia. When the American colonists fought the British in the War of Independence from 1775 to 1783, Washington became general of their army. In 1789 he became president, although he did not consider himself fit for such an important task.

MAJOR WARS

Some of the most important wars fought since the fall of the Roman Empire in AD476.

1337-1453	Hundred Years' War
1455-1485	Wars of the Roses
1618-1648	Thirty Years' War
1642-1651	English Civil War
1701-1713	War of Spanish Succession
1740-1748	War of Austrian Succession
1756-1763	Seven Years' War
1775-1783	American War of Independence
1792-1815	Napoleonic Wars
1854-1856	Crimean War
1861-1865	American Civil War
1870-1871	Franco-Prussian War
1899-1902	Boer War (South Africa)
1914-1918	World War I
1936-1939	Spanish Civil War
1939-1945	World War II
1957-1975	Vietnam War
1973	Yom Kippur War
1980-1988	Iran-Iraq War
1991	Gulf War

WASP

See BEES AND WASPS.

WATER

Water is the most precious liquid on Earth; without it, nothing can live. Water is made up of hydrogen and oxygen. Its molecules contain two atoms of hydrogen (H) to one atom of oxygen (O). We write this as the chemical formula H_2O.

Water plays an important part in our weather. The Sun warms the Earth's water, changing some of it into vapour. The vapour rises and, as it does so, condenses and falls as rain or snow. This continuous process is called the water cycle.

Water also shapes the Earth. Rain, ocean waves and rivers erode the land. Glaciers gouge paths through rocks and soil.

Great dams can harness the power of water to make electricity. We call this form of power hydroelectricity.

See also ENERGY; GLACIER; LAKE; OCEANS; RAIN AND HAIL; RIVER.

Waves: At sea, waves are caused mainly by the wind.

WATERFALL

A waterfall is caused by water wearing away rock at different speeds. If a river flows over a join between hard rock and soft rock, it wears away the soft rock more quickly and makes a deep 'step'. Some waterfalls are quite small, but in some places wide rivers fall over huge cliffs. The most famous waterfalls are Niagara, between Canada and the United States, and the Victoria Falls in Africa.

WATT, JAMES (1736-1819)

Watt was a Scottish engineer who invented a more efficient steam engine than any before. He devised a condenser and several methods of changing the motion of a piston into the rotating motion of a wheel.

WAVES

If you drop a stone into a pond, it pushes the water out of the way in a wave. The energy in this wave moves along to make another wave, and in this way moves across the water. Sound is also carried by waves. Light waves,

Wind direction

Peak of wave

Trough of wave

X-rays, radio waves, and other forms of radiation are all types of electromagnetic waves.

WEATHER

The Earth's atmosphere moves constantly, driven by the Sun's heat. Huge masses of warm and cold air flow between the tropics and the polar regions. As these air masses meet, rise and fall, and heat and cool, they cause weather. When cold and warm air masses meet, a spiral of air called a depression results. A depression brings clouds, rain, or storms. The meeting line between two air masses is called a front. Fronts usually bring changes in the weather.

WEST INDIES

See CARIBBEAN.

WHALE

Although whales spend all their lives in the sea, they are mammals, not fish. Whales are warm-blooded. They have skin, not scales. The females give birth to live young and feed them on milk. A whale

Whale: The blue whale is the largest whale and the largest mammal ever to live.

can dive to great depths, loading its blood with enough oxygen to last for up to 45 minutes, but it must surface to breathe. Whales swim by beating their tails up and down.

There are two families of whales: toothed whales, and whalebone or baleen whales.

WHEEL

The wheel is one of the most important inventions. A great deal of human and animal energy is saved through using it.

No one knows when the wheel was invented. Its first use was probably as a potter's wheel in Mesopotamia about 5,000 years ago. Wheels were next used on carts. These wheels were solid, made by cutting slices off large tree trunks.

Without wheels, advanced transport systems would not be possible. They are essential to most machines and engines.

William the Conqueror
(*c*.1027-1087)
In 1066 William, Duke of Normandy, landed with his army in Sussex and defeated and killed King Harold. He was crowned William I, the first Norman king of England.

William was an efficient administrator. He caused a great survey of the land to be made. It is known as the *Domesday Book*. William's descendants ruled England for many years after his death.

Wind
Wind is the movement of air over the Earth's surface. The chief cause of wind is the unequal heating of the Earth's surface. At the equator, which gets most heat from the Sun, air becomes warm and rises. At the poles, which are the coldest places, cold air sinks. As the warm air rises, cool air moves in to take its place. Changing temperatures over the sea and land also affect the pattern of the winds.

Winds are named after the direction from which they come; so a north wind blows from the north, and so on.

Windmill
Windmills are used to grind corn, pump water and generate electricity. Their source of power is the wind. Sails or blades are fixed to a shaft. The shaft is connected to the machinery to be driven. As other forms of energy become expensive, windmills may

Wheel: From the first time man ever rolled a log to the pneumatic (air-filled) tyres of today, the wheel has travelled a long way.

Windmill: *The most efficient modern wind machines have two or three blades like an aircraft propeller.*

again become popular. A light steel type has been devised in the USA for use on farms.

Wood
Wood is used in building, in making furniture and is burned as fuel. Cut wood is called timber. The timber we get from coniferous trees, such as pine, is called softwood. The timber we get from deciduous trees, such as oak, is called hardwood. Softwoods are used mainly in building construction, hardwoods for furniture.

Wood is also made into paper, textile fibres, plastics, explosives and several other chemicals. The main chemical substance in wood is cellulose.

Wool
Wool is the fine hair from the fleece of sheep. Wool fibres are naturally crinkled which helps woollen garments keep their shape. Each fibre is covered with tiny overlapping scales so that the fibres lock together when they are spun into yarn. A Merino ram can give up to 12kg of wool.

World War I
World War I (1914-1918) involved Europe, America and much of the Middle East, and so became known as a 'world war'. France, Britain (and her empire), the United States, and Russia were on one side. On the other were Austria-Hungary, Germany and Turkey.

The war reached a stalemate in northern France, where the front lines of both sides hardly moved for several years. In the east, the Germans fared better. Because of this and its own internal problems, Russia was forced to withdraw from the struggle in 1917.

The United States was at first reluctant to be drawn into the conflict, but after many German attacks on US shipping, the United States declared war on Germany.

The Allied armies slowly pushed the Germans back, until in November 1918 peace was agreed.

WORLD WAR II

In September 1939, Adolf Hitler's German armies invaded Poland, an early step in his planned conquest of Europe. Germany, then Italy, and eventually Japan had entered into a war against most of the major nations of the world. Before the war was over, battles had been fought from the North Atlantic and Europe to the tropical jungles of the Far East.

At first the Germans were successful in their sweep across Europe, and into North Africa and Russia. In December 1941, the United States entered the war after the Japanese bombed the Pacific Fleet at Pearl Harbor in Hawaii, and the tide began to turn. By June 1944, Allied forces had landed in France. Germany surrendered the following spring.

In the Pacific, Japan had invaded China, Malaya and Indonesia and had captured many Pacific islands. Victories by the US Navy and finally the dropping of atomic bombs on the Japanese cities of Hiroshima and Nagasaki forced Japan to surrender.

WORM

Worms are animals with soft bodies. Some live underground or in water, others as parasites inside plants or other animals.

There are about 20,000 different kinds of worms. One group includes flatworms which have flat, ribbon or leaf-shaped bodies. The harmful parasites, the tapeworm and the liver fluke are flatworms. Threadworms,

World War I: For four years, fighting centred around two lines of trenches stretching across western Europe.

roundworms and hookworms belong to another group. Many of these are also parasites.

Segmented worms are not harmful. Their bodies are made up of many segments or rings. Tiny bristles on the segments help them to move along. They include ragworms, lugworms and earthworms. Earthworms live in moist soil, and eat bits of leaves and decayed plant matter in the soil. They come to the surface to feed or after heavy rain. Earthworms help the garden by turning over the soil and breaking it up.

See also PARASITE.

WRIGHT, ORVILLE (1871-1948) AND WILBUR (1867-1912)

These two American brothers made the first motor-powered, heavier-than-air flight in 1903.

They taught themselves about flight by making and flying kites and gliders. By 1903 they were ready to attach a four-cylinder, 13 horse-power engine to a biplane glider. On December

Wright Brothers: *The world's first successful powered aeroplane,* Flyer 1, *took to the air in 1903.*

17th, Orville took off, rose to a height of nearly 3m and flew over 35m. The flight took 59 seconds.

X-RAY

X-rays are invisible waves of energy like light waves. They can pass through and into most materials. They pass through flesh, for example. In hospitals doctors take X-ray photographs to look inside the body. A patient stands in front of a photographic film and X-rays are passed through him. When the film is developed, the patient's bones show up. This is because the bones block some of the rays and cast a shadow on the film. The doctors can see if any of the bones are broken. Some new X-ray machines can photograph body organs as well.

X-rays were discovered by the German scientist Wilhelm Röntgen in 1895.

YZ

YAK
Yaks live in the cold, high mountains of central Asia. The yak can live on the poor pasture of the Himalayas. It gives milk, butter and meat, its skin is made into leather, and its long, shaggy hair is woven into cloth.

ZEBRA
The zebra is a relation of the horse. Its distinct black stripes help to camouflage it in the shadowy high grass of the African plains on which it lives. Zebras roam in herds, and gallop off at great speed if attacked by lions, their main enemy.

ZOO
A zoo is a place where wild animals are kept in captivity. People enjoy going to zoos to see animals from other countries. But more important, zoos help to save rare animals from becoming extinct.

In the past, kings collected wild animals in zoos. The first public zoos began in the 19th century. Often the cages were too small for the animals and the bars made it difficult for people to see them properly.

Today zoos have enclosures in which the animals feel more at home. Ditches, moats and glass keep the animals and visitors apart. Birds fly about inside large aviaries. Mountain goats climb artificial hills, while penguins, polar bears, seals and even elephants have pools to splash in. In special darkened builings, people can see animals which are normally active only at night.

ZOOLOGY
This is the science that deals with the study of animals. Zoologists find out about animals' bodies, their growth patterns and habits. About a million different species, or kinds, of animals have been described by zoologists and sorted into groups.

The study of zoology helps us to control animal pests and diseases, and to improve the quality of farm animals.

Yak: *The yak's shaggy hair protects it from the cold.*

Index

Page numbers in **bold** type denote main entries; page numbers in *italic* type refer to illustrations and charts.

aardvark **4**, *4*
abacus 36
aborigines **4**
abstract painting 170
Abyssinian cat *42*
abyss (ocean floor) 165
acetic acid 4
Achaemenid Empire *108*
acids **4**, 177
  acid rain *177*
Aconcagua mountain 156
acorn 95, *194*
Adventures of Huckleberry Finn (Twain) 217
Adventures of Tom Sawyer (Twain) 217
Aeneid (Virgil) 176
Aeschylus 176
Afghanistan 62
Africa **4-5**, *4*, 61, 85, *108*, *110*
  geography 68, 92, 129, *156*, 215, 225
  wildlife 10, 34, 65, *81*, 100, 107, 136, *136*, 139, 153-4, 178, 187, *187*, 231
agriculture *see* farming
AIDS 5
air **5-6**, 16, 32
aircraft **6-7**, *6*, 8, 83, 127-8
  historic planes 28, *139*, *139*, 230, *230*
  see also airship; helicopter
aircraft carrier *196*
air-cushion vessel *see* hovercraft
airships and balloons **20-1**, *21*
Akashi-Kaikyo bridge 32
Albania 60, 76
Albert, Prince 221-2
alcohol 171, 213
Alexander the Great 7, 14, *108*
Alexandria Lighthouse 195
algae 7, *7*, 10, 136, *174*, 175, 199
algebra 144
Algeria 61
alkali 200
Allah 185
alligators and crocodiles **64**, *64*, 186
alloy 8, 214
alphabet **8**
alpha particle *183*
Alps 125, 208
Alsation dog 71
aluminium 6, 8, 148
Amazon River 31, 202
America *see* Canada; Central, North and South America; United States of America
American Civil War 50, *50*, *111*, 138, *224*
American football 91
American War of Independence (Revolution) 187, 219, 224, *224*
amethyst 97
amoeba 9, 44, 186
amphibian **8**, 84, 94, 179
Amundsen, Roald 85, 192
anaesthetic 147, *147*
anatomy 26-7, 147
ANC *110*
Andes 118-19, 140, 178, 189, 202
Andorra 60
aneroid barometer 21
Anglo-Saxon **8-9**
Angola 61
Angora *101*
Anguilla 62
animal **9**
  see also amphibian; bird; insect; mammal; reptile
Anne, Queen 130
ant **9-10**, *9*
Antarctic **10**, *156*, 165, 171
anteater **10**, *10*
antelope **10**, 151
antibiotic **10**, 72, 147
antibody 118
Antigua and Barbuda 62
antiseptic 147, *147*
aorta 105, *105*
apartheid 202
ape **11**, *11*, 114
Apollo II spaceship *189*
appendix (of the body) 69
Aquino, Corazón 172
Arab *108*, 125, 151
Arabian camel 37
Arabian (Persian) Gulf 119
archaeology **11**, 180
arch bridge 32
arch dam 66
archery **12**, *12*
Archimedes **12**
architecture **12-14**, *12*, *13*, 48-9, *185*, 186
Arctic **14**, 122, 137, 191
Arctic fox 94
Arctic Ocean 14, 165
Argentina **14**, 62, 202
aria 166
Aristophanes 176
Aristotle **14-15**, *109*
arithmetic 144
armadillo **15**
Armenia 62
armour **15**, *15*
Armstrong, Neil 16, *111*
army ant 10
art *see* painting; sculpture
Art Nouveau 13
Asia **15-16**, 62, 98, *108*, *110*, 185
  geography 68, 92, *156*, 215

wildlife 10, 23, 34, 37, 65, 136, 153-4, 170, 178, 195, 214, 231
asphalt 40
Association football (soccer) 91
Assyrian civilization *108*, 124
asteroid 201
astronaut **16-17**, *17*, 204
  see also space exploration
astronomy **17**, 59-60, 96, 206, 211
Atahualpa, King 119
Athens 102, *103*, 166, 175
athletics **17**, 103
Atlantic Ocean **17-18**, 77, 84, 88, 165
atmosphere 6
  see also air
atom **18**, *18*, 28, 80, 173, 182, 190
atomic bomb 164, 220, 229
Aurelia jellyfish *126*
Austerlitz, Battle of *160*
Australia **18-19**, 56, 59, 63, *111*
  geography 46, 68
  people and animals 4, 65, 129, 132, *132*, 175
Australian Rules football 91
Austria 60, 84, 97, *160*, 184, *208*, 228
automobile *see* car
Azerbaijan 62
Aztec **19**, *19*, 60, *109*, *111*

Babylon 124
Bach, Johann Sebastian **20**, 157, *157*
bacon 173
bacteria **20**, 70, 171, *174*, 200
  ways to kill 10, 72, 118, 218
bacteriology 27
Bactrian camel 37
badger **20**, *20*
Bahamas 62
Bahrain 62
baleen whale 226
Balkans **76**
ballad 176
ballet 66
ballistic missile 152
balloons and airships **20-1**, *21*
Bangladesh 62
banjo 159
bank (for money) 153, 162, 208
Barbados 62
barley *see* cereals
barn owl *168*
barometer **21**
baroque architecture *13*, 14

baseball **22**, *22*
basketball **22**
bat (animal) **22**, *22*, 76
bauxite 40, 202
bean 54, 91, 148, 181, 221
bear 14, **23**, 231
beaver **23**, 189
Becket, Samuel *176*
Becquerel, Henri 65
beech 92, *134*
beer 33
bees **23-4**, *23*, *24*, 121
Beethoven, Ludwig van *24*, 157, *157*
beetle *121*
Belarus 60, 76
Belgium 60, 84, **162**
Belisarius *108*
Belize 46, 62
Bell, Alexander Graham **24-5**, *25*
bell (musical instrument) *158*, 159
Benelux 162
Bengal, Bay of 119
Benin 61
Benz, Karl 40, *111*
Berlioz, Hector 157
Bermuda 62
beta particle *183*
Bhutan 62
Bhutto, Benazir *110*
Bible **25**, 128, 154, 169, 176, 181
bicycle **25-6**, *25*
bimah 208
biology 192, **267**
birch 92
bird **26**, **27**, 84, 161, 180
  species **26**, 73, *73*, 115, *115*, *161*, 168, *168*, 171, *187*
bird of paradise 26
bison **27-8**, *27*, 44, 178
blackbird 26
Black Death *111*
black hole **28**, *28*
black widow spider *204*
blank verse 176
Blériot, Louis 28
blitzkrieg 209
block and tackle *141*
blood **28-9**, *29*, 30, 105, 115, *147*
bluejay 26
Boadicea **29**
boar 173
Boer War *110*, *224*
Bolívar, Simón **29**
Bolivia 29, 62
bone **29-30**
book **30**, 56, 104, 181
boomerang 4, *4*
Booth, John Wilkes 138
Bosnia-Herzegovina 60, *111*
Boston terrier 71
botany 26
Botswana 61
Botticelli, Sandro *169*
bows and arrows 12
Boxer Rebellion *110*
boxing **30**
Boyacá, Battle of 29

INDEX

Brachiosaurus 179
Brahmaputra River 119
Brahms, Johannes 30, 157, *157*
braille 30, *31*
Braille, Louis 30
brain 30-1, *31*, 73, 85, 114, 161, 199
brass 8, 214
brass section (orchestra) *167*
Brazil 31-2, 54, 60, 62
Brazilian Rhinoceros beetle *121*
Brazil nut *164*
bread 90
breathing 32, 88, 161
Brecht, Bertolt *176*
bridge 32
British Isles 8-9, 32-3, 45
Britten, Benjamin *157*
broad-leaf tree 92, 216
broccoli 221
bronze 33, *33*, 103, 214
Bronze Age 33, *33*, *109*
brown-lipped snail *152*
Brunei 62, 203
Brussels 162
brussel sprout 221
Buddha and Buddhism 16, 33-4, *34*, *108*, 119, 185
buffalo 27-8, *34*, 44
bulb 34
Bulgaria 60, 76
Bull Run, Battle of 51
bumblebee 23
Burkina Faso 61
burr (fruit) 95
Burundi 61
Butler, Edward 155
butter 33, 90, 162, 166, 223, 231
butterflies and moths 34-5, *35*, *38*, 121, 197
Byzantine Empire *13*, 35, *108*, 190

cacao 162
cactus 68
Caesar, Julius 36, 51
caesium atomic clock 52
calculator 36, 197
calculus 144, 162
calendar 36
Californian redwood 215-16
Camberwell Beauty butterfly *35*
Cambodia 62, 203
camel 36-7, *36*
camera 37-8, *37*, 172, 211, *211*
see also film; photography
Cameroon 61
camouflage 38-9, *38*
Canada 39, 56, 62, 164
farming 46
geography 92, 163, 225
sport 91, 112
see also North America
canal 39, *124*

cancer 39
cannon *see* gun
Canterbury Tales 47
Cape buffalo 34
Cape Verde Islands 61
capybara 189
car 40, 82, 83, 91-2, 177
caravel *85*, 196
carbohydrate 90, 91
carbon 8, 40, 95, 97, 181
carbon-14 dating 11
carbon dioxide 32, 105, 115, 134, 135, 172, *172*
Caribbean (West Indies) 40, 54, 62-3
caribou 151
carpel 90, *90*
carrot 221, *221*, 223
carving 192
case law 134
Caspian Sea 133
cassette 184
castle 40-1, *41*
cat 42-3, *42*, 136
catamaran 196
caterpillar 35, *38*, 121, 197
cathedral *see* church
cattle 34, 44, 86, 210
where farmed 14, 32, 99, 162, 178
cave 44, *44*
cedar 59
cell 44-5, *45*, 156, 186
cellulose 228
Celsius (centigrade) scale 213
Celts *45*, *45*
cement 129
Central African Republic 61
Central America 10, 45-6, 62-3, 153, 164
see also Aztec; Maya
cereals 46, *46*, 223
where grown 19, 78, 83, 99, 125, 163, 178, 219
cerebellum 31, *31*
cerebral cortex 31, *31*
Cézanne, Paul *169*
Chad 61
chamber music 157, 167
Champollion, Jean 107
chanterelle mushroom *157*
charcoal 95
Charlemagne 46-7, *109*
Charles I 50, 65, *130*
Charles II *130*
Chaucer, Geoffrey 47
Cheddar cheese 47
cheese 33, 47, 91, 94, 162, 181
cheetah *136*, *176*
Chekhov, Anton *176*
chemicals 33, 175, 177, 191
chemistry 47, 192
Cheshire cheese 47
chess 47
Chile 62
chimpanzee 11

China 16, 47-8, 62, *108*
ancient Chinese achievements 39, 48, 52, 124, 169, 170, 197
culture 58, 72, 133
farming 60, 210
history 57, *110*, 143, 144, 229
wildlife 170
chlorine 191
chlorophyll 135, 172, *172*, 174
chocolate 54
Chopin, Frédéric *157*
Christianity 25, 48, 119, 154, 185, 191
history 16, *108*, *109*, 127, 140, 153
chromite 172
chromium 124
chromosome 98, 148
chrysalis (pupa) 121, *121*
church and cathedral *12*, 48-9, *49*, 150
Churchill, Winston Spencer 49
cinnamon 166
cirrus cloud *53*
civilization *51*, 86, 103, 119
Civil Rights Movement 129-30, 132
Civil War 50-1, *50*, 65, *111*, 224
clarinet *158*, 159
classical music 158
Clemens, Samuel (Mark Twain) 217
Cleopatra *51*, *108*
climate 51-2, *52*
of countries 5, 32, 39, 126, 218-19
clipper (ship) 196, *196*
clocks and watches 52, 197, 214
cloud 52-3, *53*, 90, 183, 199
see also water vapour
Clovis, king of the Franks *109*
Clydesdale horse 113
coal 53, 82, 95, 151
where found 14, 16, 19, 39, 76, 83, 99, 162, 219
Coalbrookdale iron bridge 32
cochineal dye 72
cockle (shellfish) 152
cocoa 5, 32, 40, 54, *54*
coconut 95, 203
Cocteau, Jean *176*
cod 89, *89*
coffee 54
where grown 5, 16, 32, 40, 46, 129, 148
coin 153
coke 53, 124
Cold War *111*
Colobus monkey *153*
Colombia 62
Colorado beetle 121
Colossus of Rhodes 195

colour 54-5, *55*, 137, 145
see also spectrum
Columbus, Christopher 40, *55*, 84, *85*, *111*
combustion 95
comet *56*, *56*
common law 134
Common Wall lizard *140*
Commonwealth 56
communication 56-7, 133, 191, *191*
Communism *57*, 83, *111*, 143, 187
Communist countries 48, 76, 99, 135
Comoros 61
compass 57
composers 20, 24, 30, 105, 156, 157, *157*, 166
computer 57-8, *58*, 80, 122, 188
concave lens 135
concrete 188
Confucius and Confucianism 48, **58**, *108*, 185
conger eel 77
Congo 61
Congress (USA) 102
conifer 59, 92, *174*, *215*, 216, 228
conservation 59
Constantine, Emperor 35, 48
Constantinople 35, *111*, 190
constellation 59
continental shelf 165
convex lens 135
convicts 19
Cook, Captain James 19, 59, *111*
Copernicus, Nicolaus 59-60
copper 8, 33, 60
where found 16, 19, 172, 202, 208, 219
coral reef 18
coral snake 19
core, Earth's 74, 75, 188
cork 204
Cornish Rex cat *43*
Cortés, Hernan 19, 60, *60*, *111*
Costa Rica 45-6, 62
Côte d'Ivoire 61
cotton 60
where grown 5, 16, 46, 78, 125, 148, 164, 219
counterpoint (music) 157
countries of the world 60-3
coyote 71
crab 9, 63, *63*
crab spider 205
cricket 63-4
Crimean War *111*, 224
Croatia 60
crocodiles and alligators 64, *64*, 186
Cromwell, Oliver 50, **65**
crossbill 26
crossbow 12

INDEX

Crusades 65, *108*, *109*
crustacean 63
crust, Earth's 74, *74*, 166, 188, 223
crystal 97, 199
Cuba 57, 62, *111*
Cubism 173
cucumber 95, 221
cumulus cloud *53*
Curie, Marie and Pierre 65, *147*
Custer, George 65
cycad *174*
cyclone 116
cymbal *158*, 159
Cyprus 62
cytology 26
Czech Republic 60, 76

daffodil 175
Daguerre, Louis 172
Daimler, Gottlieb 40, *111*, 155
dam 66, 124, 133, 219, 225
dance **66**
dandelion 95
Darwin, Charles Robert **66-7**
Das Kapital (Marx) 144
David Copperfield (Dickens) 69
Dayton Peace Accord *111*
death cap toadstool *157*
Debussy, Claude *157*
deciduous tree 92, 216, 228
decimal system *108*
Declaration of Independence *111*, 126
deep-freeze 184
deer **67**, *67*
democracy **67**, 101, 103
Democratic Republic of Congo 110
dendrochronology 11
Denmark 60, 84, **191-2**
depression (weather feature) 226
dermis 198
desert 5, **67-8**, *68*, 151
detergent 200
deuterium 116
Dhaulagiri mountain *156*
diamond 97, *97*, 151, 202
Diana, Princess of Wales *111*
Dias, Bartolomeu 110
Dickens, Charles **68-9**
dicotyledon *174*, 175
diesel engine 83, 183, 207
digestion **69**, *69*
dinosaur **179-80**, *179*
Diplodocus *179*
disease 70, 72, 118, *147*, 171
diving, underwater **70**, 136
Djibouti 61
DNA 98
doberman 71, *71*
dog **70-1**, *70*, *71*
dolphin **72**, 143

Domesday Book 227
dominant gene 98, *98*
Dominica 62
Dominican Republic 62
dragon **72**
Drake, Sir Francis 82
dramatic poem 176
dreams **198-9**
dripstone 205
drugs 10, 70, **72**, 147
Druidism 45
Dunant, Jean Henri 184
Durer, Albrecht *169*
Dvorak, Antonin *157*
dye 53, **72**
dynamite **72**, 163

eagle **73**, *73*
ear **73**, *73*, 202
Earth **74-5**, *75*, 98, 142, 220
  Earth's motion 59-60, 193-4, 214
  see also atmosphere; crust; Solar System
earthquake **75**, *75*, 99, *111*, 126, 169
earthworm 230
Eastern Europe and the Balkans **76**
ebony 92
echo **76**
eclipse 17, **76**, *76*
ecology 27, **77**
Ecuador 62
Edison, Thomas **77**, *77*
Edward I to Edward VIII *130*
eel **77**
egg **78**, *78*, 91, 223
  birds 27, 171
  fish 77, 88
  human 115, 186, *186*
  insects 9, 10, 24, 120, 121, *121*
  mammal 175
  reptiles and amphibians 8, 64, 94, 140, 151, 186, 199
Egypt 60, 61, 78, *110*, 160
Egypt, Ancient *13*, 51, **78-9**, *79*, *108*
  culture 30, 33, 106, 169, 170, 181
  farming 44, 124
  slavery 154, 198
Einstein, Albert **79**
Elbruz, Mount *156*
electricity 57, 77, **79-80**, *80*, 210
  electric transport 40, 183, 206
  ways of making 53, 66, 82, 164, 225
  see also hydroelectricity
electromagnetic wave 226
electron 18, *18*, 28, 80, 211, *211*
electronic instrument 159
electronics 33, **80**, *80*, 122, 203, 215
electron microscope 149

elegy 176
elements and compounds 18, 40, **80**, 148, 151, 182
elephant **80-1**, *81*, 105, 231
Elgar, Edward *157*
El Greco *169*
Elizabeth I **82**, *130*
Elizabeth II 101, *130*
elk (moose) 67
elm 92
El Salvador 46, 63
e-mail 122
emerald 97, 202
Empire State Building *12*
emu 19
energy 79, **82**, *82*
  from food 90-1, 181, 207
  from fuel 95, 116, 164
  from sunlight 135, 137, 173
Engels, Friedrich 57
engine 40, **83**, 155, 183, 189, 207
  see also jet engine; steam engine
English Civil War 50, 65, *111*, *224*
ENIAC computer 58
epic poem 176
epidermis 198
equator *5*, 31, 227
Equatorial Guinea 61
Eritrea 61
erosion 83
Eskimo *see* Inuit
essential oil 166
Estonia 60
Ethiopia 61, *108*
Euclid *109*
Euripedes *176*
Europe 46, **76**, 83, *109*, *111*
  geography 92, *156*, 215
  people 45, *109*, 150, 159
  wildlife 20, *20*, 23, 67, *140*, 195
European Court of Justice 84
European Economic Community *see* European Union
European Union **84**, *111*, 162
Everest, Mount 156, *156*
evergreen tree 216
evolution 66-7, **84**
excise duty 209-10
exoskeleton 197
explorers **84-5**, *85*
explosive 53, 72, 104, 163, 224, 228
Eyck, Jan van *169*
eye **85**, *85*, 199

factory *see* industry
Falkland Islands 14, 18
farming (agriculture) 46, *46*, 51, 86, *108*, *124*, 207
  Africa 54, 202

Americas 14, 32, 40, 46, 54, 178, 219
Asia 16, *108*, 119, 125, 203
Australasia 19, 162
Europe 33, 76, 83, 94, 99, 102, *109*, 125, 162, 192, 204
Farouk, King 160
fat 90-1, 200
fatty oil 166
feather *26*
Federal Republic of West Germany 99, *111*
fennec fox 94
fern 86, *174*, 175
fertilizer 86
feudal system 150
fibre optics **86-7**, *86*
field gun 104
figure skating 118
Fiji 63
film 37-8, *37*, **87**, 181
  see also camera; photography
fingerprints **87**, *87*
Finland 60, 84, **191-2**
fir 59, 92, 216
fish 32, 38, 84, **87-8**, *88*, 161, 174, 179
  as food 6, 91, 126, 169, 181, 223
  species 77, 88, *89*, *127*, 193, 195, *195*
fishing **88-9**, *88*, *89*, 192
fission, nuclear 220
fjord 192
flag **89**
flatworm 229
flea *121*, 171
Fleming, Alexander *147*
Flemings 162
Florence *49*, 125, 146
flower 14, **89-90**, *90*, 121
flute *158*, 159
fly (insect) 120, *121*
fog **90**
folk music 158
food 16, 19, **90-1**, 115, 125, 181
  food processing 33, 184
food web 77
football **91**
Ford, Henry 40, **91-2**
forest 5, 16, 31-2, 39, 92, *92*, 99
  see also tree; wood
fossil 84, **92-3**, 114, 129, 179
fox 14, 71, **93-4**, *93*, 189
France 60, 66, 84, **94**, 223
  history 94, *111*, 128, 160, 184, 187, 228, 229
Franco-Prussian War *111*, *224*
free verse 176
French bull dog *71*
French Guiana 62
French horn *158*
French Revolution 94, *111*, 187
Freud, Sigmund **94**, *147*

234

INDEX

frogs and toads 8, **94-5**, *94*, 151
front (weather feature) 226
fructose 207
fruit **95**, *95*, 164, 223
  where grown 14, 19, 40, 78, 83, 125, 129, 162, 163, 204, 219
fuel **95**, 189
  see also oil; petroleum
fungus 136, 156, **157**, *174*, 175, 186

Gabon 61
Gaelic football 91
Gagarin, Yuri 16, 203
galaxy **96**, *96*, 220
Galileo 52, **96**, *147*, 186
galleon **196**, *196*
Gama, Vasco da **96**, *110*
Gambia 61
gamma ray *183*, 205
Gandhi, Mohandas **96-7**, *129*
Ganges River 119
Garibaldi, Giuseppe **97**
gas 144-5
  in airships 20
  in atmosphere 5-6, 9, 168
  coal gas 53
  in engines 7, 127, *127*, 128
  gas thermometer 213
  natural gas 32, 39, 76, 95, 192, 219
  in space 56, 74, 96, 201, 206
Gasherbrum mountain 156
Gautama 33-4
gem **97**, *97*, 151
genetics 26, **97-8**, *98*, 147-8, *147*
Genghis Khan **98**
Genoa 125
geology **98-9**
geometry 144, 181, *181*
George I to George VI *130*
Georgia 60
gerbil 189
German Democratic Republic 99, *111*
germanium 215
Germany 60, 84, **99**, *111*, 127-8
  see also World War I and World War II
Gettysburg, Battle of 51
geyser **99-100**, *99*
Ghana 61, *108*
gibbon 11
Gibraltar 60
gill net 89, *89*
ginkgo *174*
Giotto *169*
giraffe **100**
girder bridge 32
Giza pyramids 181
glacier 83, **100**, *100*, 117, 132, 192, 225

glass **100**
globe 143
Globe Theatre 212
glucose 207
gnat *121*
goat **101**, *101*, 231
Gobi desert 68
Godwin Austen mountain *156*
gold **101**, 151
  where found 19, 39, 149, 202, 219
Gorgonzola cheese 47
gorilla 11
Gosainthan mountain 156
Gothic architecture 13, *13*, 49, *49*
government 39, 67, **101-2**, 153, 209
Goya *169*
grain *see* cereals
gramophone *77*
Grand Canal, China 39
Grant, Ulysses S. 51
grass 14, **102**, 175
grasshopper *38*, 120
gravity 28, *28*, **102**, 162, 165
gravity dam 66
Great Barrier Reef 18
Great Diving beetle *121*
Great Lakes 133, 163
Great Rift Valley 129
Greece 60, 84, **102**, *111*
Greece, Ancient 101, **102-3**, *103*, 109
  architecture 12-13, *13*, *185*, 186
  athletics 17, 166
  culture 8, 51, 113, 159, *159*, 169, 175-6, 212
  famous people 7, 12, 14-15, 113, 175, *176*, 181, 200
  science 59, 147
  slavery 198
  warfare 15, 224
Greek Orthodox Church 35
Greenland 63, *109*, 223
Gregorian calendar 36
Gregory XIII, Pope 36
Grenada 63
greyhound *71*
Grieg, Edvard *157*
grizzly bear 23
Guadeloupe 63
Guatemala 46, 63
Guinea 61
Guinea-Bissau 61
guinea pig 189
guitar *159*
Gulf Stream 18, **103-4**, 192
Gulf War *110*, *224*
gun (cannon) 15, 41, **104**, *174*, 209, 224
gunpowder 48, 224
Gupta Empire *108*
Gutenberg, Johannes 30, 56, **104-5**, *105*, *111*, 181
Guyana 62

gymnastics **104**
gyrocompass 57

habit, monk's 152
haddock 88
hail, hailstone **183**
Haiti 63, *111*
Halicarnassus Museum 195
Halley's comet 56
ham 173
hamster 189
Handel, George Frederick **105**, *157*
Han Dynasty *108*
Hanging Gardens of Babylon 195
Hannibal **105**
Harappan civilization *108*
hardwood 228
hares and rabbits **182**
Harlequin Longhorn beetle *121*
harp *158*
Harvey, William **105**, *147*
Hawaiian Islands 59, 218, 229
Haydn, Franz 157
hazelnut *164*
H bomb 116
heart 28, **105**, *106*, 161
heat 82
hedgehog **106**
Heinkel *178* jet 128
helicopter **106**, *106*, 136
helium 20, 207
Henry I to Henry VII *130*
Henry VIII 82, 130, *130*
Hercules 106
heredity 98
herring 88, *89*
Hesiod 159
hibernation 23, **106**, 186
hieroglyphic **106-7**, *107*
Hill, Rowland 178, 206
Himalaya Mountains 119, 156, 231
Hinduism 16, 97, **107**, *107*, 119, 185
hippopotamus **107**
Hiroshima atomic bomb 229
history **107**, **108-11**, *224*, *224*
Hitler, Adolf 49, *111*, **112**, 229
Hittite civilization *108*
HIV-1 5
hockey **112**
Hollywood 87
holocaust **112-13**
Holy Roman Empire 47
Homer 103, **113**, 159, *176*
Homo erctus 180
Homo sapiens 114
Honduras 46, 63
honeybee 23
Hong Kong 48, 62, *110*
hookworm 230
horn (musical instrument) *158*, 159

horse *112*, **113**, 174, 178, 224
horse chestnut *164*
horsetail *174*
House of Representatives (USA) 102
hovercraft **113**, *113*
howitzer 104
human beings 84, **114**, 180
human body **114**, **115**, 118, 223
  see also blood; brain; breathing; digestion; heart; nervous system; senses; skeleton; skin; teeth;
humanist thinking 186
hummingbird 26, **115**, *115*
humus 200
Hundred Years' War *111*, *224*
Hungary 60, 76, 228
Huns *108*
hunting dog 71
hurricane and tornado **116**, *116*
hydrochloric acid 4
hydroelectricity 39, 66, 99, 208, 219, 225
hydrofoil **116**
hydrogen 18, 20, 95, **116**, 181, 206, 207, 225
hypothalamus 31
Hyracotherium 113

Ibsen, Henrik *176*
ice 10, 83, 183, 199
  see also glacier
Ice Age **117**, 133, 143, 180, 192
iceberg **117**, *117*
ice dancing 118
ice hockey 112
Iceland 60, 100, 191-2, 223
Iceni tribe 29
ice-skating **117-18**
igneous rock 188
iguana 140
Iliad (Homer) 103, 113, *176*
immune system **118**
impressionist painting 170
Incas *111*, **118-19**, *118*, 174
inclined plane 141, *141*
income tax 209
India 16, 56, 62, **119**
  farming 60, 124, 210
  geography and wildlife 34, 68, 81, 139
  history 47, 96-7, *108*, *110*
Indian Mutiny *110*
Indian Ocean **119**, 165
Indonesia 62, 190, 203, 229
Industrial Revolution *111*, **119-20**, *120*, 215

235

INDEX

industry (factories) 177, *177*
  Americas 119-20, 149, 164, 219, 220
  Asia 16, 126, 203
  Europe 32-3, 94, 99, 119, 125, 162, 204
  see also Industrial Revolution
influenza 70
insectivore 106
insects 32, 38, *38*, **120-1**, *121*, 161, 197
  see also ants; bees; butterflies and moths; wasps
instinct 9
International Date Line **122**, *122*
internet 58, **122**
intestine 69, 69
Inuit (Eskimo) 14, **122-3**, 164
invertebrate *see* vertebrate
Ionesco, Eugene 176
Iran 62
Iran-Iraq War *110*, 224
Iraq 62, *110*, 224
Ireland 32, 60, 84, 223
iris (of the eye) 85, *85*
iron 8, 18, 75, **123-4**, *123*, 148
  where mined 14, 16, 40, 76, 83, 99, 192, 202, 208, 219
Iron Age **123**
irrigation 78, **124**, *124*, 125
Islam 16, 78, 108, **125**, *125*, 155
  see also Koran; Muhammad; Muslim
Israel 62, *110*, **125**, 151
Israelite 154
Italy 60, 84, **125**, 146, 169, 229

jackal 71
jade 97
Jamaica 63
James I & II *130*
Janssen, Zacharias *147*
Japan 16, 62, **126**
  geography 32, 100
  history 48, *108*, *110*, 171, 229
jazz 158
Jefferson, Thomas **126-7**
jellyfish **126**, *127*
Jenner, Edward *147*
Jerusalem 65
Jesus Christ 25, 48, 108, **127**, 185
  see also Christianity
jet engine 7, 83, **127-8**, *127*, 189
jewellery 97, 101, 151, 197
Jews *see* Judaism
Joan of Arc **128**, *128*
John, King 130, *130*
Jonson, Ben 176, *176*
Jordan 62

Judaism and Jews 25, 112, **128**, 154, 185, 208
  see also Israel
Jupiter 96, 201, *201*

Kalahari desert 5
Kanchenjunga mountain *156*
Kandinsky, Vassily *169*
kangaroo 4, 19, **129**, *129*
kayak 122-3
Kazakhstan 62
Kennedy, John F. *111*, **129**
Kenya 54, 61, **129**
kerosene (paraffin) 83, 128
kettle drum *158*
Kilimanjaro, Mount 4, *156*
kinetic energy 82
King, Martin Luther **129-30**
kings and queens **130**, *130*
Kiribati 63, 169
kiwi **131**
knight **131**, *131*, 224
knot **131-2**, *132*
koala 19, **132**, *132*
Kodiak bear 23
Koran 125, **132**, 185
Korea, North 62
Korea, South 16, 62
Kremlin **132**
Kublai Khan 144
Ku Klux Klan **132**
Kuwait 62, *110*
Kyrgyzstan 62

lactic acid 4
lactose 207
ladybird 121, *121*
lake 124, **133**, *133*, 163
language 45, 51, 106, **133**
Laos 62, 203
Lao Tse 48
lapis lazuli 97, *97*
Lapp people 191
larch 59, **134**, *215*
lard 166
larva 121, *121*
laser 86, **133**, 137
lateral line 88
latitude and longitude 51-2, **133-4**
Latvia 61
lava 223, *223*
law **134**
lawyer 134
lawyer's wig toadstool *157*
lead (metal) 19, **134**, 208
leaf **134-5**, *134*, 175, 221
leaf butterfly *38*
leaf insect *38*
League of Nations 218
leather (hides) 44, 173, 231
Lebanon 62, *110*
Lee, Robert E. 51

leek *221*
legislator 134
lemon oil 166
Lenin, Vladimir **135**
lens **135**, *135*, 137
  of camera 37-8, *37*, 149, *149*, 210, 211
  in the eye 85, *85*
Leonardo da Vinci **135-6**, *169*, 186
leopard 39, **136**, *136*
Lesotho 61
letterpress 181
lettuce 223
lever 141
Liberia 61
Libya 61, *110*
lice 171
lichen 10, **136**, *137*
Liechtenstein 61
light 28, *28*, 82, **137**, 149, 225-6
  see also laser; spectrum
lightning and thunder **137-8**, *138*
lily 175
limestone 124
Lincoln, Abraham 51, **138**
Lindbergh, Charles **138-9**, *139*
linseed oil 166
lion 43, **139**, *139*, 210
Lister, Joseph **139-40**, *147*
Liszt, Franz 157
lithography 181
Lithuania 61
Little Big Horn, Battle of 65
liver 69, 223
liver fluke 229
liverwort *174*, 175
lizard **140**, *140*, 186
llama 140
lobster 88, *89*
longbow *12*, *12*
longitude and latitude 51-2, **133-4**
Low Countries 162
lugworm 230
lung 32, 105
lute 159
Luther, Martin *111*, **140**, 184
Luxembourg 61, 84, **162**
lyrics 176

M-60 tank *209*
McAdam, John 188
Macao 62
Macedonia 61
mackerel 88, *89*
McKinley mountain *156*
Madagascar 61, 119
madder dye 165
Magellan, Ferdinand 84, **142**
magic **142**
magma 223, *223*
Magna Carta 130

magnet and magnetism **142**, *142*, 173
  Earth's magnetic field 57, 75, 102
  magnetic compass 84
Mahler, Gustav *157*
mahogany 92
Maine Coon cat *42*
maize 32, 46, 148, 178, 219
Makalu mountain *156*
mako shark *195*
Malawi 61
Malaysia 62, 190, 203, 229
Maldives 62
Mali 61
Mali Empire *110*
Malta 61
Mameluks *110*
mammal 78, 84, **142-3**, 161, 180
mammoth *143*, *143*
Manchu dynasty *110*
Mandela, Nelson *110*
mandrill 153
Manet, Edouard *169*
mangrove 92
Manila hemp 172
mantle, Earth's *74*, 75
Maori *109*, 162
Mao Zedong 48, **143**
maple 92, *194*
maps and globes **143**
Marconi, Guglielmo *111*, **144**, *144*
Marco Polo 84, **144**
Marcos, Ferdinand 172
margarine 166, 223
marine iguana 140
Mark Antony 51
Marlborough, Duke of 49
Marlowe, Christopher 176
marrow (bone) 30
Mars 201, *201*, 202, 204
marsupial 19, 129, 132, *132*
Martinique 63
Marx, Karl 57, **144**
Mary I, Queen *130*
mathematics 12, 36, 96, **144**, 162, 181
Matisse, Henri *169*
matter **144-5**
Mauritania 61
Mauritius 61, 119
Mauryan Empire *108*
Maxwell, James Clerk **145**
Maya *109*, **145**, *145*
Mayflower ship *111*, **146**, *146*
measles 70
measurement **146**
meat 44, 90-1, 162, 181, 223, 231
Medici family **146**
medicine 53, **147**, *147*, 177
Mediterranean 193
medulla oblongata 30-1, *31*

INDEX

Medusa *159*
Melanesia 169
Menai Bridge 32
Mendel, Gregor **147**-8, *147*
Mercury 201, *201*
mercury barometer 21
mercury thermometer 213
meridian 122, 134
Merino sheep 228
Mesolithic period 206-7
Messiah (Handel) 105
metals 8, 33, *33*, **148**, 206
metamorphic rock 188-9
metamorphosis 121
meteor **148**, *148*
metric system 146
Mexico 19, 63, *109*, *111*, **148**-9
Michelangelo **149**, *149*, 169, 186
Micronesia 63, 169
microscope 147, 148, **149**, *149*
microwave 205
Mid-Atlantic Ridge 18
Middle Ages **150**, *150*
  buildings 13, 41, 49, *49*
  culture 47, 91, 169, 176
  monasteries 153
  trade 153
  warfare 12, 15, *15*, 41, 89, 131, 224
Middle East (Mesopotamia) 16, 33, **151**, 180, 226
midge *121*
migration, animal 88, **151**
milk 4, 44, 47, 142-3, 171, 207, 223
Milky Way 96, *96*
millet 46
mineral 148, **151**-2
  where found 5, 14, 16, 19, 39, 149, 163, 202, 219
mineral oil 166
Ming dynasty *110*
mining 32, **151**-2, *151*, 202
  see also mineral
Minoan civilization *109*
miracle play 176
missile **152**
Mississippi River 163, 217
mistletoe 171
Mobutu, President *110*
Model T Ford 40, *91*, 92
mohair 101
molar tooth *210*
Moldova 61, 76
molecule 18, 80, 202
mole (tunneling machine) **216**, 217
mollusc **152**, *152*, 165
Monaco 61
monastery **152**
money **153**
Mongolia 62
Mongols 98, *110*
monk 150, 152

monkey **153**-4, *153*
monocotyledon *174*, 175
monsoon 119, 203
Mont Blanc 156
Monteverdi, Claudio 166
Montgolfier brothers 20
month 214
Moon 102, **154**, *154*, 191, 201, 214
  eclipse 76, *76*
  effect on tides 165, 213-14, *213*
Moon landing 189
moose (elk) 67
moraine 100, *100*
morality play 176
Morocco 61
mortar (gun) 104
Morton, William 147
Moses 154
mosque **155**
mosquito 121, 171
moss 10, 14, **155**, *174*, 175
moths and butterflies **34**-5, *35*, *38*, 121, 197
motion picture *see* film
motorcycle **155**, *155*
motor nerve 161
moulding 192
mountain 4, 18, **155**-6, *156*
mouse 189
Mozambique 61
Mozart, Wolfgang **156**, *157*, 166
Mughal Empire *110*
Muhammad VI, sultan 168
Muhammad *108*, 125, *125*, 132, **156**
  see also Islam
mummy (preserved body) *181*
muscle *114*
muscle sense 195
mushrooms and toadstools **156**, *157*
music 66, **156**-9
  musical instruments *158*, *159*, 167, *167*
  see also composers; opera; orchestra
Music for the Royal Fireworks (Handel) 105
musk oxen 14
Muslim 65, 97, *109*, 119, 151, 168, 185
  see also Islam; Muhammad
mussel 152
Myanmar 62, 203
Mycenaean civilization *109*
mystery play 176
mythology **159**, *159*

Nagasaki atomic bomb 229
Namibia 61, *110*
Nanda Devi mountain *156*
Nanga Parbat mountain *156*

Napoleon Bonaparte *111*, **160**, *160*, *160*
Napoleonic Wars 224
Nasser, Gamal Abdul **160**
Native American 65, **160**-1, *161*, 164, 219
Nauru 63
Nazi party 112
neap tide *213*, 214
nebula 96
Nelson, Horatio **160**
Neolithic period 206-7
Nepal 62
Neptune 201, *201*, 204
nervous system 30-1, 73, **161**, 194
nest **161**, *161*
Netherlands (Dutch) 61, 84, *110*, **162**
neutron 28, 220
neutron star 28
New Caledonia 63
newt 8, 151
Newton, Sir Isaac 54, 102, **162**
New Zealand 59, 63, 100, *109*, *111*, 131, **162**
Niagara Falls 225
Nicaragua 46, 63
nickel 75, 124, 172
Niger 61
Nigeria 61, **162**
Niger River 162
Nile, Battle of 160
Nile River 78
nitric acid 4
nitrogen 5, 86, 181
Niue 63
Nobel, Alfred 72, 163
Nobel prize 65, 72, 130, **163**, *163*, 190
nomads **163**
Noriega, Manuel *111*
Norman conquest 33, *109*
Norse people 159
North America 62-3, **163**-4
  geography 68, 133, *156*
  wildlife 23, 64, 67, 178, 182, 195, 198
  see also Canada; Native American; United States
Northern Ireland 32
North Pole 14, 85, 193-4, 227
Norway 61, 191-2
nuclear energy **164**, 206, 207, 220
nucleus 18, **44**, *44*, 164
nut **164**, *164*
nylon 175
nymph (insect) 120

oak 92, *134*, *215*, 228
oasis *68*, **165**
oats *see* cereals
ocean 14, 52, 74, 103-4, **165**
  see also Arctic; Atlantic; Indian; Pacific Oceans; tides

ocellated lizard *140*
octopus 152, **165**-6, *165*
ode 176
Odyssey (Homer) 103, 113, 176
oil **166**, 166, 175
  where found 14, 16, 32, 39, 76, 149, 151, 162, 192, 202, 203, 219
Olaf, King of Norway *222*
olive 204
Olympic games 17, 103, *166*
Olympus, Mount 159
Oman 62
onion 34, 204, *221*
opal 97, *97*
opera 157, **166**
Opium War *110*
optic nerve *85*
orangutan 1
orchestra 158-9, *158*, **167**, *167*
Origin of Species (Darwin) 67
Osman I 168
otter **167**-8
Ottoman (Turkish) Empire 35, 102, *111*, **168**, 190
ovule 90, *90*
owl 14, **168**, *168*, 189
oxen 14, 44
oxygen 18, 88, **168**, 181, 189, 225
  in the body 5-6, 29, 32, 105, 115
oyster 88

Pacific Ocean 88, 165, **169**, 193
paddy field 187
Painted Lady butterfly *35*
painting **169**-70
  famous painters 135-6, 149, *169*, 173, 185, 186
Pakistan 62, *110*
Palaeolithic period 206-7
palaeontology 27
Palau 63
palm oil 162, 203
Panama 46, 63, *111*
Panama Canal 39, *111*
panda **170**
paper 48, **170**, *170*-1, 208, 228
Papua New Guinea 63
papyrus 170
paraffin (kerosene) 83, 128
Paraguay 61
parasite *121*, 156, **171**, 230
pasta 125
pasteurization 171
Pasteur, Louis 147, **171**
pastoral poem 176
patella 30
pea 95, 148, 175, 181, *194*, 221
pea crab 63

237

INDEX

peanut 162, *164*, 181
pear *95*
Pearl Harbor **171**, 229
Peary, Robert 85
peat *95*
Peke-faced Persian cat *43*
Peloponnesian War *109*
penguin 10, **171**, 231
penicillin 10, 72, *147*
penis 115
penny farthing bicycle 25, *25*
percussion instrument *158*, 159, *167*
perfume **171**
periscope 207
Perseus *159*
Persian (Arabian) Gulf 119
Persian Empire 7, *108*, *109*
Peru 29, 62, 118-19, 174
petal *90*
Peter the Great **172**
petroleum 40, 82, 83, 95, 129, 166, 203
pewter 134
pharaoh 78, 181
pheasant *26*
Philip of Macedonia 103
Philippines 62, 142, **172**, 203
Phoenicians 84, *109*
phonograph 77, *77*
phosphorus 86
photography 57, 145, **172**-3, 181, 197
see also camera; film
photosynthesis 135, *172*, **173**, 175
physics **173**, 192
Picasso, Pablo *169*, **173**, *173*
pig 99, **173**
Pilgrim Fathers *111*, 146
pine 59, 92, *134*, 216, 228
pink orchid mantis *38*
Pinter, Harold 176
pirate **173**-4
Pizarro, Francisco *111*, **174**
planet *see* Solar System
plankton 10, **174**
plants 34, 137, 165, **174**-5, *174*, 181
see also algae; fern; flower; grass; lichen; moss; tree
plastics 53, **175**, 183, 190, 228
plate armour 15, *15*
Plato 14, *109*, **175**, 200
platypus 19, **175**
play (theatre) **175**-6, 212-13
famous playwrights *176*, 195
plum *95*
Pluto 201, *201*
poetry **176**, 195
poison 4, 29, **177**, 199
Poland 61, 76
polar bear 14, 23, 231

pollen 59, 90, *90*
pollination 121
Pollock, Jackson *169*
pollution **177**, *177*
polonium 65
polyethylene 175
Polynesia 169
polystyrene 175
Pope **177**
pop music 158
porcupine **178**, *178*, 189
pork 173
Portugal 32, 61, 84, 96, **204**
postmark 206
Post Office **178**
potassium 86
potato 90, 99, 121, **178**, 221, *221*
potential energy 82
pottery (porcelain) 48
prairie 163, **178**, 219
prawn 88
prehistoric animals **178**-80, *179*
prehistoric people 180, *180*
President **180**
see also United States of America
pride of lions 139
primate (animal) 153
Prime Minister 102, **180**
printing 30, 48, 56, 104, *104*, **181**
prism 54, 137, 145, 205, 218
probe, space 204
projection (map) 143
propellor 7, 113
protein *45*, 90, 91, **181**
Protestant *111*, 140, 184
proton 18, *18*, 28
protoplasm 44, *45*
psychoanalysis 94, *147*
Ptolemy I *108*
Puccini, Giacomo *157*, 166
Puerto Rico 63
pug dog *70*
pulley 141, *141*
pumpkinseed fish 88
pupa (chrysalis) 121, *121*
pupil (of the eye) 85, *85*
purse-seine net 89, *89*
PVC 175
pyramid *108*, **181**, 195
Pythagoras **181**, *181*
python 199

Qatar 62
quartz crystal clock 52
Queen 101, 130
Queensberry, Marquis of 30

rabbits and hares **182**
raccoon 182
Rachmaninov, Sergei 157
Racine, Jean Baptiste 176
radar 76, **182**, *182*

radioactivity 11, 65, **182**-3, *183*, 190, 220
radio, radio wave 57, 80, *144*, 145, **182**, 205, 211, 226
radio telescope 211
radium 65, *147*, 183
ragworm 230
railway **183**
rain 52, 83, 119, **183**, 199, 225
ramjet *127*
Ramos, Fidel 172
Raphael *169*
rat 189
rates (local tax) 210
reactor, nuclear 164
recessive gene *97*, *98*
recording **183**-4
Red Cross 89, **184**, *184*
Red Point Siamese cat *42*
Red Sea 119
reflecting telescope 211
Reformation 140, **184**
refracting telescope 211
refraction 137
refrigeration **184**
refugee **185**
reindeer 14
relativity laws 79
religion 16, 45, 159, **185**
see also Buddhism; Christianity; Hinduism; Islam; Judaism
Rembrandt van Rijn *169*, **185**
Renaissance 13-14, *13*, 150, 169-70, **185**-6, *185*
reproduction 115, **186**, *186*
reptile 84, 161, 179, **186**-7
see also crocodile; lizard; snake; tortoise
Republic (Plato) 175
respiration *see* breathing
retina (of the eye) 85, *85*
revolution **187**
revolver 104
rhinoceros **187**, *187*
rice 16, 46, *46*, 90, *108*, **187**
where grown 14, 78, 126, 203
Richard I, II, III 130
rickets 223
rifle 104
Rio de Janeiro Earth Summit *111*
river *133*, **187**-8, *188*, 225
RNA 98
road **188**
Robert, Louis 171
robot **188**
rock 74-5, 98, 155, **188**-9, 200, 225
rock bass 88
rocket 152, **189**, *189*
Rocky Mountains 163
rococo architecture *13*
rodent 178, **189**, 210

Roentgen, William *147*, 230
Rogun dam 66
Roman Catholic *111*, 125, 140, 177, 184, 191
Romanesque architecture 13, *13*, 49
Romania 61, 76
Rome, ancient 51, *109*, 150, **190**
architecture and building 13, 32, 48-9, *188*
culture 8, 30, 36, 159, 169
death of Jesus 127
empire 29, 35, 36, 45, 51, 79, *108*
famous people 36, 51, 176
medicine 147
slavery 198
warfare 14, 105, 224
Rome, Treaty of *111*
Romulus and Remus 190
Roosevelt, Franklin D. **190**
Roquefort cheese 47
rose (plant) 175
Rosetta Stone 107
Rotterdam 162
Roundheads 50
roundworm 230
Rousseau, Henri *169*
Royal Academy of Dancing, France 66
rubber **190**, 203
Rubens, Peter Paul *169*
ruby *97*
Rugby football 91
Rushmore, Mount 219
Russia 46, 61, 132, **190**
history *110*, *111*, *160*, 172, 187, 205, 223, 228, 229
see also USSR
Rutherford, Ernest **190**
Rwanda 61, *110*
rye *see* cereals

Sadat, Anwar *110*
Sahara desert 5, 68
sail 196
saint **191**
St Bernadette of Lourdes 191
St Francis of Assisi 191
St Kitts-Nevis 63
St Lawrence Canal 39
St Lucia 63
St Peter 177
St Petersburg 172
St Vincent and the Grenadines 63
Saladin 65
salamander 8
salmon 88
salt 151, **191**
San Marino 61
São Tomé & Príncipe 61
sardine 88, *89*
Sardinia 125
Sassanid Empire *108*

238

INDEX

satellite *111*, **191**, *191*, 201, 204, 210
Saturn 201, *201*
Saturn rocket *189*
Saudi Arabia 62
sausage 173
Scandinavia 159, **191-2**, 198
see also Denmark; Iceland; Norway; Sweden
scapula 30
scenery 212-13
Schubert, Franz 157
Schumann, Robert 30, *157*
science **192**
branches of science 17, 26-7, 47, 97-8 98-9, 144, 173, 231
famous scientists 59-60, 65, 66-7, 77, 79, 96, 135-6, 145, 162, 171, 181, 190
Scotland 32
Scott, Robert **192**
screw 141, *141*
Scrooge 69
sculpture *149*, 186, **192-3**, *192*
scurvy 223
sea 74, 133, **193**
see also ocean
Sea of Galilee 193
sea horse 193
seals and sea lions 10, 14, *193*, 193, 231
Sears Tower *12*
sea otter 168
seasons 18, **193-4**, *194*
seaweed 7, 165, 175
sedimentary rock 188-9
seed 59, 95, 164, 175, **194**, *194*, 216, 221
segmented worm 230
seismometer 75
Senate (USA) 102
Senegal 61
senses 9, 31, **194-5**
see also ear; eye
sensory nerve 161
sepal *90*
Seven Wonders of the World **195**
Seven Years' War *111*, 224
sexual reproduction 115, 186, *186*
Seychelles 61, 119
shaduf *124*
Shakespeare, William 82, 176, *176*, **195**, *212*
Shang dynasty 108
shark 88, **195**, *195*
Shaw, George Bernard 176
sheep 14, 86, 162, **195**, 228
sheepdog 71
shellfish 88, 152, 169
shell (of mollusc) 152, 217
Sheridan, Richard 176
Shetland pony 113

Shih Huang Ti, Emperor 48
shihtzu (dog) *70*
Shintoism 185
ship 8, 76, 164, **195-6**, *196*, 207
historic ships 84, *84*, 173-4, 222
Shire horse 113
Shiva *107*
Shostakovich, Dmitri 157
shotgun 104
Sibelius, Jean 157
Siberia *110*, 214
Sicily 125
siege 41
Sierra Leone 61
Sikh 119
Sikhism 185
silicon chip 80, *80*, **196**, 215
silk and silkworm 48, 121, **197**
silver 19, 149, 151, **197**
Singapore 62, 203
skeleton *114*, **197**, *197*
skiing 197-8
skin **198**
skunk **198**, *198*
skyscrapers *12*, 14
slavery 40, *110*, 138, 164, **198**
sleep and dreams **198-9**
sleet 199
Slovakia 61, 76
Slovenia 61
slow worm 140
slug 152
Small Tortoiseshell butterfly *35*
smoking 215
snail 152, *152*
snake 186, 189, **199**, *199*
snapping turtle *217*
snow and sleet 199
soap **200**
soccer (Association football) 91
socialism **200**
Socrates 175, **200**
sodium 191
softwood 228
soil **200**, *200*
Solar System 60, 96, *96*, 181, **201-2**, *201*
see also Earth; Sun
Solomon Islands 63
Somalia 61
sonar 76
song 176
Songhai Empire *110*
sonnet 176
Sophocles 176
sound **202**
South Africa 61, 101, *110*, **202**
South America 62, *111*, **202-3**
farming 14, 32, 178
geography 31-2, 92, 156
people 29, 66, 118-19

wildlife 10, 15, 64, 140, 153-4, 182, 189, 199
South China Sea 193
Southeast Asia **203**
South Pole 10, 85, *192*, 227
Soviet Union *see* USSR
sow 173
space biology 27
space exploration *111*, **203-4**, *203*
see also astronaut
space shuttle *203*, *204*
Spain 61, 84, *109*, **204**, *224*
Spanish Empire 19, 29, 40, 55, 60, 119, 172, 174, 204, 215
spaniel 70, *70*
Sparta 103
spectrum 54-5, *55*, 145, 162, **204-5**, 218
speed skating 118
sperm 115, 186
spider 9, *197*, *204*, **205**
spider monkey 153
spinach 221
spinal cord 31, *31*
Spirit of St Louis (aeroplane) 139, *139*
spore 86, 155, 156
sport 12, 17, 22, 30, 63-4, 112, 117-18, 197-8
Spotted Short-hair cat *43*
spring tide *213*, 214
spruce 59, 216
Sputnik I 191, 203
squid 152, **165-6**, *165*
squirrel 189, 210
Sri Lanka 62, 210
Stag beetle *121*
stainless steel 124
stalactite and stalagmite **205**, *205*
Stalin, Joseph 205
stamen 90, *90*
stamp **206**
star 28, 58, 59, 96, **206**
starch 90
statute law 134
steam engine 40, 83, 119, 183, *196*, **206**, *206*, 225
steel 8, 15, **123-4**, *123*, 162, 208
Stephenson, George 183
steppes 16
stick insect *38*
stigma (of flower) 90, *90*
Stilton cheese 47
Stockton and Darlington railway 183
stomach 69, *69*
stomata 135
Stone Age 33, 169, **206-7**
stratus cloud *53*
Stravinsky, Igor 157
stringed instrument *158*, 159, *167*
submarine 76, **207**, *207*
sucrose 207
Sudan 61
Suez Canal 39, *110*, 160

sugar 90, 102, 134, 171, 173, **207**
where grown 5, 14, 16, 32, 40, 99, 129, 148, 172
Suleiman the Magnificent 168
sulphuric acid 4
sultan 168
Sumerian civilization *108*
Sun 76, 96, 137, **207-8**, *208*
effect on tides 213-14, *213*
sunlight 7, 51, 135, 137, 173, 208, 223
see also solar system
sun bear 23
Sung dynasty *108*
Sun Yat-sen *110*
Superior, Lake 133
supertanker *196*
Surinam 62
Surtsey volcano 192
suspension bridge 32
Swaziland 61
sweat gland 198
Sweden 61, 84, 172, 191-2, 198
sweet chestnut 134, *164*
Switzerland 61, 184, **208**
sycamore *95*, *134*
symphony 157
symphony orchestra *167*
synagogue **208**
Syria 62

tadpole 95
Taiwan 62
Tajikistan 62, 66
Talbot, William Fox 172
Talmud **209**
T'ang dynasty *108*
tank **209**, *209*, 224
Tanzania 61
Taoism 185
tape recording 183-4, 222
tapeworm 171, 229
tarmac 188
Tasman, Abel *111*, 162
taste bud 194
tax **209-10**
Tchaikovsky, Peter Ilyich 157
tea 5, 16, 129, 196, **210**
teeth **210**, *210*
telegraph 57, 144
telephone 24-5, *25*, 57, 87, 133, 191, **210-11**
telescope 17, 162, *210*, **211**
television 57, 80, 133, 184, 191, **211-12**, *211*
Telford, Thomas 32
Tempietto (Rome) *185*
Temple of Artemis 195
Ten Commandments 154
tennis 212
Tenochtitlán 19
tepee *161*
terrorism **212**

239

INDEX

testes 115
tetracycline 10
Thailand 62, 203
theatre 176, **212**, *212*
  see also opera; play
thermometer 147, **213**
Thirty Years' War *111*, 224
thorn-tree hopper *38*
threadworm 229-30
thunder and lightning **137**-8, *138*
tick bird *187*
tidal wave 169
tides 165, **213**-14, *213*
tiger 43, **214**, *214*
timber *see* forest; tree; wood
time **214**
tin 16, 19, 33, 162, 202, 203, 214
Titian 169
toads and frogs 8, **94**-5, *94*, 151
toadstools and mushrooms **156**, *157*
tobacco 5, 32, 40, **214**-15, 219
Toggenburg goat *101*
Togo 61
tomato 95, 221
Tonga 63
toothed whale 226
tornado and hurricane **116**, *116*
tortoise 186, **217**, *217*
toucan *26*
tourism 33, 40, 102, 203, 204, 208
tournament, medieval *131*
trade 51, 83, 153, 203
trade union 120, **215**
Trafalgar, Battle of 160
transistor 144, **215**
trapdoor spider 205
trawling 89, *89*
tree 59, 92, 175, **215**-16, *215*
tree frog *94*
trigonometry 144
trilobite 179
Trinidad and Tobago 63
tritium 116
Trojan War 113
trolling 89
troposphere 74
trumpet 158, 159
tsar 132, 172, 187
tsetse fly 121
tsunami 75
tuatara 186
tuberculosis 10, 70
Tunisia 61
tunnel **216**-17, *216*
tunny (tuna) 88, *89*
turbine 83, *127*, 127, 164
turbojet, turbofan, turboprop 127, *127*
Turkey 62, **102**, 228
Turkmenistan 62
Turner, J.M.W. 169
turnip 221
turquoise 97
turtle 186, **217**, *217*

Tuvalu 63, 169
Twain, Mark **217**
typhoid 70
typhoon 116
Typhoon submarine *207*
Tyrannosaurus 179

Uganda 61
ugly milk cap toadstool *157*
Ukraine 61, 76
Uln Cathedral *13*
ultrasonic wave 202
ultra-violet rays 205, **218**
umbrella ant 10
United Arab Emirates 62
United Kingdom 32, 61, 84
  see also British Isles
United Nations 89, *111*, 208, **218**, 218, *218*
United States of America 63, 163-4, 180, **218**-20, *219*
  civil rights 129-30, 132
  farming 46, 60
  football 91
  geography 100, 225
  history 65, **110**, 119-20, 126, 161, 171, 228, 229
  Presidents 102, 126-7, 129, 138, 190, 219, 224
  see also American Civil War; American War of Independence; North America
Universe 162, **220**, *220*
uranium 19, 39, 164, 183, 202, 219, **220**
Uranus 201, *201*
Urban II, Pope 65
Uruguay 63
USSR 57, *111*, 205
  see also Russia
Uzbekistan 62

vaccination 70, 118, 147, *147*
vagina 115
vampire bat 23
Vandals 108
van Gogh, Vincent 169
Vanuatu 63
VAT 209
Vatican City 61, 125, 177
VCR 222
Vedas 107
vegetable 126, 221, *221*, 223
  where grown 78, 83, 129, 148, 162, 163, 219
Velasquez, Diego 169
Venezuela 62, 202
Venice 39, 125
Venus 201, *201*, 204
Verdi, Giuseppe 157, 166
verse 176

vertebrates and invertebrates 9, 29, 142, 179, 197
Victor Emmanuel, King 97
Victoria Falls 225
Victoria, Queen *130*, **221**-2, *221*
videotape **222**
Vienna, Congress of *111*
Vietnam 62, *111*, 203
Vietnam War *110*, 224
Viking 84, *109*, 196, *196*, **222**, *222*
vinegar 4
Vinson Massif 156
violin 158, 159, 202
Virgil 176
virus 5, 70, 118
Vishnu 107
Visigoths *109*
vitamin 70, 218, **223**
Vivaldi, Antonio 157
vixen 93
volcano 99, 126, 169, 192, **223**, *223*

Wagner, Richard 157, 166
Wales 32
Walloon 162
Wall Street Crash *111*
walnut 95, *164*
walrus 14
war **224**, *224*
War of Austrian Succession **225**
War of Spanish Succession 224
Wars of the Roses *111*, 224
Washington, George 219, **224**
watches and clocks **52**, 197, 214
water 18, 52, 135, 173, **225**
  water cycle 225
  water vapour 6, 52, 90, 183, 225
  see also cloud; dam; irrigation; lake
waterfall **225**
Waterloo, Battle of *111*, 160
Water Music (Handel) 105
Watt, James 119, 206, *206*, **225**
waves 165, **225**-6, *225*
weasel 14
weather 154, **226**
  weather forecasting 21, 191
  see also climate
weaver bird *161*
wedge 141, *141*
Western Samoa 63
West Indies *see* Caribbean
whale 10, 14, 72, 143, **226**, *226*
wheat *see* cereals

wheel 141, *141*, **226**, 227
whiskey, Irish 33
Whittle, Frank 127
Wilde, Oscar 176
Wilhelm mountain 156
William I (the Conqueror) *130*, **227**
William II *130*
William III and Mary *130*
William IV *130*
Williams, Tennessee 176
wind 83, 116, 165, **227**
wind instrument 158, 159, 167
windmill (wind generator) *82*, **227**-8, *228*
wine 94, 99, 125, 204
wireless *see* radio; telegraph
wisent (buffalo) 28
wolf 178, 210
wolf spider 205
wombat 19
wood (timber) 95, 99, 170, *170*, 175, **228**
  where grown 39, 76, 99, 192, 203, 208, 219
  see also forest; tree
woodwind section (orchestra) 158
wool 19, 195, 196, **228**
woolly monkey 153
World Trade Centre *12*
World War I 99, *111*, 209, 224, **228**-9, *229*
World War II 49, 99, *110*, *111*, 112, 126, 171, 209, 224, **229**
World Wide Web 122
worm 9, **229**-30
Wright, Wilbur and Orville 6, **230**, *230*

X-ray 147, *147*, 205, 226, **230**

yak 44, **231**, *231*
year 214
Yemen 62
Yom Kippur War 224
Yugoslavia 61, 76, *111*

Zaire 61, *110*
Zambia 61
zebra 38, **231**
Zeus 103, 166
  Statue of Zeus 195
Zimbabwe 61
zinc 8
zodiac 59
zoo **231**
zoology 26, **231**